Treasured
from
St. George Island

Welcome to St. George Island and Florida's forgotten coast . . . Florida the way it used to be. Its beautiful, unspoiled beaches are among the top ten in the United States. Abundant fish and wildlife, sunshine and gentle breezes, make St. George Island a very special vacation spot for visitors from around the world. But it is the ever-present friendliness and graciousness of the inhabitants which make St. George Island so very special.

St. George Island, in the northwest gulf coast area of Florida, along with Little St. George, St. Vincent Island and Dog Island, protects and nurtures an estuarine system equal to none in the United States. St. George Island is a priceless inheritance and a reminder of our responsibility to preserve the fragile beauty of our barrier islands and surrounding waters.

To your culinary enjoyment and the St. George Island First Responders, a unit of the St. George Island Volunteer Fire Department, which this book will support, we dedicate *Treasured Recipes from St. George Island.*

Welcome to
St. George Island
The Uncommon Florida

Published by: St. George Island First Responders

Copyright 1994 St. George Island First Responders
St. George Island Volunteer Fire Department
P.O. Box 682
Eastpoint, Florida 32328

Library of Congress Number: 93-074988
ISBN: 0-9659979-0-1
Previously ISBN: 0-87197-397-9

Designed, edited and manufactured by:
Favorite Recipes® Press
an imprint of

FRP™

P.O. Box 305142
Nashville, Tennessee 37230
1-800-358-0560

Manufactured in the United States of America
First Printing: 1994   5,000 copies
Second Printing: 1997   7,500 copies

Contents

Acknowledgements

The proceeds from the sale of *Treasured Recipes from St. George Island* will be used to benefit the St. George Island First Responders, a unit of the St. George Island Volunteer Fire Department.

The St. George Island First Responder Unit expresses grateful appreciation to all of our friends who contributed their recipes, their time, and their efforts, all of which have made this book possible.

Cookbook Committee

Alice Collins   Judi Little   Mary Lou Short

Cover by

Carol Mitchell

Illustrations by

Marilyn Bean   Karen Dingler   Linda Holzhausen
Carolyn Bassett   John Ficklen   Bill Short
Jim Grosvenor

Stories by

Alice Collins   Woody Miley
Shaun Donahoe   Mary Lou Short

First Responder Unit Commander

Judi Little

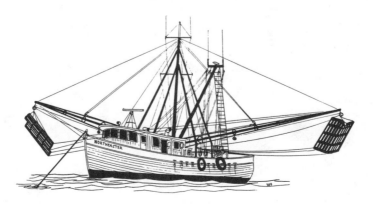

Contributors

Ann Abbey
Ann Abbott and Wes
 Johnson
Jay Abbott
Joan and John Ackerly
Pamela Amato
Jolene Armistead
Linda Arnold
Katherine Autrey
Scottie Baker
Jayne Bamburg
Dominic Baragona
Vilma Baragona
Todd Baroody
Doris Barrett
Marilyn Bean
Mason Bean
Alice Bell
Bill Bell
Frannie Beman
Tomie Jean Blanton
Nancy Watts-Bloom
Edna Bono
Sharon Bono
Jane and Sue Booth
Jennifer Ficklen-Bucci
Janie Burke
Cathy Buzzett
Jean Carson
Dottie Cassel
Ane Cates
Mike Cates
Cheryl Cianciolo
Rachel L. Clague
Sharen Clark
Maxine Cobb
Alice D. Collins
Ken Collins
Nora Collins
B. L. Cosey
Dot Crozier
Jeanne Crozier
Jane E. Davis
Josie Davis
Betty Day
Connie Dehner
Verna Dekle
Claire Dews
Louise Dickerson
Rose Drye
Patty Durham
Polly Edmiston
Nick and Becky Eppes

Bobbie Felice
Susan Ficklen
Susan Florin
Azilee Drake Foy
Marti Fraker
David Fulmer
Hobson Fulmer, DVM
Martha Fulmer
Howard Gann
Alma Garrett
Shirley Gelch
Martha Gherardi
Kathy Gilbert
Clarence Gissendanner
Virginia Glass
Conrad Gleber and
 Gail Rubini
Lucy Goldman
Elaine Good
Jean Gross
Tom Gross
Ruth Guernsey
Ollie Gunn
Shirley Gunn
Kathy Gunter
Gerri Guyon
Carol Haberkern
Clem and JoAnna
 Hallman
Peggy Hamm
Darlyne Harper
Eunice Hartmann
Don and Barbara
 Hartsfield
Lana Heady
Chris Healy
Gwen Henkel
Alec and Jane Hinson
Frankie Hodgson
Liz Hoffman
Roy Hoffman, Jr.
Bernice Holmes
Norma Hoopes
Diane Hunt
Barry Isenberg
Mary Isenberg
Charlotte James
Lora James
Ellie Jones
Pauline Jordy
Peggy Juppé
Dana Troutman Keith
Paula Kemp

Larry Kienzle
Molly Kirkland
Lorraine Knight
Beth Krontz
Laura LaFleur
Rhonda and Jim
 Lambert
Eddie Lardent
Irene LaSlavic
Frank Latham
Sue Latham
Fred Lawhon
Margaret Lawhon
Richard and Shelia
 Lawrence
Phyllis Vitale-Lewis
Ticia Lipscomb
Arthur Little
Judi Little
Jean Lively
Teresa Lobenburg
Sally Lonbom
Helen Marsh
B. Marty
Sweet Mary
Marion Miley
Carol Mitchell
Pat Morrison
Kathy Morton
Beth Mosely
Jackie Mossburg
Chef Cole Nelson
Kim Norgren
Virginia Norris
Sharon O'Dell
Jan Pendleton
Virginia Pendleton
Margaret Pfeifer
Melanie Pinkerton
Jane Pitts
Jerry Plowden
Katrina Plumblee
Elaine Poindexter
Alice Powell
Karen C. Powers
Diana Prickett
Linda Protsman
Karen Rabinowitz
Shirley Redd
Sue Reitinger
Marcia Rentz
Anna Johnson Riedel
Karen Riedle

Libby Ringold
Beatrice Ritchey
Ann Robuck
Mary Rodgers
Sara Rodrigue
Edna Rudasill
Babs Ruhl
Linda Russell
Betty Sankey
Vicki Sayle
Gladys Scudder
Lola Seager
Ann Sharp
John Shelby
Kristen Shelby
Neil Sherman
Bill Short
Mary Lou Short
H. Lee Simmons
Marsha Smith
Helen Solomon
Helen Townsend
 Spohrer
John B. Spohrer, Jr.
John Henry and Nelle
 Spratt
Lawanna Stansell
Cass Stark
Phyllis Stanley
 Stephens
Evelyn Stripling
Bo Suber
Sandra Thaxton
Marta Thompson
Movitia Toomey
Barbara Travis
Beverly Troutman
Carol "Woody"
 Troutman
Harry Tucker, MD
Mildred R. Tucker
Joan Valenti
Patty Valentine
Pam Vest
Helene Wagner
JoEllen Ward
Betty Webb
Dr. Andrew Weil
Kathleen Whalen
Ellen Whitlock
Barbara Yonclas
Barbara Young

The History of St. George Island

The Creek Indians first inhabited St. George Island around the 10th century A.D. The expedition of Pánfilo de Narváez may have been the first Europeans to see the island.

In the mid 17th century, the Spanish had occupied the Gulf area and built a fort at St. Marks. Pirates roamed the Gulf waters preying on ships transporting gold back to Spain.

In the late 1700s, the pirate William Augustus Bowles figured prominently in Florida political affairs. People believe that he buried treasure on the western tip of St. George Island, now Little St. George Island, after beaching his ship to avoid capture by the Spanish. Another pirate, Billy Bowlegs Rodgers, also raided the waters of the Gulf in his ship "Mysterio," and reportedly buried treasure in the area.

St. George Island, once a part of Indian territory, was sold in 1803 by the Creek and Seminole Indians along with almost 2,000,000 acres of land to the John Forbes Company ("the Forbes Purchase") to settle debts.

During the 18th century, pirates are believed to have had camps on nearby St. Vincent Island, and treasure chests are reportedly buried there. There are also reports of shipwrecks from the Spanish Grand Fleet.

After the late 1800s, St. George Island had quite a succession of colorful and flamboyant owners. The Island's pine forests were turpentined; cattle were grazed there, cottages, a hotel and boardwalk that ran from the bay to the gulf were built.

During World War II the island was used for training exercises, and today you can still find brass shell casings washed up along the bay.

In 1965, the four-mile-long Bryant Patton Bridge and Causeway was built. Since then, visitors have enjoyed the miles of pristine beaches and natural beauty. Shell enthusiasts come to collect shells, and bird watchers are thrilled by the more than 200 species of birds.

To many who live on and visit the Island, St. George Island truly is paradise found.

Map of
St. George Island

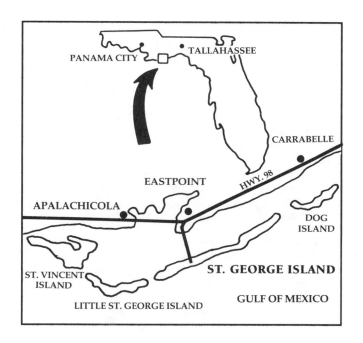

St. George Island is approximately four miles off the coast of Apalachicola, Florida, and is accessed by the Bryant Patton Bridge. The Island is 65 miles from Panama City and 75 miles from Tallahassee. With a length of 28 miles, it is one of the longest barrier islands in Florida, but it is only a mile and a half at its widest point. Visitors are charmed by St. George Island's beautiful unspoiled beaches and quiet atmosphere, and many feel that the Island is Florida's best kept secret.

Nutritional Guidelines

*T*he editors have attempted to present these family recipes in a form that allows approximate nutritional values to be computed. Persons with dietary or health problems or whose diets require close monitoring should not rely solely on the nutritional information provided. They should consult their physicians or a registered dietitian for specific information.

Abbreviations for Nutritional Profile

Cal — Calories

Prot — Protein

Carbo — Carbohydrates

Fiber — Dietary Fiber

T Fat — Total Fat

Chol — Cholesterol

Sod — Sodium

g — grams

mg — milligrams

Nutritional information for these recipes is computed from information derived from many sources, including materials supplied by the United States Department of Agriculture, computer databanks and journals in which the information is assumed to be in the public domain. However, many specialty items, new products and processed foods may not be available from these sources or may vary from the average values used in these profiles. More information on new and/or specific products may be obtained by reading the nutrient labels. Unless otherwise specified, the nutritional profile of these recipes is based on all measurements being level.

- **Artificial sweeteners** vary in use and strength so should be used "to taste," using the recipe ingredients as a guideline. Sweeteners using aspartame (NutraSweet and Equal) should not be used as a sweetener in recipes involving prolonged heating which reduces the sweet taste. For further information on the use of these sweeteners, refer to package information.
- **Alcoholic ingredients** have been analyzed for basic ingredients, although cooking causes the evaporation of alcohol, thus decreasing caloric content.
- **Buttermilk, sour cream** and **yogurt** are the types available commercially.
- **Cake mixes** which are prepared using package directions include 3 eggs and ½ cup oil.
- **Chicken**, cooked for boning and chopping, has been roasted; this method yields the lowest caloric values.
- **Cottage cheese** is cream-style with 4.2% creaming mixture. Dry curd cottage cheese has no creaming mixture.
- **Eggs** are all large. To avoid raw eggs that may carry salmonella as in eggnog or 6-week muffin batter, use an equivalent amount of commercial egg substitute.
- **Flour** is unsifted all-purpose flour.
- **Garnishes**, serving suggestions and other optional additions and variations are not included in the profile.
- **Margarine** and **butter** are regular, not whipped or presoftened.
- **Milk** is whole milk, 3.5% butterfat. Lowfat milk is 1% butterfat. Evaporated milk is whole milk with 60% of the water removed.
- **Oil** is any type of vegetable cooking oil. Shortening is hydrogenated vegetable shortening.
- **Salt** and other ingredients to taste as noted in the ingredients have not been included in the nutritional profile.
- If a choice of ingredients has been given, the nutritional profile information reflects the first option. If a choice of amounts has been given, the nutritional profile reflects the greater amount.

Appetizers

St. George Island Volunteer Fire Department
by Linda Holzhausen

Volunteer Fire Department and First Responder Unit

The St. George Island Volunteer Fire Department and First Responder Unit is ranked as one of the best in Florida. This highly trained, dedicated group of Island residents volunteer hundreds of hours towards the safety and well-being of Island residents and visitors.

The fire department, originally started in 1974, received its charter in 1977. The firehouse, nestled in a pine thicket, and overlooking St. George Sound, was constructed from volunteer labor and contributed materials. It was completed in 1982 and now serves as the fire station and civic hall.

The original fire truck, dubbed "woogidy woogidy," was a converted 1953 army transport vehicle with a crank start and three gear speeds: slope, hilly and level. Held together by sheer determination of the firemen, the old truck finally snapped a steering cable on the way to a fire, sending truck and firemen careening off the road through a marsh thicket.

Through the years, donations and proceeds from the St. George Island Annual Chili Cookoff and Auction have supported the fire department, providing funding for new fire trucks and state of the art equipment.

The Island is located 20 miles from medical facilities, and in 1987 the First Responder Unit was formed to provide emergency medical aid for St. George Island. All first responders are certified and several volunteers in the unit are EMT's and Paramedics.

In 1989, funds raised by the Chili Cookoff provided for a rescue truck, and the community rallied to raise funds for equipment and supplies.

The unit daily fulfills their commitment to offer emergency medical aid 24 hours a day, 7 days a week. Our first responder unit is a vital link with the medical community in Franklin County.

The St. George Island Volunteer Fire Department and First Responder Unit, the Chili Cookoff and Auction Committee, and the residents of St. George Island proudly received the 1992 Rural Community of the Year Award. St. George Island...people helping people!

Cheese Puffs

3 eggs
8 ounces cream cheese, softened
16 ounces feta cheese, crumbled
1 1-pound package phyllo pastry, cut into 1½-inch strips
½ cup melted butter

Yield: 24 servings

Beat eggs in mixer bowl until foamy. Add cream cheese and feta cheese gradually, beating well after each addition. Brush phyllo strips with melted butter. Place 1 teaspoonful of cheese mixture on each strip. Fold end diagonally to enclose filling. Continue to fold strip to form triangle. Place on nonstick baking sheet. Bake at 350 degrees until puffed and brown. May substitute margarine for butter.

Approx Per Serving: Cal 181; Prot 5 g; Carbo 11 g; Fiber <1 g; T Fat 13 g; 64% Calories from Fat; Chol 61 mg; Sod 375 mg.

Beatrice Ritchey

Morton Wings

1 5-pound package chicken wings, thawed
¼ cup hot sauce
¼ cup melted butter
1 teaspoon minced garlic
1½ tablespoons Worcestershire sauce
½ teaspoon seasoned salt
Kitchen Bouquet to taste

Yield: 50 servings

Rinse chicken and pat dry. Place on rack in baking pan. Broil until brown on both sides, turning occasionally; drain. Combine chicken with mixture of hot sauce, butter, garlic, Worcestershire sauce, salt and Kitchen Bouquet in bowl, tossing to coat.

Approx Per Serving: Cal 107; Prot 9 g; Carbo <1 g; Fiber <1 g; T Fat 8 g; 65% Calories from Fat; Chol 31 mg; Sod 65 mg.

Kathy Morton

Party Ham Rolls

2 cups butter
3 tablespoons prepared
  mustard
3 tablespoons poppy seeds
1 medium onion, grated
1 teaspoon Worcestershire
  sauce
3 8-ounce packages party
  rolls
1 pound boiled ham,
  shredded
1 pound Swiss cheese,
  shredded

Yield: 36 servings

Melt butter in skillet. Stir in mustard, poppy seeds, onion and Worcestershire sauce. Cook over low heat until onions are tender, stirring constantly. Remove rolls from foil-lined container; do not separate. Slice into halves horizontally. Spread each half with prepared sauce. Return bottom half of rolls to pan. Layer ham, cheese and remaining layer of rolls on top. Wrap with foil. Bake at 400 degrees for 15 minutes; cut into rolls.

Approx Per Serving: Cal 220; Prot 9 g; Carbo 11 g;
  Fiber 1 g; T Fat 16 g; 65% Calories from Fat;
  Chol 46 mg; Sod 421 mg.

Sandra Thaxton

Dominic's Meatballs

5 pounds ground beef
16 ounces soft bread crumbs
10 to 12 eggs, beaten
8 ounces grated Parmesan
  cheese
3 tablespoons salt
1 tablespoon pepper
1 clove of garlic, minced
1/2 cup parsley

Yield: 160 servings

Combine ground beef, bread crumbs, eggs, Parmesan cheese, salt, pepper, garlic and parsley in bowl; mix well. Shape into small balls. Place in baking pan. Bake at 400 degrees for 15 minutes; drain.

Approx Per Serving: Cal 50; Prot 4 g; Carbo 2 g;
  Fiber <1 g; T Fat 3 g; 51% Calories from Fat;
  Chol 26 mg; Sod 172 mg.

Dominic Baragona

German Sweet and Sour Meatballs

1 envelope onion soup mix
1/4 cup water
2 eggs, beaten
2 pounds ground beef
1   16-ounce can sauerkraut
1   8-ounce can whole berry
    cranberry sauce
3/4 cup water
1/3 cup packed brown sugar
1/2 cup chili sauce
1 tablespoon parsley flakes
1/2 teaspoon garlic powder

Yield: 64 servings

Combine soup mix, 1/4 cup water, eggs and ground beef in bowl; mix well. Shape into small balls. Cook in skillet until brown on all sides, stirring occasionally; drain. Combine sauerkraut, cranberry sauce, 3/4 cup water, brown sugar, chili sauce, parsley and garlic powder in bowl; mix well. Add meatballs, tossing to coat. Pour mixture into baking pan. Bake at 325 degrees for 30 minutes. May cook in slow cooker using manufacturer's instructions.

Approx Per Serving: Cal 46; Prot 3 g; Carbo 3 g;
    Fiber <1 g; T Fat 2 g; 42% Calories from Fat;
    Chol 16 mg; Sod 96 mg.

Bobbie Felice

Swedish Meatballs

1 pound coarsely ground
    beef
1/2 cup bread crumbs
1 egg, beaten
Salt and pepper to taste
Garlic powder to taste
1   12-ounce bottle of chili
    sauce
1   8-ounce jar grape jelly

Yield: 32 servings

Combine ground beef, bread crumbs, egg, salt, pepper and garlic powder in bowl; mix well. Shape into small balls. Combine chili sauce and grape jelly in large saucepan. Cook over low heat until blended, stirring frequently. Add meatballs. Cook over low heat until meatballs test done, stirring frequently.

Approx Per Serving: Cal 70; Prot 4 g; Carbo 9 g;
    Fiber <1 g; T Fat 2 g; 28% Calories from Fat;
    Chol 16 mg; Sod 167 mg.

Libby Ringold

Sausage Balls

3 cups baking mix
1 pound hot pork sausage
10 to 12 ounces Cheddar
   cheese, shredded

Yield: 40 servings

Combine baking mix, sausage and cheese in bowl; mix well. Shape into bite-sized balls. Place on ungreased baking sheet. Bake at 375 degrees for 15 minutes or until brown.

Approx Per Serving: Cal 90; Prot 4 g; Carbo 6 g;
   Fiber <1 g; T Fat 6 g; 58% Calories from Fat;
   Chol 14 mg; Sod 230 mg.

Jayne Bamburg

Spinach Balls

2 10-ounce packages
   frozen spinach, cooked,
   drained
2 cups herb-seasoned
   stuffing mix
6 eggs, beaten
1 tablespoon minced onion
1/2 teaspoon pepper
1 tablespoon MSG
1/2 teaspoon thyme
3/4 teaspoon garlic powder
1/2 cup grated Parmesan
   cheese
3/4 cup melted butter

Yield: 48 servings

Combine spinach, stuffing mix, eggs, onion, pepper, MSG, thyme, garlic powder, Parmesan cheese and melted butter in bowl; mix well. Shape into balls. Place on nonstick baking sheet. Bake at 350 degrees for 20 minutes. May use egg substitute for eggs and margarine for butter. May omit MSG.

Approx Per Serving: Cal 52; Prot 2 g; Carbo 3 g;
   Fiber <1 g; T Fat 4 g; 65% Calories from Fat;
   Chol 32 mg; Sod 379 mg.

Helen Solomon

Toast Cups with Mushroom Spread

1 loaf sandwich bread
1/2 cup butter, softened
1 12-ounce can mushroom
  caps, drained, finely
  chopped
1 small onion, finely
  chopped
2 tablespoons butter
1 teaspoon sherry
8 ounces cream cheese,
  softened
2 tablespoons mayonnaise
Salt and pepper to taste

Yield: 60 servings

Trim crust from bread; roll to flatten. Spread 1 side of each bread slice with 1/2 cup butter. Cut into 1 1/4-inch rounds. Place butter side up in miniature muffin cups. Bake at 325 degrees for 10 to 15 minutes or until light brown. Remove to wire rack to cool. Sauté mushrooms and onion in 2 tablespoons butter in skillet until tender. Stir in sherry. Add mixture of cream cheese and mayonnaise; mix well. Season with salt and pepper. Spoon into toast cups. Place on baking sheet. Bake just until heated through. May fill toast cups with chicken, tuna or crab salad.

Approx Per Serving: Cal 48; Prot 1 g; Carbo 3 g;
    Fiber <1 g; T Fat 4 g; 71% Calories from Fat;
    Chol 10 mg; Sod 81 mg.

Jane Pitts

Stuffed Mushrooms

4 ounces spinach, cooked,
  drained, chopped
4 ounces feta cheese,
  crumbled
Nutmeg to taste
1/4 cup melted butter
Salt and pepper to taste
20 large mushrooms, stems
  removed, blanched

Yield: 20 servings

Combine spinach, feta cheese, nutmeg, melted butter, salt and pepper in bowl; mix well. Stuff each mushroom cap with mixture. Place on nonstick baking sheet. Bake at 350 degrees for 10 minutes or until heated through.

Approx Per Serving: Cal 41; Prot 1 g; Carbo 1 g;
    Fiber <1 g; T Fat 4 g; 75% Calories from Fat;
    Chol 11 mg; Sod 92 mg.

Harry L. Tucker, M.D.

Party Pinwheels

16 ounces cream cheese, softened
1 envelope ranch-style dressing mix
2 green onions, minced
4 12-inch flour tortillas
1/2 cup chopped red bell pepper
1/2 cup chopped celery
1 2-ounce can sliced black olives, drained

Yield: 36 servings

Combine cream cheese, dressing mix and green onions in bowl; mix well. Spread mixture on tortillas. Sprinkle with red pepper, celery and olives. Roll to enclose filling; wrap in foil or plastic wrap. Chill for 2 hours. Cut off ends. Cut rolls into 1-inch slices.

Approx Per Serving: Cal 68; Prot 2 g; Carbo 4 g; Fiber <1 g; T Fat 5 g; 66% Calories from Fat; Chol 14 mg; Sod 131 mg.

Norma Hoopes

Edam-Shrimp Appetizer

15 ounces Edam cheese, cut into 1/4-inch slices
8 ounces shrimp, finely chopped
1/4 cup minced onion
2 tablespoons margarine
1 medium tomato, chopped
1 cup soft bread crumbs
1/3 cup raisins
2 tablespoons capers
1/4 teaspoon salt
1/8 teaspoon pepper
1 egg, beaten

Yield: 30 servings

Reserve 1/3 of cheese slices; chop. Line bottom and side of 1-quart round baking dish with remaining cheese slices. Sauté shrimp and onion in margarine in skillet until shrimp turns pink. Stir in 1/2 cup of reserved cheese, tomato, bread crumbs, raisins, capers, salt, pepper and egg. Spoon into prepared dish. Sprinkle with remaining cheese. Bake at 350 degrees for 30 minutes. Let cool in dish for 15 minutes. Invert onto serving platter. Garnish with lemon slices and watercress. Cut into wedges.

Approx Per Serving: Cal 76; Prot 5 g; Carbo 3 g; Fiber <1 g; T Fat 5 g; 58% Calories from Fat; Chol 31 mg; Sod 187 mg.
Nutritional information does not include capers.

Karen C. Powers

Shrimp French Pizza

3 slices bacon, cut into
   halves
3 green onions, chopped
2 tablespoons chopped
   parsley
4 ounces sliced mushrooms
4 eggs
1/2 cup half and half
1 teaspoon seasoned salt
Pepper to taste
1 cup shredded Swiss cheese
4 ounces shrimp, cooked
Paprika to taste

Yield: 3 servings

Fry bacon in skillet until partially cooked, stirring constantly. Drain; reserving drippings. Sauté onions, parsley and mushrooms in reserved drippings in skillet until onions and mushrooms are tender, stirring frequently. Spoon into round shallow baking dish. Beat eggs, half and half, seasoned salt and pepper in mixer bowl until blended. Pour over sautéed mixture. Top with bacon, cheese and shrimp. Sprinkle with paprika. Bake at 350 degrees for 17 minutes or until set. May substitute Gruyère cheese for Swiss cheese.

Approx Per Serving: Cal 446; Prot 28 g; Carbo 7 g;
   Fiber 1 g; T Fat 34 g; 69% Calories from Fat;
   Chol 372 mg; Sod 845 mg.

Ellen Whitlock

My Best Pickled Shrimp

3 pounds shrimp, cooked,
   peeled
2 small onions, thinly sliced
3 bay leaves
2 tablespoons green
   peppercorns in vinegar
2 teaspoons salt
2 teaspoons dry mustard
1/2 cup oil
2 cloves of garlic, minced
6 tablespoons white wine
   vinegar
1/2 cup white wine

Yield: 50 servings

Layer shrimp, onions, bay leaves and peppercorns in glass container. Pour mixture of salt, dry mustard, oil, garlic, wine vinegar and wine over layers. Marinate, covered, in refrigerator overnight, turning occasionally; drain. May store leftovers in marinade in refrigerator for several days. May substitute 1 tablespoon whole black peppercorns for green peppercorns in vinegar.

Approx Per Serving: Cal 42; Prot 4 g; Carbo <1 g;
   Fiber <1 g; T Fat 2 g; 52% Calories from Fat;
   Chol 38 mg; Sod 129 mg.
   Nutritional information does not include green peppercorns in vinegar.

Nancy Watts-Bloom

Nicaraguan Ceviche

Juice of 3 limes
1/4 cup vinegar
1 tablespoon sugar
2 tablespoons chopped
   parsley
1 clove of garlic, minced
Chopped cilantro to taste
2 green bell peppers,
   chopped
2 stalks celery with tops,
   chopped
1 onion, chopped
2 pounds fresh grouper, cut
   into 1/2-inch pieces
Salt, pepper and sugar to
   taste
Tabasco sauce to taste

Yield: 32 servings

Combine lime juice, vinegar, 1 tablespoon sugar, parsley, garlic and cilantro in glass bowl; mix well. Add green peppers, celery and onion; mix well. Stir in grouper; press fish into liquid. Add just enough water to cover fish. Chill, covered, for 24 to 48 hours or until grouper is opaque. Season with salt, pepper, sugar and Tabasco sauce. Serve cold with club or butter crackers. May substitute snapper or cobia for grouper. Even though ceviche is not cooked conventionally, the acid "cooks" the fish. You will not believe this fish is cooked without heat!

Approx Per Serving: Cal 33; Prot 6 g; Carbo 1 g;
   Fiber <1 g; T Fat <1 g; 9% Calories from Fat;
   Chol 11 mg; Sod 15 mg.

Diane Hunt

Crab Swiss Bites

12 flaky refrigerator rolls
8 ounces crab meat
1 tablespoon chopped green
   onions
4 ounces Swiss cheese,
   shredded
1/2 cup mayonnaise
1 teaspoon lemon juice
1/4 teaspoon curry powder
1   8-ounce can water
   chestnuts, drained

Yield: 36 servings

Separate each roll into 3 layers. Place on ungreased baking sheet. Combine crab meat, green onions, cheese, mayonnaise, lemon juice and curry powder in bowl; mix well. Spread on each roll layer. Top each with water chestnut. Bake at 400 degrees for 10 to 12 minutes or until brown.

Approx Per Serving: Cal 70; Prot 3 g; Carbo 5 g;
   Fiber <1 g; T Fat 5 g; 57% Calories from Fat;
   Chol 11 mg; Sod 144 mg.

Beverly Troutman

Island Crab Puffs

1/4 cup finely chopped onion
12 ounces crab meat
2 eggs, beaten
1/2 cup dry bread crumbs
2 tablespoons parsley flakes
1 1/2 teaspoons dry mustard
1/4 teaspoon black pepper
1/4 teaspoon red pepper
Oil for frying

Yield: 48 servings

Combine onion, crab meat, eggs, bread crumbs, parsley flakes, dry mustard, black pepper and red pepper in bowl; mix well. Shape into 1-inch balls. Fry in oil in skillet for 1 minute or until brown on all sides; drain. Serve immediately or keep warm in 250-degree oven for 30 minutes.

Approx Per Serving: Cal 15; Prot 2 g; Carbo 1 g;
    Fiber <1 g; T Fat <1 g; 25% Calories from Fat;
    Chol 15 mg; Sod 31 mg.
    Nutritional information does not include oil for frying.

Ane Cates

Crab Rolls

20 slices white sandwich
    bread
8 ounces Velveeta cheese
1 cup butter
2   7-ounce cans flaked crab
    meat, drained
1 cup melted butter
1 cup sesame seeds

Yield: 60 servings

Trim crusts from bread; roll to flatten. Combine Velveeta cheese and 1 cup butter in double boiler. Cook over boiling water until blended, stirring frequently. Cool. Stir in crab meat. Cook until of spreading consistency, stirring constantly. Cool. Spread mixture on bread slices; roll to enclose filling. Dip rolls in 1 cup melted butter; roll in sesame seeds. Place seam side down in baking pan. Freeze, covered, until firm. Thaw slightly; cut into thirds. Place on baking sheet. Bake at 400 degrees until brown.

Approx Per Serving: Cal 107; Prot 3 g; Carbo 4 g;
    Fiber <1 g; T Fat 9 g; 74% Calories from Fat;
    Chol 26 mg; Sod 173 mg.

Jean Carson

Helen's Oysters Rockefeller

1 small onion
1 bunch green onions
1/2 bunch fresh parsley,
  stems removed
3 large lettuce leaves
1 stalk celery
1/2 package fresh spinach,
  rinsed, drained
1/2 cup margarine
Anise seeds to taste
Juice of 1 lemon
Tabasco sauce and Beau
  Monde seasoning to taste
Salt and pepper to taste
3/4 cup (or more) bread
  crumbs
3 1/2 dozen oysters on the
  half shell

Yield: 42 servings

Chop onion, green onions, parsley, lettuce, celery and spinach in food processor. Melt margarine in saucepan. Stir in chopped vegetables and anise seeds. Cook over low heat for 10 minutes or until onions are tender, stirring frequently. Stir in lemon juice, Tabasco sauce, Beau Monde seasoning, salt and pepper. Cook for 2 minutes, stirring constantly. Remove from heat. Stir in bread crumbs. Line bottom of baking pan with rock salt. Place oysters on shell with oyster liquid over salt. Bake at 375 degrees until oyster edges begin to curl; drain liquid. Spoon prepared sauce over oysters. Broil just until brown. Serve immediately. May substitute 2 baby food jars of spinach for fresh spinach.

Approx Per Serving: Cal 39; Prot 1 g; Carbo 3 g;
  Fiber <1 g; T Fat 3 g; 60% Calories from Fat;
  Chol 7 mg; Sod 75 mg.

Helen Townsend Spohrer

Artichoke-Cheese Appetizer

2 16-ounce cans artichoke
  hearts, drained, finely
  chopped
2 cups grated Parmesan
  cheese
2 cups mayonnaise
Garlic powder to taste

Yield: 30 servings

Combine chopped artichoke hearts, Parmesan cheese, mayonnaise and garlic powder in bowl; mix well. Spoon into baking dish. Bake at 350 degrees for 30 minutes. Serve with rye toast or assorted party crackers.

Approx Per Serving: Cal 144; Prot 3 g; Carbo 2 g;
  Fiber 0 g; T Fat 14 g; 84% Calories from Fat;
  Chol 14 mg; Sod 306 mg.

Molly Kirkland

Artichoke Spread

1/2 cup California Chenin
    Blanc
1 cup mayonnaise
1 cup grated Parmesan
    cheese
1/2 cup plain bread crumbs
1/4 teaspoon white pepper
1/4 teaspoon oregano
1   9-ounce can artichoke
    hearts or bottoms,
    drained, finely chopped
1 cup shredded Cheddar
    cheese

Yield: 8 servings

Add Chenin Blanc to mayonnaise in bowl, stirring until blended. Stir in Parmesan cheese, bread crumbs, white pepper, oregano and chopped artichokes. Spoon into ungreased 1-quart baking dish. Sprinkle with Cheddar cheese. Bake at 350 degrees for 25 to 30 minutes or until bubbly. Broil until cheese is brown. Serve hot with party bread, crackers or raw vegetables. May spoon into mushroom caps.

Approx Per Serving: Cal 354; Prot 10 g; Carbo 8 g;
    Fiber <1 g; T Fat 31 g; 77% Calories from Fat;
    Chol 41 mg; Sod 636 mg.

Patty Durham

Banana Dip

8 ounces cream cheese,
    softened
1   13-ounce jar
    marshmallow creme
10 bananas, sliced

Yield: 40 servings

Beat cream cheese and marshmallow creme in mixer bowl until smooth. Spoon into serving bowl. Serve with sliced bananas.

Approx Per Serving: Cal 75; Prot 1 g; Carbo 14 g;
    Fiber 1 g; T Fat 2 g; 24% Calories from Fat;
    Chol 6 mg; Sod 24 mg.

Sweet Mary

St. George Island State Park

Nine miles of undeveloped beaches and dunes, surrounded by the Gulf of Mexico and Apalachicola Bay, provide the perfect setting for this beautiful state park. Occupying 1,962 acres at the end of the Island, the park is a combination of sandy coves, shady pines and oak forests. The park also includes extensive beaches, dunes, forests of slash pines and live oak hammocks. Wildlife is abundant and you frequently may see osprey, raccoons, ghost crabs, salt-marsh snakes and diamondback terrapins. With the presence of such birds as the snowy plover, least tern, black skimmer, willet and many other species, bird watching is a favorite pastime.

Baked Cheese Dip

1 cup shredded sharp
   Cheddar cheese
3/4 cup mayonnaise
1/2 teaspoon grated onion
   with juice
1/2 teaspoon prepared
   mustard
Worcestershire sauce to
   taste
MSG to taste
1/2 teaspoon chopped parsley
1 egg white, stiffly beaten

Yield: 32 servings

Combine cheese, mayonnaise, onion, mustard, Worcestershire sauce, MSG and parsley in bowl; mix well. Fold in beaten egg white. Spoon into soufflé dish. Place in pan of water. Bake at 350 degrees for 30 minutes or until set.

Approx Per Serving: Cal 52; Prot 1 g; Carbo <1 g; Fiber <1 g; T Fat 5 g; 90% Calories from Fat; Chol 7 mg; Sod 54 mg.

Kathy Gilbert

Emergency Pâté

1 1/4 pounds braunschweiger
1/2 cup butter, softened
1/4 cup finely chopped onion
2 tablespoons minced chives
3 tablespoons brandy

Yield: 20 servings

Beat braunschweiger and butter in mixer bowl until blended. Add onion, chives and brandy; mix well. Spoon into mold. Chill until set. Invert onto serving platter. Garnish with olives and sliced tomatoes.

Approx Per Serving: Cal 94; Prot 2 g; Carbo 1 g; Fiber <1 g; T Fat 9 g; 84% Calories from Fat; Chol 33 mg; Sod 199 mg.

Chris Healy

Mexican Layer Dip

8 ounces cream cheese, sliced
1 4-ounce can green
   chilies, drained
2 16-ounce cans refried
   beans
16 ounces Cheddar cheese,
   sliced
2 8-ounce jars salsa

Yield: 50 servings

Layer cream cheese, green chilies, refried beans, half the Cheddar cheese, salsa and remaining Cheddar cheese in order listed in baking pan. Bake at 350 degrees until cheese melts. Serve with tortilla chips.

Approx Per Serving: Cal 75; Prot 4 g; Carbo 4 g; Fiber 1 g; T Fat 5 g; 58% Calories from Fat; Chol 15 mg; Sod 209 mg.

JoEllen Ward

Salsa Supreme

3 large tomatoes, finely
   chopped
1 large onion, finely
   chopped
6 tablespoons chopped
   fresh cilantro
Juice of 2 limes
3 cloves of garlic, crushed
2 teaspoons oil
1 teaspoon salt
1/2 teaspoon pepper
1 to 2 tablespoons chopped
   jalapeño peppers
2 teaspoons sugar

Yield: 12 servings

Combine tomatoes, onion, cilantro, lime juice, garlic, oil, salt, pepper, jalapeño peppers and sugar in bowl; mix well. Spoon 1/2 of the undrained tomato mixture into blender container. Process on high until tomatoes and onion are 1/3 original size. Combine with remaining tomato mixture; mix well. Chill, covered, in refrigerator for 2 to 4 hours. May substitute 1 teaspoon minced garlic for garlic cloves.

Approx Per Serving: Cal 27; Prot 1 g; Carbo 5 g; Fiber 1 g; T Fat 1 g; 29% Calories from Fat; Chol 0 mg; Sod 203 mg.

Helen Solomon

Marilyn's Vidalia Onion Dip

2 cups chopped Vidalia
  onions
2 cups shredded Swiss
  cheese
2 cups mayonnaise

Yield: 50 servings

Combine onions, cheese and mayonnaise in bowl; mix well. Spoon into shallow baking dish. Bake at 325 degrees for 20 minutes. Serve with assorted crackers.

Approx Per Serving: Cal 82; Prot 1 g; Carbo 1 g; Fiber <1 g; T Fat 8 g; 89% Calories from Fat; Chol 9 mg; Sod 62 mg.

Marilyn Bean

Reuben Ball

1 round loaf rye bread
1 12-ounce can corned
  beef, shredded
1 small onion, finely
  chopped
1 16-ounce can sauerkraut
1/2 cup shredded Swiss
  cheese
2 to 4 tablespoons sour
  cream

Yield: 15 servings

Scoop out center of bread loaf to form shell; cut center into pieces. Combine corned beef, onion, sauerkraut and cheese in bowl; mix well. Stir in just enough sour cream to make of spreading consistency. Spoon mixture into bread shell. Serve with bread pieces. May substitute pumpernickel bread for rye bread.

Approx Per Serving: Cal 164; Prot 10 g; Carbo 17 g; Fiber 3 g; T Fat 6 g; 34% Calories from Fat; Chol 24 mg; Sod 639 mg.

Beatrice Ritchey

Spinach Dip

1 10-ounce package frozen
  chopped spinach, thawed
1/2 cup mayonnaise
1 1/2 cups sour cream
1 envelope vegetable soup
  mix
3 green onions, chopped

Yield: 40 servings

Squeeze moisture from spinach. Mix spinach with mayonnaise, sour cream, soup mix and green onions in bowl. Serve with raw vegetables or assorted crackers.

Approx Per Serving: Cal 42; Prot 1 g; Carbo 1 g; Fiber <1 g; T Fat 4 g; 85% Calories from Fat; Chol 5 mg; Sod 57 mg.

Teresa Lobenburg

Hot Crab Meat Dip

8 ounces cream cheese, softened
6 ounces fresh crab meat
1 tablespoon Worcestershire sauce
Tabasco sauce to taste
1/4 cup finely chopped onion
1 tablespoon lemon juice
1 tablespoon crumbled bleu cheese
1/4 cup sherry

Yield: 12 servings

Combine cream cheese, crab meat, Worcestershire sauce, Tabasco sauce, onion, lemon juice, bleu cheese and sherry in bowl; mix well. Spoon into baking dish. Bake at 350 degrees for 30 minutes. May substitute canned crab meat for fresh.

Approx Per Serving: Cal 86; Prot 4 g; Carbo 1 g; Fiber <1 g; T Fat 7 g; 73% Calories from Fat; Chol 33 mg; Sod 112 mg.

Joan and John Ackerly

Favorite Hot Crab Dip

1/4 cup butter
1/4 cup flour
1 1/2 cups milk
8 ounces cream cheese, softened
1/2 teaspoon salt
2 tablespoons mayonnaise
1/2 teaspoon parsley flakes
16 ounces crab meat
1 tablespoon Worcestershire sauce
1/2 teaspoon Tabasco sauce
1/4 teaspoon pepper
1/2 teaspoon dry mustard
1 tablespoon lemon juice

Yield: 24 servings

Melt butter in saucepan. Stir in flour and milk. Cook until thickened, stirring constantly. Add cream cheese; mix well. Add salt, mayonnaise, parsley flakes, crab meat, Worcestershire sauce, Tabasco sauce, pepper, dry mustard and lemon juice; mix well. Cook over low heat until blended, stirring constantly. Spoon into chafing dish. Serve with toast points or sesame crackers. May substitute margarine for butter and half and half for milk.

Approx Per Serving: Cal 92; Prot 5 g; Carbo 2 g; Fiber <1 g; T Fat 7 g; 68% Calories from Fat; Chol 37 mg; Sod 166 mg.

Josie Davis

The Quilting Group

Every Tuesday morning ladies from the Island gather at the Civic Club to quilt. They are not quilting just any quilt, but THE Seafood Festival Quilt. This stunning work of art is raffled off each year on the first weekend in November at the Florida Seafood Festival held in Apalachicola. Proceeds from the raffle benefit the St. George Island Volunteer Fire Department and First Responder Unit and the raffle has raised thousands of dollars. The one of a kind quilts, lovingly stitched by the quilting group, are designed by a local artist and depict something concerning the Island. Each year everyone says the quilts can't get any better, but somehow they do!

Hot Curried Crab Dip

8 ounces king crab meat
8 ounces cream cheese with
    chives, softened
1 tablespoon mayonnaise
1/2 onion, grated
1 tablespoon horseradish
2 tablespoons milk
1 tablespoon
    Worcestershire sauce
1/2 teaspoon curry powder
Salt and pepper to taste

Yield: 16 servings

Combine crab meat, cream cheese, mayonnaise, onion, horseradish, milk, Worcestershire sauce, curry powder, salt and pepper in double boiler. Cook over boiling water until heated through, stirring constantly. Spoon into chafing dish. Serve with assorted chips.

Approx Per Serving: Cal 74; Prot 4 g; Carbo 1 g; Fiber <1 g; T Fat 6 g; 72% Calories from Fat; Chol 31 mg; Sod 99 mg.

Claire Dews

Betty's Crab Meat Dip

16 ounces cream cheese,
    softened
3 tablespoons sour cream
2 tablespoons grated onion
2 tablespoons horseradish
16 ounces crab meat
Salt and pepper to taste
Tabasco sauce to taste
1 cup sliced almonds, toasted
2 tablespoons sherry

Yield: 32 servings

Combine all ingredients in bowl; mix well. Spoon into baking dish. Bake at 350 degrees until bubbly. Spoon into chafing dish. Serve with assorted crackers.

Approx Per Serving: Cal 85; Prot 5 g; Carbo 1 g; Fiber <1 g; T Fat 7 g; 73% Calories from Fat; Chol 30 mg; Sod 83 mg.

Alec and Jane Hinson

St. George Island's First Inhabitants

The Apalachicola River is the largest river in Florida and the 21st largest river in the United States. With its rich resources and opportunity for expanded travel, it is no wonder it played a key part in the lives of Native Americans. Bay crossings were made in dugout canoes. A campsite midden located near what is now the Bob Sike's Cut area on St. George Island has been pillaged over the years due to exposure by wave action and, more recently, development. Fortunately, amateur archaeologists have saved some of the artifacts by beachcombing after high tides and storms. Many fine examples of Indian pottery are found in private collections.

Hot Crab Dip

8 ounces cream cheese,
  softened
1 teaspoon finely chopped
  onion
1 teaspoon Worcestershire
  sauce
1 tablespoon milk
1 6-ounce can white crab
  meat, drained
2 tablespoons slivered
  almonds

Yield: 16 servings

Beat first 4 ingredients in bowl until blended. Stir in crab meat. Spoon into small baking dish; sprinkle with almonds. Bake at 350 degrees for 15 to 20 minutes or until bubbly. Serve with assorted crackers.

Approx Per Serving: Cal 67; Prot 4 g; Carbo 1 g; Fiber <1 g; T Fat 6 g; 75% Calories from Fat; Chol 25 mg; Sod 81 mg.

Linda Russell

Crab Meat and Cheese Spread

8 ounces cream cheese,
  softened
1 teaspoon sour cream
2 tablespoons grated onion
1 cup cocktail sauce
1 6-ounce can crab meat,
  drained, shredded
Fresh chopped parsley to
  taste

Yield: 16 servings

Mix first 3 ingredients in bowl. Spread in baking dish. Spread 1/2 cup cocktail sauce over layer. Spoon crab meat over sauce. Top with 1/2 cup cocktail sauce; sprinkle with parsley. Serve with melba toast rounds.

Approx Per Serving: Cal 81; Prot 4 g; Carbo 5 g; Fiber <1 g; T Fat 5 g; 58% Calories from Fat; Chol 25 mg; Sod 203 mg.

Louise Dickerson

Smoked Mullet Spread

5 smoked mullet, deboned,
  flaked
1 envelope Italian salad
  dressing mix
Buttermilk

Yield: 16 servings

Combine flaked mullet and dressing mix in bowl. Stir in buttermilk until of desired consistency. Serve with assorted crackers.

Nutritional information for this recipe is not available.

Alice D. Collins

Smoked Oyster Dip

16 ounces cream cheese,
  softened
1 teaspoon Worcestershire
  sauce
2 teaspoons lemon juice
1 cup sour cream
1   3-ounce can smoked
  oysters

Yield: 12 servings

Combine cream cheese, Worcestershire sauce, lemon juice and sour cream in bowl; mix well. Stir in undrained oysters. Serve with corn chips.

Approx Per Serving: Cal 186; Prot 4 g; Carbo 2 g;
    Fiber <1 g; T Fat 18 g; 86% Calories from Fat;
    Chol 53 mg; Sod 149 mg.

Alice D. Collins

Smoky Salmon-Cheese Spread

1   7-ounce can red salmon
8 ounces cream cheese,
  softened
2 tablespoons finely
  chopped onion
1/2 teaspoon liquid smoke
Fresh chopped parsley

Yield: 16 servings

Drain salmon, reserving 2 teaspoons liquid; flake. Combine salmon, reserved liquid, cream cheese, onion and liquid smoke in bowl; mix well. Chill, covered, until firm. Shape into a log; roll in chopped parsley. Serve with assorted crackers. May roll log in chopped pimento instead of parsley. May substitute fresh salmon for canned salmon.

Approx Per Serving: Cal 69; Prot 4 g; Carbo <1 g;
    Fiber <1 g; T Fat 6 g; 76% Calories from Fat;
    Chol 21 mg; Sod 109 mg.

Mary Rodgers

Salmon Spread

2 cups canned red salmon,
   drained
1/3 cup mayonnaise
1/4 cup finely chopped onion
1 envelope onion and bacon
   dip mix
2 tablespoons dry sherry
2 tablespoons finely
   chopped parsley
1 teaspoon Dijon mustard
2 cloves of garlic, crushed
1/4 teaspoon soy sauce
1/4 teaspoon lime juice
Salt and pepper to taste

Yield: 48 servings

Combine salmon, mayonnaise, onion, dip mix, sherry, parsley, Dijon mustard, garlic, soy sauce, lime juice, salt and pepper in bowl; mix well. Chill, covered, in refrigerator. Spread on rye bread; cut into finger sandwiches.

Approx Per Serving: Cal 22; Prot 1 g; Carbo <1 g;
   Fiber <1 g; T Fat 2 g; 69% Calories from Fat;
   Chol 4 mg; Sod 60 mg.

Claire Dews

Cream Cheese-Shrimp Dip

1/4 cup milk
8 ounces cream cheese,
   softened
1/2 cup mayonnaise
1/4 cup chopped green
   onions with tops
2 teaspoons horseradish
1/8 teaspoon red pepper sauce
Worcestershire sauce to taste
1   4-ounce can popcorn
   shrimp, drained

Yield: 40 servings

Stir milk 1 tablespoon at a time into cream cheese in bowl until smooth. Add mayonnaise, green onions, horseradish, red pepper sauce and Worcestershire sauce; mix well. Stir in shrimp. Chill, covered, for 1 hour. may substitute mayonnaise-type salad dressing for mayonnaise.

Approx Per Serving: Cal 44; Prot 1 g; Carbo <1 g;
   Fiber <1 g; T Fat 4 g; 86% Calories from Fat;
   Chol 13 mg; Sod 38 mg.

Barbara Travis

Margaret Ann's Shrimp Dip

8 ounces cream cheese,
  softened
1/2 onion, finely chopped
1 12-ounce bottle of chili
  sauce
Lemon juice to taste
Horseradish to taste
8 ounces popcorn shrimp,
  cooked, drained

Yield: 10 servings

Combine cream cheese and onion in bowl; mix well.
Spread mixture over bottom of round dish. Spread with
mixture of chili sauce, lemon juice and horseradish.
Top with shrimp. Serve with butter crackers.

Approx Per Serving: Cal 135; Prot 6 g; Carbo 10 g;
    Fiber 1 g; T Fat 8 g; 54% Calories from Fat;
    Chol 60 mg; Sod 563 mg.

Jean Carson

Shrimp Dip

16 ounces cream cheese,
  softened
10 green onions, chopped
3 tablespoons mayonnaise
1 tablespoon
  Worcestershire sauce
1 tablespoon lemon juice
2 pounds shrimp, cooked,
  chopped

Yield: 32 servings

Combine cream cheese, green onions, mayonnaise,
Worcestershire sauce and lemon juice in bowl; mix
well. Stir in shrimp. Serve with crackers.

Approx Per Serving: Cal 83; Prot 6 g; Carbo 1 g;
    Fiber <1 g; T Fat 6 g; 68% Calories from Fat;
    Chol 61 mg; Sod 106 mg.

Jim and Rhonda Lambert

Curried Tuna Spread

1 6-ounce can tuna, drained
1/2 cup mayonnaise
1/2 teaspoon onion salt
1/2 teaspoon curry powder

Yield: 12 servings

Combine tuna, mayonnaise, onion salt and curry powder in bowl; mix well. Spread on assorted crackers; top with sliced olives.

Approx Per Serving: Cal 83; Prot 4 g; Carbo <1 g; Fiber 0 g; T Fat 7 g; 81% Calories from Fat; Chol 10 mg; Sod 166 mg.

Cass Stark

Vegetable Sandwich Spread

3 small carrots, grated
1 small onion, chopped
1 small cucumber, chopped
8 ounces cream cheese, softened
3 tablespoons mayonnaise
1/2 teaspoon salt
Red pepper to taste

Yield: 16 servings

Drain carrots, onion and cucumber for 1 hour. Combine vegetables with cream cheese, mayonnaise, salt and red pepper in bowl; mix well. Chill, covered, in refrigerator. Spread on your favorite sandwich bread.

Approx Per Serving: Cal 76; Prot 1 g; Carbo 2 g; Fiber 1 g; T Fat 7 g; 82% Calories from Fat; Chol 17 mg; Sod 127 mg.

Judi Little

Kahlua

3 cups sugar
3 cups water
10 tablespoons Yuban
   instant coffee granules
1 tablespoon vanilla extract
1 quart vodka

Yield: 9 servings

Combine sugar, water and coffee granules in saucepan; mix well. Simmer for 1 hour, stirring occasionally. Stir in vanilla and vodka. Cool.

Approx Per Serving: Cal 502; Prot <1 g; Carbo 69 g;
   Fiber 0 g; T Fat <1 g; <1% Calories from Fat;
   Chol 0 mg; Sod 3 mg.

Jane M. Burke

Homemade Irish Cream

1 tablespoon instant coffee
   granules
2 tablespoons boiling water
1   14-ounce can sweetened
   condensed milk
2 cups half and half
1 teaspoon vanilla extract
1 cup whiskey

Yield: 5 servings

Dissolve coffee in boiling water in small bowl; mix well. Combine coffee, condensed milk, half and half, vanilla and whiskey in blender container. Process until combined. May substitute nondairy liquid creamer for half and half.

Approx Per Serving: Cal 486; Prot 9 g; Carbo 48 g;
   Fiber 0 g; T Fat 18 g; 33% Calories from Fat;
   Chol 62 mg; Sod 141 mg.

Patty Valentine

Soups
and Salads

Shore Birds of St. George Island
by Linda Holzhausen

Birds of St. George Island

The St. George Island area boasts an incredible bird species inventory. There are 315 different species that can be found here. This total is a very high species count for such a relatively small area but may be explained by the natural elements of the Apalachicola system. Habitats within the area include cypress swamplands and deciduous and coniferous forests of the Apalachicola River floodplain. Delicate brackish marshes which are the basis for the estuarine system, extensive dunes, beaches and savannahs are found in the barrier island system. All of these habitats support an amazing variety of plant communities (1,162 species around the bay) and are thus capable of supporting large animal populations. Indeed, an even 100 species of birds nest in our area. The least terns and black skimmers that nest on the causeway to St. George typically represent the largest nesting colony of both species in Florida. The major threat to their survival is speeding cars, which take a great toll each year.

The remaining 215 bird species are what make up the bulk of our bird diversity. The Apalachicola River estuary lies on the eastern fringe of the Mississippi migratory flyway and thus receives large numbers of birds from both the Midwest and the Atlantic Seaboard which use the Gulf of Mexico and peninsular Florida in migration. The barrier islands and the Apalachicola River form a very unique system that creates landmarks to bird migration. Both in spring and fall, the barrier islands serve as vital nesting areas for birds flying across the Gulf states. Birding on St. George is exceptional, particularly in the spring. We are first landfall for the trans-gulf migrants. They are more tired and hungry than fearful of man. Spring bird counts of 150 species a day are possible. The first waves as early as February are typically warblers. These are soon followed by tanagers, buntings, grossbeaks and hummingbirds.

The Apalachicola Bay's strategic location between two major migratory flyways at the mouth of a major river system with a large barrier island system and the diversity of habitats make possible a dynamic bird haven during all times of the year.

Black Bean Soup

2 slices bacon, crisp-fried,
    crumbled
1 onion, chopped
1 carrot, finely chopped
1 rib celery, finely chopped
1   16-ounce package black
    beans
1 bay leaf
1 teaspoon thyme
1½ tablespoons cumin
½ teaspoon oregano
½ teaspoon parsley
¼ teaspoon cayenne pepper
¼ teaspoon garlic powder
Salt and black pepper to
    taste
10 cups chicken broth
2 ham hocks
1½ tablespoons cumin
¼ cup lime juice

Yield: 12 servings

Combine bacon, onion, carrot and celery in large saucepan. Sauté for 5 minutes or until onion is translucent. Add beans, bay leaf, thyme, 1½ tablespoons cumin, oregano, parsley, cayenne pepper, garlic powder, salt and black pepper. Cook for 5 minutes. Add chicken broth and ham hocks. Bring to a boil. Simmer for 2½ hours. Remove ham hocks; scrape meat from bone. Add meat to saucepan. Stir in remaining 1½ tablespoons cumin and lime juice. Remove bay leaf. Ladle into soup bowls. May add a small amount of sherry at serving time. May garnish with dollop of sour cream and chopped chives.

Approx Per Serving: Cal 208; Prot 16 g; Carbo 26 g;
    Fiber 9 g; T Fat 4 g; 19% Calories from Fat;
    Chol 8 mg; Sod 814 mg.

Bobbie Felice

Woody's Favorite Black Bean Soup

1   16-ounce package black
    beans
1 onion, cut into quarters
3 pounds hot sausage, cut
    into bite-sized pieces
½ cup olive oil
3 or 4 tablespoons minced
    garlic
3 onions, coarsely chopped
1 green bell pepper,
    coarsely chopped
3 tablespoons sugar
Hot sauce to taste
Pepper sauce to taste

Yield: 8 servings

Sort and rinse beans. Soak beans in cold water to cover in large stockpot overnight; do not drain. Add onion quarters. Bring to a boil. Simmer over low heat for 6 hours. Add sausage, olive oil, garlic, remaining onions and green pepper. Simmer over medium heat for 1 hour or until sausage is done. Stir in sugar, hot sauce and pepper sauce. Serve over yellow rice in soup bowl. Garnish with finely chopped onion.

Approx Per Serving: Cal 657; Prot 30 g; Carbo 48 g;
    Fiber 14 g; T Fat 39 g; 53% Calories from Fat;
    Chol 66 mg; Sod 1043 mg.

Marion Miley

Gazpacho

1/2 cup olive oil
4 teaspoons lemon juice
6 cups V-8 juice
2 cups beef broth
1/2 cup grated onion
2 tomatoes, peeled, chopped
2 cups chopped green bell
    peppers
2 cucumbers, chopped
2 cups chopped celery
Tabasco sauce to taste
Salt and pepper to taste

Yield: 4 servings

Mix olive oil and lemon juice in bowl. Add V-8 juice, broth, onion, tomatoes, green peppers, cucumbers and celery; mix well. Stir in Tabasco sauce, salt and pepper. Chill for 4 hours or longer. Ladle into soup bowls. Garnish with croutons.

Approx Per Serving: Cal 380; Prot 6 g; Carbo 31 g;
    Fiber 7 g; T Fat 28 g; 63% Calories from Fat;
    Chol 0 mg; Sod 1778 mg.

Mary Lou Short

Lentil Soup

2 cups dried lentils
8 cups vegetable stock or
    water
1/2 onion, chopped
1 small carrot, chopped
1 stalk celery, chopped
1 small potato, chopped
2 tablespoons oil
2 bay leaves
1 1/2 teaspoons salt
2 teaspoons vinegar or
    lemon juice

Yield: 8 servings

Rinse and sort lentils. Combine lentils, vegetable stock, onion, carrot, celery, potato, oil, bay leaves and salt in large saucepan. Cook for 1 hour or until lentils are tender. Stir in vinegar. Remove bay leaves. Ladle into soup bowls.

Approx Per Serving: Cal 229; Prot 14 g; Carbo 34 g;
    Fiber 6 g; T Fat 5 g; 19% Calories from Fat;
    Chol 0 mg; Sod 1427 mg.

Cass Stark

Minestrone

3 slices bacon, chopped
1 cup chopped onion
2 large cloves of garlic,
 minced
1/2 cup chopped celery
1 14-ounce can beef broth
1 10-ounce can bean and
 bacon soup
1 teaspoon dried basil
1 1/2 soup cans water
1 16-ounce can stewed
 tomatoes
1/4 to 1/2 cup uncooked
 ditalini noodles
1/2 teaspoon salt
1 cup shredded cabbage
1 cup chopped zucchini

Yield: 8 servings

Brown bacon in large saucepan. Add onion, garlic and celery. Cook until vegetables are tender. Stir in broth, soup, basil, water, tomatoes, noodles and salt. Bring to a boil. Reduce heat. Simmer, covered, for 15 minutes. Add cabbage and zucchini. Cook for 10 minutes or until zucchini is tender-crisp, stirring occasionally. Ladle into soup bowls. Serve with Italian garlic bread or corn bread. This minestrone may be stored in refrigerator or freezer before adding cabbage and zucchini. I like to make it the day before serving.

Approx Per Serving: Cal 116; Prot 6 g; Carbo 17 g;
 Fiber 4 g; T Fat 3 g; 25% Calories from Fat;
 Chol 3 mg; Sod 977 mg.

Irene LaSlavic

French Onion Soup

1 pound onions, thinly
 sliced
2 tablespoons butter
2 cups beef broth
2 cups chicken broth
1 ounce sherry
1 cup toasted Italian bread
 croutons
3 ounces Gruyère or Swiss
 cheese, shredded

Yield: 4 servings

Brown onions in butter in large saucepan. Stir in beef broth and chicken broth. Simmer for 45 minutes, skimming top occasionally. Stir in sherry. Simmer for 10 minutes longer. Spoon into 4 ovenproof cups or bowls. Top with croutons and cheese. Broil until cheese is melted and golden brown.

Approx Per Serving: Cal 249; Prot 12 g; Carbo 15 g;
 Fiber 2 g; T Fat 15 g; 54% Calories from Fat;
 Chol 39 mg; Sod 1006 mg.

Sharon Bono

Split Pea and Potato Soup

1 pound dried split peas
2 1/2 quarts water
1 cup finely chopped carrots
1 cup finely chopped celery
1 cup finely chopped onions
2 tablespoons tomato paste
3/4 teaspoon garlic powder
1/2 teaspoon marjoram
1 bay leaf
2 potatoes, peeled, cut into
  1/2-inch pieces
Salt and pepper to taste

Yield: 8 servings

Sort and rinse peas. Combine peas and water in 6-quart stockpot. Bring to a boil slowly, skimming foam from top. Add carrots, celery, onions, tomato paste, garlic powder, marjoram and bay leaf. Simmer, partially covered, for 45 minutes. Add potatoes. Simmer for 30 to 40 minutes or until potatoes are tender. Remove bay leaf. Add salt and pepper. May purèe a small amount of peas and return to soup to thicken. Ladle into soup bowls. Garnish with fresh parsley, dill or basil.

Approx Per Serving: Cal 239; Prot 15 g; Carbo 45 g; Fiber 10 g; T Fat 1 g; 3% Calories from Fat; Chol 0 mg; Sod 59 mg.

Nancy Watts-Bloom

Bahamian Fish Chowder

1 pound mackerel
2 cups fish stock
1/2 pound salt pork or 6
  slices bacon, cut into
  1/2-inch pieces
1 large yellow onion,
  chopped
1 green bell pepper, chopped
3 ribs celery, chopped
1 teaspoon dried thyme
4 cups canned tomatoes
1   6-ounce can tomato paste
4 potatoes, peeled, chopped
1/4 cup Worcestershire sauce
3/4 cup lime juice

Yield: 4 servings

Poach mackerel in fish stock in deep saucepan. Debone cooled mackerel; cut into 2-inch pieces. Reserve poaching liquid. Sauté pork in same saucepan. Add onion, green pepper and celery. Sauté until tender and browned. Add thyme, tomatoes, tomato paste, potatoes and reserved liquid. Reduce heat. Simmer for 1 hour or until potatoes are tender. Add mackerel. Stir in Worcestershire sauce and lime juice. Adjust seasonings to taste. May add 1 teaspoon honey or sugar if seasonings are too strong. May substitute 2 pounds flounder for 1 pound mackerel. May add 1/4 cup brandy or sherry if desired.

Approx Per Serving: Cal 548; Prot 34 g; Carbo 55 g; Fiber 8 g; T Fat 23 g; 37% Calories from Fat; Chol 76 mg; Sod 1542 mg.

Harry L. Tucker, M.D.

St. George Island Chowder

3 potatoes, peeled, chopped
3 cloves of garlic, minced
1 large onion, chopped
1 stalk celery, finely
  chopped
1/8 cup butter
1 tablespoon flour
1/2 cup finely chopped
  Kielbasa
1 14-ounce can chicken
  broth
25 oysters
1 1/2 quarts milk
2 cups whipping cream
1/2 cup minced parsley

Yield: 10 servings

Cook potatoes in water to cover in saucepan until tender; drain and set aside. Sauté garlic, onion and celery in butter in large saucepan. Mix in flour. Add Kielbasa and potatoes. Stir in broth. Cook until thickened, stirring frequently. Add oysters, milk, whipping cream and parsley. Simmer for 20 minutes. Ladle into soup bowls.

Approx Per Serving: Cal 371; Prot 12 g; Carbo 20 g;
    Fiber 1 g; T Fat 28 g; 66% Calories from Fat;
    Chol 113 mg; Sod 496 mg.

Bill Bell

Nicaraguan Crab Soup

4 quarts water
1 teaspoon salt
1 teaspoon sage
1/2 to 1 teaspoon red pepper
  flakes
24 blue crabs
1 large onion, chopped
4 or 5 potatoes, scrubbed,
  chopped
2 carrots, sliced
2 stalks celery, sliced
2 green bell peppers, chopped
4 large tomatoes, chopped
1 tablespoon minced garlic
6 tablespoons flour
1/4 cup catsup
2 cups sour cream
Hot sauce to taste
Salt and black pepper to
  taste

Yield: 15 servings

Bring water to a boil in large stockpot. Add salt, sage, red pepper and crabs. Boil until crabs are red. Remove crabs. Clean and pick cooled crabs. Return to stockpot. Add vegetables and garlic. Simmer until potatoes are tender. Mix flour with enough water to make smooth paste. Add flour mixture to soup 1 tablespoon at a time to thicken, mixing well after each addition. All the flour paste may not be needed. Stir in catsup and sour cream. Add remaining seasonings. Ladle into soup bowls. Serve with additional sour cream and hot sauce. This soup is served in restaurants in Central America with the whole crab floating in the soup. May substitute canned tomatoes for fresh tomatoes.

Approx Per Serving: Cal 220; Prot 19 g; Carbo 19 g;
    Fiber 2 g; T Fat 8 g; 33% Calories from Fat;
    Chol 90 mg; Sod 436 mg.

Diane Hunt

Cream of Crab Soup

1 tablespoon flour
2 tablespoons butter,
  softened
2 quarts milk
1/2 onion, chopped
1/2 cup chopped parsley
1/2 teaspoon celery salt
1 teaspoon onion salt
1 teaspoon white pepper
2 cups crab meat
1 cup whipping cream,
  whipped

Yield: 8 servings

Cream flour and butter in mixer bowl until light and fluffy. Combine with milk in double boiler over hot water. Add onion, parsley, celery salt, onion salt and white pepper. Bring to a boil; reduce heat. Simmer until thickened, stirring constantly. Stir in crab meat. Simmer until flavors are blended. Spoon into soups bowls. Top with whipped cream.

Approx Per Serving: Cal 315; Prot 15 g; Carbo 14 g; Fiber <1 g; T Fat 23 g; 64% Calories from Fat; Chol 111 mg; Sod 537 mg.

Peggy Hamm

Cajun Shrimp Gumbo

1/3 cup oil
1/3 cup flour
2 cups chopped onions
1 cup chopped green bell
  pepper
1   10-ounce package frozen
  cut okra, thawed
1   8-ounce can tomato sauce
2 cups water
1   14-ounce can chicken broth
1 cup chopped fresh parsley
3 bay leaves
2 tablespoons
  Worcestershire sauce
1 tablespoon thyme
1 tablespoon Kitchen Bouquet
2 tablespoons each garlic
  salt, pepper and hot
  pepper sauce
2 pounds peeled shrimp
1 pound crab meat, flaked

Yield: 12 servings

Heat oil in large heavy pot. Add 1/2 of the flour, stirring constantly. Add remaining flour, stirring constantly. Cook until dark brown, stirring constantly. Add onions, green pepper and okra; mix well. Cook until vegetables are tender. Stir in tomato sauce, water and chicken broth. Simmer for 1 hour, stirring frequently. Add parsley, bay leaves, Worcestershire sauce, thyme, Kitchen Bouquet, garlic salt, pepper, hot pepper sauce, shrimp and crab meat. Simmer for 15 minutes, stirring occasionally. Discard bay leaves. Ladle over hot cooked rice in soup bowls.

Approx Per Serving: Cal 207; Prot 23 g; Carbo 10 g; Fiber 2 g; T Fat 8 g; 35% Calories from Fat; Chol 156 mg; Sod 1637 mg.
Nutritional information does not include Kitchen Bouquet.

John Henry and Nelle Spratt

Seafood and Okra Gumbo

1/4 cup bacon drippings
3 tablespoons flour
3 large onions
6 cloves of garlic
6 stalks celery
2 pounds okra
2 large green bell peppers
1   16-ounce can tomatoes
5 ounces Worcestershire
    sauce
1/4 teaspoon ground thyme
1 tablespoon ground oregano
1/4 cup Greek seasoning
2 tablespoons parsley flakes
Salt and pepper to taste
3 pounds small shrimp
2 quarts water
2 pounds boneless fish
8 ounces uncooked rice
1 pound crab meat, rinsed

Yield: 18 servings

Heat bacon drippings in large heavy stockpot. Add flour. Cook until lightly browned, stirring frequently. Chop onions, garlic, celery, okra and green peppers. Add to stockpot. Cook until vegetables are tender, stirring frequently. Add tomatoes, Worcestershire sauce, thyme, oregano, Greek seasoning, parsley, salt and pepper. Simmer for 30 minutes. Peel shrimp and cut into 1-inch pieces. Add water, shrimp and fish. Simmer for 1 hour. Stir in rice and crab meat. Simmer for 45 minutes. Garnish with green onion tops. This gumbo tastes even better the second day.

Approx Per Serving: Cal 272; Prot 29 g; Carbo 21 g;
    Fiber 3 g; T Fat 8 g; 25% Calories from Fat;
    Chol 165 mg; Sod 369 mg.
    Nutritional information does not include Greek seasoning.

David Fulmer

Seafood Gumbo

1/2 cup oil
1/2 cup flour
2 cups finely chopped
    onions
1 cup finely chopped celery
1 gallon water
4 cloves of garlic, minced
Salt and black pepper to
    taste
Red pepper to taste
2 pounds shrimp, peeled,
    deveined
1/2 teaspoon parsley flakes
8 ounces catfish fillets, cut
    into bite-sized pieces
1/2 pint raw oysters
Gumbo filé to taste

Yield: 6 servings

Heat oil in heavy stockpot. Stir in flour gradually. Cook until color of a copper penny, stirring constantly. Add onions and celery; mix well. Cook until onions are tender. Stir in water and garlic. Cook over medium heat for 1 hour, stirring frequently. Season with salt, black pepper and red pepper. Stir in shrimp, parsley and catfish. Cook for 10 to 15 minutes or until catfish and shrimp test done. Stir in oysters. Bring gumbo to a boil; remove from heat. Ladle over hot cooked rice in soup bowls; sprinkle with gumbo filé.

Approx Per Serving: Cal 422; Prot 36 g; Carbo 17 g;
    Fiber 2 g; T Fat 23 g; 49% Calories from Fat;
    Chol 268 mg; Sod 424 mg.

Marion Miley

Ollie's "Chili Cookoff" Seafood Gumbo

1½ cups water
6 large onions, peeled,
   chopped
1   12-ounce can tomato
   purée
1 gallon crushed tomatoes
1   12-ounce can tomato
   paste
12 green bell peppers,
   chopped
2 stalks celery with leaves,
   chopped
Salt and pepper to taste
1 gallon crushed tomatoes
6   14-ounce cans stewed
   tomatoes
10 pounds potatoes, peeled,
   coarsely chopped
12 packages gumbo mix
1 gallon crushed tomatoes
2   12-ounce cans tomato
   purée
10 pounds popcorn shrimp
16 pounds grouper, cut into
   1½-inch pieces
2 pounds crab meat, rinsed,
   picked
½ gallon oysters

Yield: 75 servings

Warm 4-gallon stockpot over low heat. Add water, onions, 1 can tomato purée, 1 gallon crushed tomatoes, tomato paste, bell peppers, celery, salt and pepper. Cook until onions and bell peppers are tender. Add 1 gallon crushed tomatoes. Simmer for 30 minutes. Add stewed tomatoes and potatoes. Simmer for 20 minutes or until potatoes are tender. Stir in gumbo mix. Add remaining can crushed tomatoes and 2 cans tomato purée. Simmer until liquid is somewhat reduced. Add shrimp. Simmer until shrimp is tender. Stir in grouper. Simmer until grouper is cooked through. Stir in crab meat and oysters. Simmer until cooked through. Ladle into soup bowls. May add 1 bottle of Louisiana hot sauce if desired.

Approx Per Serving: Cal 293; Prot 38 g; Carbo 27 g;
   Fiber 4 g; T Fat 3 g; 10% Calories from Fat;
   Chol 165 mg; Sod 598 mg.
   Nutritional information does not include
   gumbo mix.

Ollie Gunn

Apalachicola National Estuarine Sanctuary

Encompassing approximately 200,000 acres of mostly submerged lands, the Apalachicola National Estuarine Sanctuary is the largest United States estuarine sanctuary. Apalachicola Bay is characterized by a series of rivers, bayous, tidal creeks, salt marshes and barrier islands, including St. George Island. Each of these elements is essential to the integrity of the system which supports major fisheries for oysters, shrimp, blue crabs and finfish. This area serves as a spawning ground for over 100 species of fish and is vital to the life of the Gulf of Mexico.

Hartsfield's Cajun Seafood Gumbo

3 tablespoons margarine
1½ cups chopped onions
3 tablespoons flour
3 scallions, chopped
³/₈ cup chopped parsley
1   16-ounce can chopped
    tomatoes
³/₄ cup sliced carrots
¹/₂ cup chopped celery
1 clove of garlic, pressed
³/₄ cup chopped green bell
    pepper
2 tablespoons chopped
    jalapeño pepper
³/₄ pound okra, sliced
³/₄ teaspoon thyme
1½ bay leaves
¹/₃ teaspoon mace
3 cloves
7 cups water
³/₄ pound crab meat, rinsed,
    picked
¹/₄ pound fish
³/₄ pound shrimp, deveined
³/₈ cup chopped parsley
³/₄ pound shrimp, deveined
Lemon juice to taste
¹/₂ pint oysters, shucked
V-8 juice to taste
Salt and pepper to taste
Tabasco sauce to taste
10 cups cooked long grain
    rice

Yield: 10 servings

Melt margarine in large stockpot over high heat. Add onions. Sauté until translucent, stirring constantly with wooden spoon. Stir in flour. Cook until dark beige in color, stirring constantly. Add scallions, ³/₈ cup parsley, tomatoes, carrots, celery, pressed garlic, bell pepper and jalapeño pepper. Simmer for 10 minutes, stirring frequently. Add okra, thyme, bay leaves, mace, cloves, water, crab meat, fish and ³/₄ pound shrimp. Bring to a rolling boil; reduce heat. Simmer, covered, for 1 hour or until well blended, stirring frequently. Add remaining ³/₈ cup parsley and ³/₄ pound shrimp. Return to a boil. Stir in lemon juice until okra is neutralized. Add oysters. Stir in V-8 juice if needed to obtain desired consistency. Season with salt, pepper and Tabasco sauce. Remove bay leaves. Serve over rice in soup bowls.

Approx Per Serving: Cal 460; Prot 29 g; Carbo 69 g;
    Fiber 4 g; T Fat 7 g; 13% Calories from Fat;
    Chol 156 mg; Sod 411 mg.

Don and Barbara Hartsfield

Sand Dunes

Beaches and sand dunes confront tremendous energies from storm waves, tides and winds. They act as shock absorbers to protect the coastal environment. Dunes accumulate sand in normal conditions and release it to the beach during major storms. This sand reserve helps beaches resist wave energy and provides material to help rebuild the beaches after storms. Protected by Florida law, the most prolific and valuable dune vegetation is the sea oat.

Helen's Seafood Gumbo

1 cup shortening
1 cup flour
2 large onions, chopped
1 green bell pepper, chopped
4 stalks celery, chopped
3 cloves of garlic, minced
1 pound okra, sliced
1   8-ounce can tomato sauce
2 bay leaves
1 tablespoon liquid crab boil
1/3 cup parsley flakes
1 teaspoon each thyme, basil
1/2 teaspoon marjoram
Cayenne pepper and salt to
    taste
2 to 4 pounds shrimp, peeled
1 bunch green onions, sliced
1 pound crab meat
1 pint oysters
1/3 cup parsley flakes
Gumbo filé to taste

Yield: 16 servings

Melt shortening in black cast-iron skillet. Add flour gradually, stirring constantly. Cook over low heat for 20 to 25 minutes or until mixture is color of copper penny, stirring constantly. Combine roux with next 4 vegetables in stockpot; mix well. Simmer for 15 minutes or until vegetables are tender, stirring frequently. Stir in 3 to 4 quarts water slowly. Bring to a boil. Add okra, tomato sauce and next 8 seasonings. Cook over low heat for 1 hour. Add shrimp and green onions. Cook over medium-low heat for 15 minutes. Add crab meat, undrained oysters and parsley. Cook for 5 minutes. Discard bay leaves. Ladle over hot cooked rice in soup bowls. Sprinkle with gumbo filé. Serve with French bread and tossed green salad.

Approx Per Serving: Cal 312; Prot 28 g; Carbo 14 g;
    Fiber 2 g; T Fat 16 g; 45% Calories from Fat;
    Chol 213 mg; Sod 465 mg.

Helen Townsend Spohrer

Ann's Award-Winning Cajun Seafood Gumbo

1 to 2 pints oysters
1 to 2 pounds scallops
2/3 cup bacon drippings
1 cup flour
1 onion, finely chopped
1 clove of garlic, minced
1/4 cup chopped parsley
1/8 teaspoon cayenne pepper
1 cup chopped okra
2 tablespoons tomato paste
Salt and pepper to taste
1/2 cup chopped green onion
    tops
1 pound small shrimp,
    peeled, deveined
1 pint crab meat
8 cups cooked rice

Yield: 8 servings

Drain oysters and scallops, reserving stock. Combine stock with enough water to measure 9 cups. Combine bacon drippings and flour in 5-quart stockpot. Cook over medium heat for 20 to 25 minutes or until mixture is color of chocolate, stirring constantly. Add onion and garlic. Sauté for 2 to 3 minutes or until tender. Add fish stock mixture, parsley, cayenne pepper, okra, tomato paste, salt and pepper. Simmer for 30 minutes. Add green onion tops, shrimp and crab meat. Simmer for 15 minutes. Add scallops and oysters. Simmer for 15 minutes. Serve in soup bowls over cooked rice.

Approx Per Serving: Cal 746; Prot 44 g; Carbo 80 g;
    Fiber 3 g; T Fat 26 g; 32% Calories from Fat;
    Chol 209 mg; Sod 692 mg.

Wes Johnson and Ann Abbott

Oyster Bisque

1¹/2 pints oysters
2   8-ounce bottles of clam
    juice
1¹/2 cups dry white wine
2 stalks celery, sliced
2 medium onions, sliced
2 carrots, sliced
3 slices lemon
2 teaspoons parsley flakes
1 bay leaf
2 tablespoons finely
    chopped fresh parsley
2 teaspoons salt
¹/2 teaspoon whole
    peppercorns
¹/3 cup butter
¹/3 cup flour
2 eggs
3 cups light cream
¹/4 cup dry sherry
Cayenne pepper to taste
¹/4 teaspoon nutmeg
Chopped parsley to taste

Yield: 10 servings

Chop oysters, reserving liquid. Bring oysters, reserved liquid, clam juice, white wine, celery, onions, carrots, lemon slices, parsley flakes, bay leaf, fresh parsley, salt and peppercorns to a boil in large saucepan; reduce heat. Simmer for 45 minutes, stirring occasionally. Strain through a fine sieve or cheesecloth into large measuring cup. Add enough water to measure 5 cups. Melt butter in large saucepan. Stir in flour. Cook until blended, stirring constantly. Stir in oyster stock. Cook until thickened, stirring constantly. Beat eggs with ¹/2 cup cream in bowl until blended. Stir 1 cup hot oyster bisque into egg mixture; stir egg mixture into hot bisque. Add remaining cream; mix well. Cook just until heated through, stirring constantly. Discard bay leaf. Stir in sherry and cayenne pepper just before serving. Ladle into soup bowls. Sprinkle with nutmeg and chopped parsley.

Approx Per Serving: Cal 421; Prot 13 g; Carbo 14 g;
    Fiber 1 g; T Fat 32 g; 69% Calories from Fat;
    Chol 203 mg; Sod 893 mg.

Pamela Amato

Joyce's CoCo Fruit Salad

2 cups fresh strawberries
2 cups grapes
2 cups chopped honeydew
    melon or cantaloupe
2 cups seeded watermelon
2 cups chopped fresh
    pineapple, blueberries or
    raspberries
8 ounces cream of coconut
8 ounces cream cheese,
    softened
2 cups whipping cream

Yield: 12 servings

Layer fruit in order listed in clear glass bowl. Chill for several hours. Spoon into small bowls. Mix cream of coconut, cream cheese and whipping cream in bowl; beat well. Spoon over fruit.

Approx Per Serving: Cal 297; Prot 3 g; Carbo 16 g;
    Fiber 2 g; T Fat 26 g; 75% Calories from Fat;
    Chol 75 mg; Sod 78 mg.

Shirley Gelch

Fruit Salad

1   8-ounce can crushed
    pineapple
1   16-ounce can fruit
    cocktail, drained
1 cup sliced red seedless
    grapes
1 cup chopped pecans
1   4-ounce jar maraschino
    cherries, drained, sliced
1   4-ounce package vanilla
    instant pudding mix
2 or 3 bananas, sliced,
    sprinkled with Fruit Fresh

Yield: 8 servings

Drain pineapple, reserving juice. Combine fruit cock-tail, grapes, pecans and maraschino cherries in large bowl; mix well. Mix pudding mix and pineapple juice in small bowl. Pour over fruit in large bowl. Add bananas. Chill thoroughly.

Approx Per Serving: Cal 298; Prot 2 g; Carbo 54 g;
    Fiber 3 g; T Fat 11 g; 30% Calories from Fat;
    Chol 0 mg; Sod 209 mg.

Jim and Rhonda Lambert

Ferne's Frozen Fruit Salad

6 ounces cream cheese,
    softened
1 cup Queen Anne cherries,
    cut into halves
1   8-ounce can crushed
    pineapple
3 tablespoons mayonnaise
1 cup whipping cream,
    whipped
6 lettuce leaves
2 tablespoons mayonnaise

Yield: 6 servings

Whip cream cheese with fork. Add cherries, pineapple and 3 tablespoons mayonnaise. Fold in whipped cream. Freeze until firm. Cut into slices. Serve on lettuce leaves. Top with remaining mayonnaise.

Approx Per Serving: Cal 368; Prot 4 g; Carbo 14 g;
    Fiber 1 g; T Fat 34 g; 81% Calories from Fat;
    Chol 92 mg; Sod 166 mg.

Gladys Scudder

Wild Rice-Chicken Salad

2 6-ounce packages long
    grain wild rice
3 1/2 cups chopped cooked
    chicken
1 4-ounce jar green olives,
    drained, chopped
1/2 cup chopped green
    onions
1/2 cup chopped pecans
1 cup chopped celery
1 1/2 cups mayonnaise
Salt and pepper to taste

Yield: 10 servings

Cook rice using package directions; drain. Combine cooled rice and remaining ingredients in bowl; mix well. Chill in refrigerator thoroughly. Let stand for 20 minutes before serving.

Approx Per Serving: Cal 507; Prot 20 g; Carbo 29 g; Fiber 1 g; T Fat 36 g; 62% Calories from Fat; Chol 63 mg; Sod 516 mg.

Nick and Becky Eppes

Chicken Caesar Salad

1 tablespoon chopped fresh
    garlic
1/2 tablespoon pepper
1 8-ounce bottle of red
    wine oil and vinegar salad
    dressing
4 chicken breasts, boned,
    skinned
2 heads romaine lettuce,
    torn into bite-sized pieces
1 8-ounce bottle of Caesar
    salad dressing
2 cups seasoned croutons
1 cup grated Parmesan
    cheese

Yield: 8 servings

Mix garlic, pepper and oil and vinegar dressing in bowl. Pour over chicken breasts in shallow dish. Marinate in refrigerator overnight. Grill chicken over medium coals until done. Cool completely. Cut into 1/2-inch strips. Combine chicken, lettuce, Caesar salad dressing, croutons and Parmesan cheese in large bowl; toss to mix. Serve with toasted garlic bread or rolls.

Approx Per Serving: Cal 429; Prot 24 g; Carbo 9 g; Fiber 1 g; T Fat 34 g; 70% Calories from Fat; Chol 75 mg; Sod 840 mg.

Ane Cates

Black Bean and Turkey Salad

2 cups dried black beans
5 cups chicken broth
1 cup chopped red onion
1/4 cup chopped green
   onions
1 red bell pepper, chopped,
   blanched, drained
1 green bell pepper,
   chopped, blanched,
   drained
3 cups chopped roasted or
   smoked turkey breast
2 cups cooked corn kernels
1/2 cup red wine vinegar
1/4 cup Dijon mustard
2 teaspoons minced garlic
1 teaspoon crumbled dried
   thyme
2 tablespoons honey
1/4 teaspoon cayenne pepper
1/2 tablespoon salt
1 cup olive oil
1/4 cup chopped cilantro

Yield: 8 servings

Sort and rinse beans. Bring beans and 4 cups broth to a boil in saucepan. Simmer for 2 minutes. Remove from heat. Let stand, covered, for 1 hour. Bring to a second boil. Add remaining broth. Simmer for 1 1/2 hours or until tender, stirring occasionally; drain. Combine with onion, green onions, bell peppers, turkey and corn in large bowl; mix well. Combine vinegar, mustard, garlic, thyme, honey, cayenne pepper and salt in food processor container. Add olive oil in a stream, processing until emulsified. Pour over salad. Stir in cilantro. Toss well; drain. Serve chilled on lettuce-lined platter. Surround with tomato wedges.

Approx Per Serving: Cal 582; Prot 32 g; Carbo 48 g;
   Fiber 13 g; T Fat 31 g; 46% Calories from Fat;
   Chol 45 mg; Sod 1129 mg.

Nancy Watts-Bloom

Bahama Shrimp Salad

1 cup rice, cooked
2 tablespoons French salad
   dressing
1 pound shrimp, cooked,
   chopped
1 tablespoon lemon juice
1/3 cup mayonnaise
3/4 teaspoon salt
1/4 cup chopped celery
3/4 cup chopped cauliflower
1 tablespoon chopped onion
1/4 cup chopped green bell
   pepper

Yield: 6 servings

Marinate rice in dressing. Combine with remaining ingredients in large bowl; mix well. Chill until serving time. Serve with hot corn bread muffins.

Approx Per Serving: Cal 289; Prot 15 g; Carbo 27 g;
   Fiber 1 g; T Fat 13 g; 40% Calories from Fat;
   Chol 128 mg; Sod 553 mg.

Babs Ruhl

Marinated Shrimp and Artichokes

5 tablespoons chili sauce
1 tablespoon horseradish
1/4 teaspoon hot sauce
13/4 cups chopped celery
2 9-ounce cans artichoke
   hearts
2 large onions, sliced
3/4 cup mayonnaise
1/2 cup French salad
   dressing
1 pound shrimp, peeled,
   cooked, deveined

Yield: 6 servings

Combine chili sauce, horseradish, hot sauce, celery, artichoke hearts, onions, mayonnaise and salad dressing in bowl; mix well. Add shrimp. Marinate in refrigerator overnight. Serve chilled. May use light mayonnaise if preferred. Do not substitute mayonnaise-type salad dressing for mayonnaise in this recipe.

Approx Per Serving: Cal 404; Prot 14 g; Carbo 18 g; Fiber 2 g; T Fat 31 g; 68% Calories from Fat; Chol 134 mg; Sod 1067 mg.

Chris Healy

Pink Shrimp Mousse

1 envelope unflavored
   gelatin
1/2 cup cold water
8 ounces cream cheese,
   softened
1 8-ounce bottle of
   Thousand Island salad
   dressing
1 tablespoon lemon juice
1/2 teaspoon salt
2 cups finely chopped
   cooked shrimp
1/2 cup chopped celery
1/4 cup chopped green bell
   pepper

Yield: 6 servings

Soften gelatin in cold water in saucepan. Heat until gelatin is dissolved, stirring constantly. Combine with cream cheese and salad dressing in bowl. Add lemon juice, salt, shrimp, celery and green pepper; mix well. Spoon into greased 1-quart mold. Chill until firm. Unmold onto serving plate. Garnish with whole shrimp. Serve with crackers.

Approx Per Serving: Cal 335; Prot 16 g; Carbo 8 g; Fiber <1 g; T Fat 27 g; 73% Calories from Fat; Chol 155 mg; Sod 684 mg.

Alice Bell

How to Find a Sand Dollar

Sand dollars can be found on the beaches and the shallow sand flats. The best time to find them is at low tide or after a storm. Wade in ankle to waist deep across the sand bottom. Look for the top of the sand dollar just protruding from the sand. Carefully gather the sand dollar and place it in a flat bucket. To clean your sand dollars, place in a solution of 50% bleach and 50% water. Soak until they turn white. Rinse with fresh water and let dry in the sun.

Molded Shrimp Salad

2 tablespoons unflavored
  gelatin
1 cup cold water
1   10-ounce can cream of
  tomato soup
9 ounces cream cheese,
  softened
1/2 cup mayonnaise
3/4 cup chopped celery
3/4 cup chopped green bell
  pepper
2 tablespoons grated onion
Salt to taste
2 cups finely chopped
  cooked shrimp

Yield: 6 servings

Soften gelatin in cold water. Bring soup to a boil in saucepan. Stir in cream cheese and gelatin. Cook until gelatin is dissolved, stirring constantly. Chill until partially set. Add mayonnaise, celery, green pepper, onion and salt; mix well. Stir in shrimp. Spoon into 1-quart mold. Chill until firm. Unmold onto serving plate.

Approx Per Serving: Cal 398; Prot 18 g; Carbo 13 g;
    Fiber 1 g; T Fat 31 g; 70% Calories from Fat;
    Chol 164 mg; Sod 792 mg.

Cathy Buzzett

Seafood Slaw

2 cups chopped cooked
  shrimp
4 cups finely shredded
  cabbage
1/4 cup chopped green
  onions
1/2 cup mayonnaise
1/4 cup lemon juice
2 teaspoons sugar
1 teaspoon seasoned salt
1 teaspoon prepared
  mustard
1/4 teaspoon hot pepper
  sauce
1/4 teaspoon Worcestershire
  sauce

Yield: 8 servings

Mix shrimp, cabbage and green onions in large bowl; set aside. Combine mayonnaise, lemon juice, sugar, seasoned salt, mustard, hot sauce and Worcestershire sauce in small bowl; mix well. Pour over shrimp mixture, stirring to toss. Chill thoroughly. May substitute cooked flaked crab meat or flaked tuna for shrimp.

Approx Per Serving: Cal 155; Prot 9 g; Carbo 4 g;
    Fiber 1 g; T Fat 12 g; 66% Calories from Fat;
    Chol 86 mg; Sod 348 mg.

Alice D. Collins

Antipasto Salad

2 plum tomatoes, sliced
1/2 cup pitted black olives,
  cut into quarters
1 small head romaine
  lettuce, torn into
  bite-sized pieces
2 6-ounce jars marinated
  artichoke hearts

Yield: 4 servings

Combine tomatoes, olives, lettuce and undrained artichoke hearts in bowl. Toss to mix.

Approx Per Serving: Cal 110; Prot 3 g; Carbo 9 g;
    Fiber 5 g; T Fat 8 g; 60% Calories from Fat;
    Chol 0 mg; Sod 711 mg.

Diana Prickett

Asparagus with Rosemary-Lemon Vinaigrette

Rind of 1 lemon, cut into
  very thin strips
Salt to taste
2 pounds asparagus,
  trimmed
1/3 cup fresh lemon juice
2 tablespoons finely
  chopped fresh rosemary
2 cloves of garlic, minced
1 cup olive oil
Pepper to taste

Yield: 6 servings

Cook lemon rind in boiling salted water in large
saucepan for 3 minutes. Remove with slotted spoon.
Return water to a boil. Add asparagus. Cook for 4
minutes or until tender-crisp; drain. Rinse under cold
water; drain. Cool. Arrange on plates. Whisk lemon
juice, rosemary and garlic in small bowl. Whisk in oil
gradually. Season with salt and pepper. Spoon over
asparagus. Sprinkle with lemon rind.

Approx Per Serving: Cal 358; Prot 4 g; Carbo 9 g;
    Fiber 3 g; T Fat 36 g; 87% Calories from Fat;
    Chol 0 mg; Sod 3 mg.

Conrad Gleber and Gail Rubini

The Brown Pelican

The best fisherman in the world! Not long ago, the pelican population dwindled to a
handful due to pesticides, but today the pelican population is healthy and increasing in
numbers. An incredible sight is to watch a pelican "dive bomb" and hit the water with
a great impact. The pelican has a special air sack under the flesh on the front of the
body to cushion it from the constant pounding against the water surface. The pelican
does not spear its catch, but uses its pouch much like a fish net.

V-8 Aspic

1   12-ounce can V-8 juice
1/2 cup water
1   3-ounce package lemon
    gelatin
2 teaspoons Worcestershire
    sauce
2 teaspoons horseradish
1 cup minced onion
1 cup minced green bell
    pepper
1 cup minced celery

Yield: 6 servings

Heat juice and water in saucepan. Add gelatin, stirring until dissolved. Let stand to cool. Stir in Worcestershire sauce and horseradish. Add onion, green pepper and celery; mix well. Chill until set. Serve on bed of lettuce. Garnish with dollop of mayonnaise, sour cream or a mixture of both.

Approx Per Serving: Cal 85; Prot 2 g; Carbo 20 g;
    Fiber 1 g; T Fat <1 g; 2% Calories from Fat;
    Chol 0 mg; Sod 282 mg.

Irene LaSlavic

Bean Salad

1   16-ounce can red beans
1   16-ounce can black beans
1   16-ounce can cut green
    beans
1   16-ounce can wax beans
1 cup chopped celery
3 or 4 chopped green
    onions with tops
1/2 cup oil
1/2 cup vinegar
1/2 cup sugar
Juice of 1 lemon
Salt and pepper to taste

Yield: 20 servings

Rinse beans; drain well in colander. Combine with celery and green onions in large bowl; mix well. Mix oil, vinegar, sugar, lemon juice, salt and pepper in medium bowl. Pour over bean mixture. Marinate, covered, in refrigerator for several hours to overnight, stirring occasionally.

Approx Per Serving: Cal 120; Prot 3 g; Carbo 15 g;
    Fiber 3 g; T Fat 6 g; 41% Calories from Fat;
    Chol 0 mg; Sod 284 mg.

Virginia Norris

The Mighty Oyster

Ninety percent of Florida's oyster crop is grown in Apalachicola Bay, one of the most ideal environments for the growth and culture of oysters. The Apalachicola Bay oyster is medium sized with a round, pointed green shell and a large cup. The oyster is firm with a mild, slightly sweet flavor...the best in the world!

Cucumber Pickles

7 cups thinly sliced
  cucumbers
1 onion, chopped
1 cup chopped green bell
  pepper
2 cups sugar
1¼ cups white vinegar
1 teaspoon celery seed

Yield: 15 servings

Combine cucumbers, onion, green pepper, sugar, vinegar and celery seed in bowl; mix well. Chill until serving time.

Approx Per Serving: Cal 117; Prot 1 g; Carbo 30 g;
    Fiber 1 g; T Fat <1 g; 1% Calories from Fat;
    Chol 0 mg; Sod 2 mg.

Sweet Mary

Melissa's Cucumber Slaw

2 cups thinly sliced
  cucumbers
1 onion, chopped
2 tablespoons mayonnaise
1 tablespoon vinegar
Dillweed, salt and pepper to
  taste

Yield: 6 servings

Combine cucumbers, onion, mayonnaise, vinegar and spices in bowl; mix well. Serve with fish.

Approx Per Serving: Cal 45; Prot 1 g; Carbo 3 g;
    Fiber 1 g; T Fat 4 g; 72% Calories from Fat;
    Chol 3 mg; Sod 27 mg.

Judi Little

Mother Mary Elvira's Slaw

1 head cabbage, coarsely
  chopped
3 tablespoons horseradish
3 to 4 tablespoons
  mayonnaise
3 tablespoons sugar
½ teaspoon celery seeds
Salt and pepper to taste

Yield: 6 servings

Combine all ingredients in bowl; mix well. May add chopped onion to taste.

Approx Per Serving: Cal 131; Prot 2 g; Carbo 16 g;
    Fiber 3 g; T Fat 8 g; 49% Calories from Fat;
    Chol 5 mg; Sod 87 mg.

Arthur Little

New York Coleslaw

1 head cabbage, chopped
1 green bell pepper, chopped
1 white onion, chopped
2 carrots, shredded
1 cup white vinegar
1/4 cup oil
1/2 cup sugar
1 teaspoon salt

Yield: 8 servings

Mix vegetables in bowl. Bring vinegar, oil, sugar and salt to a boil in saucepan. Simmer for 2 minutes. Pour over mixture. Let stand, covered, for 2 hours or longer.

Approx Per Serving: Cal 157; Prot 2 g; Carbo 24 g; Fiber 3 g; T Fat 7 g; 38% Calories from Fat; Chol 0 mg; Sod 294 mg.

Margaret Pfeifer

Orange Coleslaw

1   11-ounce can mandarin oranges
2 eggs, slightly beaten
1 tablespoon sugar
1 teaspoon salt
1 teaspoon dry mustard
1/4 teaspoon pepper
2 tablespoons butter
1/2 cup cider vinegar
6 cups finely chopped cabbage

Yield: 15 servings

Drain mandarin oranges, reserving juice. Cut approximately 2/3 of the oranges into halves. Mix next 6 ingredients in double boiler over hot water. Stir in orange juice and vinegar. Cook, stirring constantly, until slightly thickened. Chill in refrigerator. Mix egg mixture, sliced oranges and cabbage in bowl. Arrange in bowl lined with cabbage leaves. Top with remaining oranges. Chill until serving time.

Approx Per Serving: Cal 44; Prot 1 g; Carbo 5 g; Fiber 1 g; T Fat 2 g; 45% Calories from Fat; Chol 32 mg; Sod 172 mg.

Gwen Henkel

Lettuce-Bleu Cheese Salad

1 large head lettuce,
shredded
1 large red onion, thinly
sliced
8 ounces bleu cheese,
crumbled
2 cups sour cream

Yield: 8 servings

Combine lettuce, onion, cheese and sour cream in bowl. Toss to coat. Chill until serving time.

Approx Per Serving: Cal 236; Prot 9 g; Carbo 6 g;
Fiber 1 g; T Fat 20 g; 76% Calories from Fat;
Chol 47 mg; Sod 432 mg.

Jeanne Crozier

Marinated Mushroom Salad

1 pound mushrooms, sliced
1 cup white vinegar
2 cups water
1/2 cup sliced carrots
1/2 cup sliced celery
1/2 cup green bell pepper
strips
1/2 cup red bell pepper strips
1/3 cup olive oil
3/4 teaspoon salt
1/4 teaspoon pepper
1/4 teaspoon garlic powder
1 teaspoon crushed oregano
leaves

Yield: 12 servings

Bring mushrooms and vinegar to a boil in saucepan; reduce heat. Simmer, covered, for 2 minutes. Drain and set aside. Bring water to a boil in saucepan. Add carrots and celery. Return to a boil; reduce heat. Simmer for 3 minutes. Add peppers. Simmer for 3 minutes longer. Drain and set aside. Mix oil, salt, pepper, garlic powder and oregano in bowl. Combine with vegetables in large bowl; mix well. Chill, covered, for 2 hours or longer.

Approx Per Serving: Cal 69; Prot 1 g; Carbo 4 g;
Fiber 1 g; T Fat 6 g; 75% Calories from Fat;
Chol 0 mg; Sod 140 mg.

Helen Solomon

Marinated Vegetables

1 red onion, chopped
1 16-ounce can baby green peas
1 16-ounce can Shoe Peg corn
1 4-ounce jar pimentos, chopped
3/4 cup chopped celery
1/2 cup chopped green bell pepper
1/2 cup vinegar
3/4 cup sugar
1 teaspoon salt
1 teaspoon pepper
1/2 cup oil

Yield: 15 servings

Mix onion, peas, corn, pimentos, celery and green pepper in bowl. Combine vinegar, sugar, salt, pepper and oil in saucepan. Bring to a boil. Pour over vegetables. Marinate in refrigerator overnight.

Approx Per Serving: Cal 154; Prot 2 g; Carbo 21 g; Fiber 2 g; T Fat 8 g; 42% Calories from Fat; Chol 0 mg; Sod 245 mg.

Doris Barrett

Neapolitan Vegetable Mold

2 3-ounce packages lemon gelatin
1 teaspoon salt
1 1/2 cups boiling water
2 cups cold water
3 tablespoons vinegar
1 1/2 cups chopped carrots
1 3/4 cups finely chopped cabbage
1 teaspoon finely chopped scallions
1 1/2 cups finely chopped spinach

Yield: 10 servings

Dissolve gelatin and salt in boiling water. Add cold water and vinegar. Divide equally among 3 bowls. Chill until slightly thickened. Stir carrots into 1 bowl. Spoon into 4x8-inch loaf pan. Chill until set. Stir cabbage into second bowl. Spoon over carrot layer. Chill until set. Stir scallions and spinach into third bowl. Spoon over cabbage layer. Chill until firm. Unmold onto serving plate. Garnish as desired.

Approx Per Serving: Cal 75; Prot 2 g; Carbo 18 g; Fiber 1 g; T Fat <1 g; 1% Calories from Fat; Chol 0 mg; Sod 269 mg.

Helen Marsh

Glorified Onions

1/2 cup cider vinegar
1 cup sugar
2 cups water
5 or 6 Vidalia onions, thinly
  sliced
1/2 cup fat-free mayonnaise
1 tablespoon celery salt
1 tablespoon celery seeds

Yield: 8 servings

Combine vinegar, sugar and water in saucepan. Heat until sugar is dissolved. Pour over onions in bowl. Marinate in refrigerator for 4 hours or overnight; drain. Add mayonnaise, celery salt and celery seeds; mix gently or toss to mix. May serve cold with Triscuits as an appetizer.

Approx Per Serving: Cal 145; Prot 1 g; Carbo 36 g;
    Fiber 2 g; T Fat <1 g; 2% Calories from Fat;
    Chol 0 mg; Sod 736 mg.

Doris Barrett

Fire and Ice Tomatoes

6 large tomatoes, peeled,
  cut into quarters
1 large green bell pepper,
  cut into strips
1 large onion, cut into rings
3/4 cup vinegar
1 1/2 teaspoons celery salt
1 1/2 teaspoons mustard
  seeds
1/2 teaspoon salt
4 1/2 teaspoons sugar
1/8 teaspoon red pepper
1/8 teaspoon black pepper
1/4 cup cold water

Yield: 10 servings

Combine tomatoes, green pepper and onion in bowl; mix well. Combine vinegar, celery salt, mustard seeds, salt, sugar, red pepper, black pepper and water in saucepan. Bring to a boil; reduce heat. Simmer for 1 minute. Pour over vegetables. Store in tightly covered container in refrigerator for several days. May add 1 sliced cucumber.

Approx Per Serving: Cal 43; Prot 1 g; Carbo 10 g;
    Fiber 2 g; T Fat 1 g; 10% Calories from Fat;
    Chol 0 mg; Sod 342 mg.

Lora James

Poppy Seed Salad Dressing

1/2 cup sugar
1 teaspoon dry mustard
1 teaspoon salt
3 tablespoons vinegar
2 teaspoons poppy seeds
1 tablespoon lemon juice
1 teaspoon paprika
1 cup oil

Yield: 25 servings

Combine sugar, mustard, salt, vinegar, poppy seeds, lemon juice and paprika in bowl. Add oil gradually, mixing with wire whisk.

Approx Per Serving: Cal 95; Prot <1 g; Carbo 4 g; Fiber <1 g; T Fat 9 g; 82% Calories from Fat; Chol 0 mg; Sod 85 mg.

Mary Lou Short

Roquefort Dressing

1/2 pound Roquefort cheese, crumbled
1/2 cup sour cream
1 cup mayonnaise
1/3 cup sweet pickle vinegar
1/2 teaspoon garlic powder
1/2 teaspoon Worcestershire sauce
1/4 teaspoon MSG
Salt and pepper to taste

Yield: 35 servings

Combine cheese, sour cream, mayonnaise, vinegar, garlic powder, Worcestershire sauce and MSG in bowl; mix well. Season with salt and pepper. Chill overnight.

Approx Per Serving: Cal 76; Prot 2 g; Carbo 1 g; Fiber 0 g; T Fat 8 g; 89% Calories from Fat; Chol 11 mg; Sod 186 mg.

Babs Ruhl

Dressing for Tossed Salad

1/2 cup sugar
1 small onion, grated
1/2 cup vinegar
Juice of 1 lemon
1/2 cup chili sauce
1 cup oil
1 teaspoon salt
1/4 teaspoon pepper
1/2 teaspoon paprika

Yield: 25 servings

Combine sugar, grated onion, vinegar, lemon juice, chili sauce, oil, salt, pepper and paprika in blender container. Process until mixed. Pour dressing into 1-quart jar; cover and shake well.

Approx Per Serving: Cal 100; Prot <1 g; Carbo 6 g; Fiber <1 g; T Fat 9 g; 76% Calories from Fat; Chol 0 mg; Sod 158 mg.

Jane C. Hinson

Meat and Meatless Entrées

ST. GEORGE ISLAND CHARITY CHILI COOKOFF AND AUCTION, INC.
St. George Island, Fla.

St. George Island Charity Cookoff and Auction
by Jim Grosvenor

St. George Island Charity Chili Cookoff and Auction, Inc.

In 1983, Jack and Margarita Pilkinton organized the first-ever chili cookoff at the Happy Pelican restaurant, as a fund raiser for the Fire Department. Chili was sold for $2.50 per bowl and approximately 50 people attended. Alice Collins won first prize which was a case of beer. She donated it to the Fire Department and Buddy Crawford said "I'll auction it off." It was sold for $50. Many other items were donated and the final tabulation showed that $800 had been raised. An annual event was founded!

The Second Annual Cookoff was expanded to include an auction and raised $7,000, the third $8,000, the fourth $18,000, the fifth $27,000. In 1987, a non-profit corporation was formed with the first Board of Directors: Harry Arnold, Gary Cates, Alice Collins, Ollie Gunn, Sr. and John Lee. Later that same year the event was sanctioned by the International Chili Society as the Gulf Coast Regional Competition. The winner is automatically eligible for the international cookoff held in California each year. Even though the next year brought heavy rains, the gross income soared to $38,000. The event has grossed over $266,000 through the 1993 event. Now the largest regional cookoff in the U.S., 16 states and Canada were represented the last two years; however, the Crock•Pot category is still a vital part of the event.

Long before the event is to be held, the quest for antiques, art, collectables and that unique auction item that will capture the imagination of generous bidders begins; for instance, a baby goat produced the most spirited bidding war ever and earned $1,500.

Through totally volunteer efforts, the St. George Island Charity Chili Cookoff continues to be staged the first Saturday in March every year to raise funds for the St. George Island Volunteer Fire Department and First Responders. There's fun for everyone, as the event now includes the cookoff competition, a 200 item plus auction, country store, 5K run and many different kinds of foods.

Grilled Pot Roast

1   3- or 4-pound pot roast
Meat tenderizer to taste
1/2 cup soy sauce
1 tablespoon lemon juice
1/4 cup whiskey
1/4 cup packed brown sugar

Yield: 6 servings

*P*ierce pot roast with fork; sprinkle with tenderizer. Place in bowl. Let stand for 1 hour. Pour mixture of soy sauce, lemon juice, whiskey and brown sugar over beef. Marinate, covered, in refrigerator for 6 hours to overnight, turning occasionally; drain. Grill, covered, over hot coals for 15 minutes on each side or to desired degree of doneness.

Approx Per Serving: Cal 449; Prot 60 g; Carbo 10 g;
    Fiber <1 g; T Fat 15 g; 31% Calories from Fat;
    Chol 180 mg; Sod 1490 mg.

Helen Marsh

Olive Pot Roast

2 medium onions, sliced
2 tablespoons oil
1   3- or 4-pound boneless
    pot roast
Salt to taste
1   8-ounce can tomato sauce
1 cup water
1 clove of garlic, finely
    chopped
1/4 teaspoon pepper
6 medium potatoes, peeled
1 pound carrots, cut into
    2-inch pieces
1 cup sliced stuffed olives
2 to 3 tablespoons
    cornstarch
1/4 cup water

Yield: 6 servings

*S*auté onions in oil in large heavy saucepan until tender. Sprinkle roast with salt. Brown on all sides in saucepan. Stir in tomato sauce, 1 cup water, garlic and pepper. Cook, covered, over low heat for 1 1/2 to 2 hours. Add potatoes, carrots and olives. Cook until vegetables are tender, basting frequently with tomato sauce mixture. Transfer meat and vegetables to serving platter. Skim fat from tomato sauce mixture. Stir in mixture of cornstarch and 1/4 cup water. Simmer for 1 minute or until slightly thickened, stirring constantly. Spoon sauce over roast and vegetables.

Approx Per Serving: Cal 642; Prot 64 g; Carbo 44 g;
    Fiber 6 g; T Fat 23 g; 32% Calories from Fat;
    Chol 180 mg; Sod 967 mg.

Edna Rudasill

Sauerbraten

1 cup vinegar
1 stalk celery
1 parsnip
2 carrots
1 onion
Salt to taste
Peppercorns to taste
Whole cloves to taste
Bay leaves to taste
1 1-pound top round steak
1 tablespoon lard
1/4 cup butter
1 cup sour cream

Yield: 4 servings

Bring vinegar, celery, parsnip, carrots, onion, salt, peppercorns, cloves and bay leaves to a boil in stockpot. Remove from heat. Let stand to cool. Pound steak lightly with meat mallet. Transfer steak to vinegar mixture. Marinate, covered, in refrigerator for 3 days. Remove steak from marinade; pat dry with cloth and spread with lard. Strain marinade into measuring cup. Stir in equal quantity of water. Brown steak on both sides in butter in skillet. Add diluted marinade. Simmer until of desired degree of doneness, basting frequently. Stir in sour cream. Simmer until flavors have enhanced beef. Serve steak with sauce. Serve with red cabbage and mashed potatoes.

Approx Per Serving: Cal 435; Prot 24 g; Carbo 18 g; Fiber 3 g; T Fat 30 g; 61% Calories from Fat; Chol 116 mg; Sod 215 mg.

Marta Thompson

Barciola

1 1-pound flank steak, butterflied
1/2 cup grated Romano cheese
1/2 cup chopped parsley
1 clove of garlic, crushed
2 cups chopped spinach
4 tablespoons oil
1 clove of garlic; crushed
1 28-ounce can tomatoes
1/4 teaspoon salt
1/4 teaspoon pepper
1/2 teaspoon oregano
1 teaspoon parsley flakes
2 teaspoons water

Yield: 4 servings

Sprinkle flank steak with cheese, parsley, 1 clove of garlic and spinach. Roll to enclose filling; tie with string in 3 places. Brown in 2 tablespoons oil in skillet. Remove to heavy saucepan. Combine 2 tablespoons oil, 1 clove of garlic, tomatoes, salt, pepper, oregano, parsley flakes and water in saucepan; mix well. Simmer for 30 minutes, stirring occasionally. Pour sauce over beef. Simmer for 15 minutes.

Approx Per Serving: Cal 357; Prot 25 g; Carbo 11 g; Fiber 4 g; T Fat 24 g; 60% Calories from Fat; Chol 58 mg; Sod 688 mg.

Patty Valentine

Steak with Sauce Laffite

1   12-ounce can beer
1/2 cup chili sauce
1/4 cup oil
2 tablespoons soy sauce
1 tablespoon Dijon mustard
1/2 teaspoon Tabasco sauce
1/8 teaspoon liquid smoke
1 medium onion, coarsely
   chopped
2 cloves of garlic, crushed
1   3-pound sirloin steak,
   1 1/2 to 2 inches thick
Salt and pepper to taste

Yield: 8 servings

Combine beer, chili sauce, oil, soy sauce, Dijon mustard, Tabasco sauce, liquid smoke, onion and garlic in saucepan; mix well. Simmer for 30 minutes, stirring occasionally. Brush steak with sauce. Grill steak over medium-hot coals for 15 minutes on 1 side, basting with sauce frequently. Season with salt and pepper. Turn steak over. Grill for 15 minutes, basting frequently. Remove to serving platter; season with salt and pepper. Reheat remaining sauce. Serve with steak.

Approx Per Serving: Cal 309; Prot 32 g; Carbo 8 g;
   Fiber 1 g; T Fat 15 g; 45% Calories from Fat;
   Chol 89 mg; Sod 606 mg.
   Nutritional information does not include liquid
   smoke.

Lawanna Stansell

Sunday Swiss Steak

3 or 4 pounds round steak,
   cut into bite-sized pieces
1/4 cup flour
Salt and pepper to taste
1 tablespoon oil
1 large onion, sliced
1   10-ounce can tomato
   soup
1   10-ounce can cream of
   mushroom soup
3/4 soup can water

Yield: 10 servings

Dredge round steak in flour; season with salt and pepper. Fry in oil in skillet until brown on both sides. Add onion, soups and water; mix well. Simmer, covered, for 1 hour. Serve with mashed potatoes, a green vegetable and a salad.

Approx Per Serving: Cal 274; Prot 35 g; Carbo 10 g;
   Fiber 1 g; T Fat 9 g; 32% Calories from Fat;
   Chol 90 mg; Sod 525 mg.

Ruth Guernsey

...undy

...irloin
... bite-sized
  pieces
2 tablespoons oil
1 envelope onion soup mix
1   10-ounce can cream of
    mushroom soup
1/2 soup can water
1/2 cup Burgundy

Yield: 6 servings

Brown steak on all sides in oil in skillet. Add soup mix, soup, water and Burgundy; mix well. Spoon into baking dish. Chill, covered, for 8 hours. Bake at 350 degrees for 1 3/4 hours.

Approx Per Serving: Cal 290; Prot 28 g; Carbo 5 g; Fiber <1 g; T Fat 16 g; 49% Calories from Fat; Chol 80 mg; Sod 578 mg.

Joan Valenti

Three/Three/Three Beef Stew

1 pound stew beef
1   10-ounce can golden
    mushroom soup
1   10-ounce can French
    onion soup

Yield: 3 servings

Combine stew beef and soups in bowl; mix well. Spoon into baking dish. Bake at 300 degrees for 3 hours. Serve over hot cooked noodles.

Approx Per Serving: Cal 322; Prot 32 g; Carbo 15 g; Fiber <1 g; T Fat 14 g; 40% Calories from Fat; Chol 91 mg; Sod 1880 mg.

Kristen Shelby

Sunsets

Island sunsets can only be described as breathtaking!
Standing on St. George's Island
Every voice and penciled shell
Blending with the Ocean's music
Seemed to me a story tell.
And the love of every lover
Seemed to speak in love to me—
When I saw the golden sunset
Sinking o'er the Florida sea.

—from poetry by William Lee Popham, circa 1918

Swedish Stew

2 pounds stew beef
2 large carrots, sliced
1 large onion, sliced
1   16-ounce can tomatoes
1   16-ounce can peas
6 or 8 whole cloves
1 teaspoon salt
1 tablespoon tapioca
1 tablespoon bread crumbs

Yield: 6 servings

Layer stew beef, carrots, onion, tomatoes, peas, cloves, salt, tapioca and bread crumbs ½ at a time in baking dish. Bake, covered, at 300 degrees for 5 hours, stirring occasionally. May add water to moisten.

Approx Per Serving: Cal 291; Prot 31 g; Carbo 17 g; Fiber 4 g; T Fat 11 g; 33% Calories from Fat; Chol 91 mg; Sod 969 mg.

Laura LaFleur

Black Bean Chili

2 red bell peppers, cut into
   ¼x2-inch strips
1 tablespoon chili powder
1 tablespoon cumin
½ teaspoon garlic powder
2   15-ounce cans black
   beans
1   15-ounce can black
   beans, drained
¼ cup catsup

Yield: 6 servings

Microwave red peppers in microwave-safe dish for 2 to 3 minutes or until soft. Combine red peppers, chili powder, cumin, garlic powder, 2 cans undrained black beans, 1 can drained black beans and catsup in large saucepan; mix well. Simmer for 30 minutes, stirring frequently. Serve with sour cream, shredded Cheddar cheese, chopped cilantro, sliced green onions and salsa. May sauté red peppers in 1 tablespoon olive oil until soft. May add ½ to 1 pound browned ground beef or turkey to chili.

Approx Per Serving: Cal 218; Prot 14 g; Carbo 41 g; Fiber 11 g; T Fat 1 g; 4% Calories from Fat; Chol 0 mg; Sod 953 mg.

Nancy Watts-Bloom

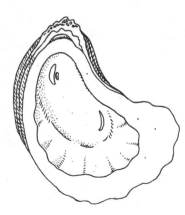

Super Beefy Enchiladas

1¹/2 cups ground beef
¹/2 cup chopped onion
1　4-ounce can green
　chilies, drained, chopped
¹/2 cup shredded Cheddar
　cheese
1　10-ounce can cream of
　mushroom soup
1　10-ounce can tomato
　soup
1　10-ounce can mild
　enchilada sauce
12 corn tortillas
Oil for frying
1 cup shredded Cheddar
　cheese

Yield: 12 servings

Brown ground beef with onion and chilies, stirring until ground beef is crumbly; drain. Stir in ¹/2 cup cheese. Combine soups and enchilada sauce in saucepan; mix well. Cook until smooth, stirring constantly. Soften tortillas in hot oil; drain. Spoon ground beef mixture in each tortilla; roll to enclose filling. Place seam side down in 9x13-inch baking dish. Pour soup mixture over tortillas; sprinkle with 1 cup cheese. Bake at 350 degrees for 25 minutes.

Approx Per Serving: Cal 237; Prot 10 g; Carbo 22 g;
　　Fiber 2 g; T Fat 13 g; 47% Calories from Fat;
　　Chol 35 mg; Sod 665 mg.
　　Nutritional information does not include oil
　　for frying.

Carol "Woody" Troutman

Manual Maloof Hamburger

4 ounces lean ground beef
1 tablespoon butter
1 thick onion slice
¹/4 cup shredded Cheddar
　cheese
2 slices bread, toasted
3 bread and butter pickles

Yield: 1 serving

Shape ground beef into patty. Fry in nonstick skillet until of desired degree of doneness; drain. Melt butter in skillet. Add sliced onion. Place ground beef patty on top of onion. Cook over medium-low heat until onion is tender. Sprinkle with cheese. Cook until cheese melts. Serve on toasted bread slices with pickles and choice of condiments.

Approx Per Serving: Cal 638; Prot 38 g; Carbo 34 g;
　　Fiber 1 g; T Fat 38 g; 55% Calories from Fat;
　　Chol 147 mg; Sod 791 mg.

Tom Gross

Shepherd's Pie

1 1/2 pounds lean ground beef
1 large onion, chopped
5 medium potatoes, peeled,
   cooked
1/2 cup milk
2 tablespoons butter
1 16-ounce package frozen
   corn, thawed
Salt and pepper to taste
2 tablespoons butter

Yield: 4 servings

Brown ground beef in skillet, stirring until crumbly. Drain ground beef in colander. Sauté onion in pan drippings until tender; drain. Combine ground beef and onion in baking dish. Beat potatoes, milk and 2 tablespoons butter in mixer bowl until smooth. Spread over ground beef mixture. Sprinkle with corn; season with salt and pepper. Dot with 2 tablespoons butter. Bake at 375 degrees for 20 minutes or until corn is tender and potatoes are light brown.

Approx Per Serving: Cal 740; Prot 46 g; Carbo 61 g; Fiber 6 g; T Fat 36 g; 43% Calories from Fat; Chol 162 mg; Sod 237 mg.

Jean Gross

Impossible Taco Pie

1 pound ground beef
1/2 cup chopped onion
1 clove of garlic, finely
   chopped
1 envelope taco seasoning
   mix
1 4-ounce can green
   chilies, drained, cut into
   quarters
1 1/4 cups milk
3/4 cup baking mix
3 eggs
2 tomatoes, sliced
1 cup shredded Monterey
   Jack cheese

Yield: 6 servings

Brown ground beef with onion and garlic in skillet, stirring until ground beef is crumbly; drain. Stir in taco seasoning. Spread mixture loosely in 10-inch greased quiche pan or pie plate. Sprinkle with chilies. Beat milk, baking mix and eggs in mixer bowl for 1 minute or until smooth. Pour over prepared layers. Bake at 400 degrees for 25 minutes. Top with sliced tomatoes; sprinkle with cheese. Bake for 8 to 10 minutes or until set. Cool for 5 minutes. Cut into wedges. Serve with sour cream, chopped lettuce and corn chips. May substitute ground turkey for ground beef. May substitute Cheddar cheese for Monterey Jack cheese.

Approx Per Serving: Cal 411; Prot 29 g; Carbo 22 g; Fiber 1 g; T Fat 23 g; 51% Calories from Fat; Chol 186 mg; Sod 1186 mg.

Jane M. Burke

Pumpkin Surprise

1　6- to 7-inch pumpkin
1 pound ground round
1 clove of garlic, chopped
1 medium onion, chopped
1 teaspoon thyme
1　6-ounce can whole pitted
　　black olives, drained
1　8-ounce can tomato sauce
1½ tablespoons oil

Yield: 4 servings

Slice top from pumpkin, reserving top; remove seeds. Parboil pumpkin in boiling water in stockpot for 20 minutes; drain. Brown ground round with garlic and onion, stirring until ground round is crumbly; drain. Stir in thyme, olives and tomato sauce. Spoon into pumpkin; replace top. Brush pumpkin with oil. Place in shallow baking pan. Bake at 350 degrees for 1 hour. Remove to serving platter; cut into wedges.

Approx Per Serving: Cal 396; Prot 28 g; Carbo 15 g;
　　Fiber 5 g; T Fat 26 g; 57% Calories from Fat;
　　Chol 84 mg; Sod 682 mg.

Kathy Morton

Texas Hash

2 cups sliced onions
¾ cup chopped green bell
　　pepper
3 tablespoons oil
1 pound lean ground beef
1　16-ounce can tomatoes
1 teaspoon salt
1 tablespoon chili powder
½ cup uncooked rice

Yield: 4 servings

Sauté onions and green pepper in oil in skillet until brown; drain. Stir in ground beef, tomatoes, salt, chili powder and rice; mix well. Spoon into greased baking dish or mold. Bake, covered, at 350 degrees for 1 hour.

Approx Per Serving: Cal 479; Prot 29 g; Carbo 30 g;
　　Fiber 4 g; T Fat 27 g; 50% Calories from Fat;
　　Chol 84 mg; Sod 800 mg.

Claire Dews

Chalupa

1 1-pound package dried
   pinto beans
1 3-pound beef roast
5 to 7 cups water
1/2 cup chopped onion
2 teaspoons garlic salt
1 tablespoon salt
2 tablespoons chili powder
1 tablespoon cumin seeds
1 teaspoon oregano
1 4-ounce can chopped
   green chilies, drained
1 2-ounce jar chopped
   pimento, drained

Yield: 10 servings

Sort beans; rinse. Combine beans, beef roast, water, chopped onion, garlic salt, salt, chili powder, cumin seeds, oregano, chilies and chopped pimento in stockpot; mix well. Cook over low heat for 5 to 7 hours or until beef is tender. Remove roast; shred. Return shredded meat to stockpot; mix well. Cook over low heat until thickened, stirring constantly. Spoon into large serving bowl. Serve with corn chips, shredded lettuce, chopped tomatoes, shredded cheese, chopped onion and sour cream.

Approx Per Serving: Cal 324; Prot 36 g; Carbo 31 g;
    Fiber 11 g; T Fat 6 g; 18% Calories from Fat;
    Chol 77 mg; Sod 1246 mg.

Jane Pitts

Teriyaki Pork with Orange Sauce

1 2-pound pork steak,
   trimmed, thinly sliced
1/2 cup soy sauce
1 tablespoon wine vinegar
2 tablespoons lemon juice
1/4 cup water
1 tablespoon sugar
1 1/2 teaspoons ginger
1/2 teaspoon garlic powder
1/2 teaspoon cornstarch
2 tablespoons cold water
1/2 cup orange juice
2 teaspoons sugar

Yield: 6 servings

Arrange pork in shallow baking dish. Pour mixture of soy sauce, wine vinegar, lemon juice, water, sugar, ginger and garlic powder over pork. Marinate in refrigerator for 1 to 2 hours, turning once. Broil or grill for 3 minutes on each side. Combine mixture of cornstarch and water with orange juice and sugar in saucepan; mix well. Cook over medium heat until thickened, stirring constantly. Serve with pork.

Approx Per Serving: Cal 148; Prot 19 g; Carbo 9 g;
    Fiber <1 g; T Fat 4 g; 24% Calories from Fat;
    Chol 52 mg; Sod 1401 mg.

Pat Morrison

Ham Balls

8 ounces ham, ground
8 ounces fresh pork, ground
1/2 cup cracker crumbs
1 egg, beaten
1 onion, chopped
1/2 to 3/4 cup milk
Salt and pepper to taste
1 cup packed brown sugar
2 tablespoons cider vinegar
1 teaspoon prepared
    mustard

Yield: 8 servings

Combine ground ham, ground pork, cracker crumbs, beaten egg, onion, milk, salt and pepper in bowl; mix well. Shape into 8 balls. Place in baking pan; flatten slightly. Bake at 325 degrees for 20 minutes. Combine brown sugar, cider vinegar and prepared mustard in saucepan; mix well. Bring to a boil, stirring constantly. Pour over ham balls. Bake for 20 minutes. Remove ham balls to serving platter; drizzle with sauce. May place 1 pineapple slice on each ham ball 5 minutes before end of baking cycle. Serve with baked sweet potatoes and wilted lettuce salad. Ask your butcher to grind the ham and pork together.

Approx Per Serving: Cal 222; Prot 15 g; Carbo 28 g;
    Fiber <1 g; T Fat 5 g; 22% Calories from Fat;
    Chol 62 mg; Sod 494 mg.

Ruth Guernsey

Cheesy Ham and Potato Casserole

6 medium potatoes, peeled,
    sliced
1 cup chopped cooked ham
1/4 cup butter, softened
1 cup evaporated milk
1/2 cup water
1 cup shredded Cheddar
    cheese

Yield: 4 servings

Combine potatoes, ham, butter, milk and water; mix well. Spoon into baking dish. Bake at 350 degrees until potatoes are tender; sprinkle with cheese. Bake until cheese melts. May add additional vegetables.

Approx Per Serving: Cal 523; Prot 24 g; Carbo 46 g;
    Fiber 3 g; T Fat 28 g; 47% Calories from Fat;
    Chol 99 mg; Sod 832 mg.

Dot Crozier

Breakfast of Champions

1 pound sausage
1 16-ounce loaf sourdough French bread, cut into cubes
2 cups shredded Cheddar cheese
12 eggs
1³/₄ cups milk
Salt and pepper to taste

Yield: 8 servings

Brown sausage in skillet, stirring until crumbly; drain. Line 9x13-inch baking dish with bread cubes. Sprinkle with 1 cup cheese. Spread with crumbled sausage; sprinkle with remaining 1 cup cheese. Beat eggs, milk, salt and pepper in mixer bowl until blended. Pour over prepared layers. Chill, covered, overnight. Bake, uncovered, at 350 degrees for 45 to 60 minutes or until set.

Approx Per Serving: Cal 511; Prot 28 g; Carbo 34 g; Fiber 2 g; T Fat 29 g; 51% Calories from Fat; Chol 377 mg; Sod 985 mg.

Cathy Buzzett

Dominic's Sausage

10 to 12 pounds pork butt, coarsely ground
5 tablespoons salt
2¹/₂ tablespoons fennel seeds
1¹/₂ tablespoons coriander
1 tablespoon peppercorns, crushed
1 tablespoon cayenne pepper
1 tablespoon Italian pepper
1 tablespoon white pepper
1 tablespoon paprika
Chopped parsley to taste
2 cloves of garlic, finely chopped

Yield: 96 servings

Combine pork, salt, fennel seeds, coriander, crushed peppercorns, cayenne pepper, Italian pepper, white pepper, paprika, chopped parsley and garlic in large bowl; mix well. Shape into patties or stuff into casings. May omit coriander.

Approx Per Serving: Cal 100; Prot 9 g; Carbo <1 g; Fiber <1 g; T Fat 7 g; 63% Calories from Fat; Chol 31 mg; Sod 357 mg.

Dominic Baragona

Brunswick Stew

2 cups chopped onion
1 tablespoon oil
1 large can Castleberry's
　pork
1 large can Castleberry's
　beef
3　8-ounce cans tomato
　sauce
1　17-ounce can cream-style
　corn
1　16-ounce can whole
　kernel corn, drained
2 cans Sweet Sue barbecue
　chicken
Tabasco sauce to taste

Yield: 10 servings

Sauté onion in oil in skillet until tender; drain. Combine onion, pork, beef, tomato sauce, cream-style corn, whole kernel corn, barbecue chicken and Tabasco sauce; mix well. Spoon into baking dish. Bake at 350 degrees for 1 hour or until bubbly.

Nutritional information for this recipe is not available.

Beverly Troutman

Miley's Mexican Brunch

2 teaspoons olive oil
1　16-ounce can refried
　beans
2 tablespoons water
1　10-ounce package frozen
　chopped spinach, thawed,
　drained
2 medium onions, finely
　chopped
1/2 cup sour cream
1 cup shredded jalapeño
　pepper cheese
5 eggs
3/4 cup salsa
1 cup guacamole
1/2 cup sour cream

Yield: 5 servings

Brush baking dish with olive oil. Spread mixture of refried beans and water over bottom. Layer with spinach, 3/4 of the chopped onions, 1/2 cup sour cream and cheese. Make 5 indentations with spoon in mixture. Break 1 egg into each indentation. Spoon salsa around eggs. Bake at 400 degrees for 20 minutes. Top with guacamole, 1/2 cup sour cream and remaining onions. May serve over corn chips or tortillas.

Approx Per Serving: Cal 468; Prot 22 g; Carbo 31 g;
　　Fiber 9 g; T Fat 30 g; 56% Calories from Fat;
　　Chol 253 mg; Sod 864 mg.

Marion Miley

Egg Muffins

8 to 10 slices crisp-fried bacon, crumbled
8 to 10 hard-cooked eggs, finely chopped
8 ounces cream cheese, softened
Salt and pepper to taste
Celery salt to taste
1 teaspoon (rounded) mayonnaise
10 English muffins, sliced into halves
1 cup shredded Cheddar cheese
1/2 cup grated Parmesan cheese

Yield: 20 servings

Combine bacon, eggs, cream cheese, salt, pepper, celery salt and mayonnaise in bowl; mix well. Spread mixture on English muffin halves. Sprinkle with Cheddar cheese and Parmesan cheese. Place on baking sheet. May freeze at this point or bake at 350 degrees until cheese melts. May also cut into quarters and serve as hors d'oeuvres. Great to serve on Thanksgiving or Christmas morning.

Approx Per Serving: Cal 199; Prot 10 g; Carbo 14 g; Fiber 1 g; T Fat 12 g; 52% Calories from Fat; Chol 129 mg; Sod 330 mg.

Linda Arnold

Skillet Potatoes and Eggs

6 medium potatoes, peeled
Salt to taste
6 slices bacon, chopped
1 cup finely chopped onion
8 eggs, beaten
1 teaspoon salt
1/4 teaspoon pepper

Yield: 8 servings

Combine potatoes, salt and enough water to cover in saucepan. Bring to a boil; reduce heat. Cook, covered, for 20 minutes or until potatoes are tender-crisp; drain. Cut into 1/8-inch slices. Fry bacon in skillet until crisp; drain, reserving drippings. Sauté onion in 2 tablespoons reserved drippings in skillet until tender. Cook potatoes 1/3 at a time in onion and drippings until brown. Remove to plate; keep warm. Return potatoes and onion to skillet, adding drippings if desired. Pour mixture of eggs, 1 teaspoon salt and pepper over potatoes; sprinkle with bacon. Cook, covered, over low heat for 5 to 6 minutes or until eggs are set. Serve immediately.

Approx Per Serving: Cal 194; Prot 10 g; Carbo 22 g; Fiber 2 g; T Fat 7 g; 35% Calories from Fat; Chol 216 mg; Sod 410 mg.

Alma Garrett

Pizza Supreme

1 tablespoon olive oil
1 package hot roll mix
1 1/4 cups hot water
2 tablespoons olive oil
8 ounces shredded nonfat
    mozzarella cheese
8 ounces shredded low-fat
    mozzarella cheese
1 tablespoon basil
1 tablespoon oregano
1/2 teaspoon garlic powder
6 to 8 plum tomatoes, seeds
    removed, chopped,
    drained
8 ounces mushrooms,
    chopped

Yield: 6 servings

Brush 11x16-inch baking pan with 1 tablespoon olive oil. Combine contents of hot roll mix with yeast packet in bowl; mix well. Stir in hot water and 2 tablespoons olive oil, stirring until dough pulls from sides of bowl. Turn dough onto lightly floured surface. Pat into prepared pan with greased hands; pierce dough with fork. Let rise, covered, in warm place for 15 minutes. Sprinkle with cheeses, basil, oregano and garlic powder. Sprinkle with tomatoes and mushrooms. Bake at 425 degrees for 20 to 25 minutes or until cheese melts and crust is light brown.

Approx Per Serving: Cal 519; Prot 32 g; Carbo 66 g;
    Fiber 2 g; T Fat 14 g; 24% Calories from Fat;
    Chol 27 mg; Sod 1013 mg.

Karen Riedle

Southern Japanese Stir-Fry

1/3 cup peanut oil
1/3 cup soy sauce
1/3 cup water
3 or 4 cloves of garlic,
    finely chopped
1 cup chopped carrots
2 potatoes, peeled, chopped
2 medium onions, sliced
4 ounces tofu, crumbled
1 cup sliced mushrooms
1 cup sliced zucchini
1 cup broccoli flowerets
8 ounces spinach leaves
2 cups shredded mozzarella
    cheese

Yield: 6 servings

Heat peanut oil, soy sauce and water in wok. Stir-fry garlic, carrots, potatoes, onions, tofu, mushrooms, zucchini and broccoli until tender-crisp. Cover with spinach; sprinkle with cheese. Steam, covered, until cheese melts. Serve over hot cooked brown rice. May use any assortment of chopped fresh vegetables.

Approx Per Serving: Cal 313; Prot 13 g; Carbo 20 g;
    Fiber 4 g; T Fat 21 g; 60% Calories from Fat;
    Chol 30 mg; Sod 1095 mg.

Cass Stark

Poultry Entrées

The Arbors
by Carolyn Bassett

The Arbors

Each summer from 1971 to 1980, seminarians would come to the Island on preaching missions. The Arbors was located approximately one-half mile east of the public beach area on the north side of Gorrie Drive. A rustic sign announced: St. George Island Community Church. Cut trees of all heights held up a flat thatched roof and people sat on milk crates with boards laid across them. Behind the rustic pulpit stood a cross made of trees.

Sunday worshippers arrived at the makeshift church not only with Bibles in hand, but fans, insect repellent and wide-brimmed straw hats. Sunday finery included everything from shorts to the traditional Sunday attire...however, shoes, if worn, were flip flops or tennis shoes, regardless of what you wore. Even now, both of the Island churches encourage people to "come as you are, God loves you that way."

Children loved the Church service and while the seminarians preached the children gathered together to play in the sand.

One of the most unusual weddings on the Island occurred at the Arbors. This was the second marriage for the bride who did not think it appropriate to wear white. To the astonishment of the wedding party and guests, down the aisle walked the bride dressed entirely in black, and, of course, shoeless.

In the early 1980s, Island residents formed the First Baptist Church of St. George Island and the First United Methodist Church of St. George Island. Both churches now serve Island residents and visitors.

Tasty Baked Chicken

1 3-pound chicken, cut up
2 teaspoons seasoned salt
1½ cups uncooked rice
1 4-ounce can mushrooms
1 10-ounce can cream of
  mushroom soup
1 10-ounce can cream of
  celery soup
1 envelope onion soup mix
1½ teaspoons savory
2 cups chicken broth

Yield: 4 servings

Rinse chicken and pat dry; season with seasoned salt. Let stand for 30 minutes. Spread rice in greased 3-quart casserole. Layer with undrained mushrooms and chicken. Pour soups over layers. Sprinkle with onion soup mix and savory. Pour chicken broth around sides of chicken. Bake, covered, at 350 degrees for 1½ hours.

Approx Per Serving: Cal 744; Prot 60 g; Carbo 69 g;
    Fiber 2 g; T Fat 23 g; 29% Calories from Fat;
    Chol 160 mg; Sod 2661 mg.

Chris Healy

No-Salt Country Captain

1 3-pound chicken, cut up
½ cup flour
½ teaspoon paprika
¼ teaspoon pepper
2 tablespoons oil
1 cup chopped onion
1 cup chopped mushrooms
1 cup chopped green bell
  pepper
2 cloves of garlic, finely
  chopped
¼ cup chopped parsley
1 cup chopped tomatoes
1 8-ounce can tomato sauce
1 tablespoon lime juice
½ teaspoon curry powder
¼ teaspoon thyme
¼ teaspoon tarragon

Yield: 6 servings

Rinse chicken and pat dry. Coat in mixture of flour, paprika and pepper. Sauté chicken in oil in skillet until brown on all sides. Transfer to plate. Cook onion, mushrooms, green pepper and garlic in skillet for 10 minutes or until tender, stirring frequently. Stir in parsley, tomatoes, tomato sauce, lime juice, curry powder, thyme and tarragon. Add chicken; mix well. Simmer for 30 to 40 minutes or until chicken is tender, stirring occasionally.

Approx Per Serving: Cal 333; Prot 36 g; Carbo 17 g;
    Fiber 3 g; T Fat 13 g; 37% Calories from Fat;
    Chol 100 mg; Sod 333 mg.

Evelyn Stripling

Honey Chicken

1   3-pound chicken, cut up,
      skinned
Salt and pepper to taste
1/4 cup margarine
1/2 cup honey
1/4 cup prepared mustard
1 teaspoon curry powder

Yield: 6 servings

Rinse chicken and pat dry. Season with salt and pepper. Arrange in baking dish. Place margarine in microwave-safe dish. Microwave on High until melted. Stir in honey, mustard and curry powder. Pour mixture over chicken, coating each piece. Bake at 350 degrees for 1 hour.

Approx Per Serving: Cal 378; Prot 34 g; Carbo 24 g;
      Fiber <1 g; T Fat 17 g; 39% Calories from Fat;
      Chol 100 mg; Sod 318 mg.

Jan Pendleton

Italian Oven-Fried Chicken

1   3-pound chicken, cut up
1/2 cup French dressing
1 cup cornflake crumbs
1/2 cup grated Parmesan
      cheese
1/2 cup chopped parsley
1 clove of garlic, finely
      chopped
1 1/2 teaspoons salt
1/4 teaspoon pepper

Yield: 6 servings

Rinse chicken and pat dry. Marinate chicken in French dressing in bowl for 1 1/2 hours. Combine cornflake crumbs, Parmesan cheese, parsley, garlic, salt and pepper in bowl; mix well. Coat chicken in cornflake mixture. Arrange in lightly greased baking pan. Bake at 350 degrees for 1 hour or until chicken is tender.

Approx Per Serving: Cal 394; Prot 38 g; Carbo 15 g;
      Fiber 1 g; T Fat 20 g; 45% Calories from Fat;
      Chol 119 mg; Sod 1201 mg.

Jean Lively

Chicken à la Orange

1   3-pound chicken, cut up,
    skinned
2 tablespoons oil
1   6-ounce can frozen
    orange juice concentrate,
    thawed
1/2 cup golden raisins
1/2 cup grated coconut

Yield: 6 servings

Rinse chicken and pat dry. Sauté chicken in oil in skillet until brown on all sides; drain. Arrange in baking dish. Pour orange juice concentrate over chicken. Sprinkle with raisins and grated coconut. Bake at 300 degrees for 40 minutes. Serve with hot cooked wild rice.

Approx Per Serving: Cal 366; Prot 34 g; Carbo 23 g;
    Fiber 2 g; T Fat 15 g; 38% Calories from Fat;
    Chol 100 mg; Sod 101 mg.

Dot Crozier

Spanish Chicken and Rice

4 chicken breasts
2 tablespoons butter
1/2 cup chopped onion
1/4 cup chopped green bell
    pepper
2 cloves of garlic, finely
    chopped
1 cup uncooked rice
1/2 cup frozen English peas
3 tablespoons chopped
    parsley
1/2 cup chopped black olives
1 cup chopped tomatoes
2 cups water
Salt and pepper to taste
1 1/2 tablespoons olive oil

Yield: 4 servings

Rinse chicken and pat dry. Sauté chicken in butter in skillet until brown on all sides. Remove to platter. Add onion, green pepper and garlic to skillet. Cook just until onion and green pepper are tender, stirring frequently. Add rice; mix well. Sauté for several minutes. Stir in peas, parsley, olives, tomatoes, water, salt and pepper. Simmer, covered, until water is absorbed and chicken is tender. Pour olive oil over mixture. Serve immediately. May substitute margarine for butter. May substitute chicken broth for water.

Approx Per Serving: Cal 464; Prot 32 g; Carbo 45 g;
    Fiber 3 g; T Fat 17 g; 33% Calories from Fat;
    Chol 88 mg; Sod 289 mg.

Martha Gherardi

Chicken Alouette with Dill Butter Sauce

4   6-ounce chicken breast
    filets
8 ounces herb-garlic cheese,
    cut into quarters
3 eggs, beaten
1/4 cup milk
1/2 cup flour
2 cups dry bread crumbs
2 tablespoons oil
Dill Butter Sauce

Yield: 4 servings

Rinse chicken and pat dry. Pound filets 1/2 inch thick between sheets of waxed paper. Spread each filet with herb-garlic cheese; fold in half, tucking ends under. Place on baking sheet. Chill, covered, for 1 hour. Beat eggs and milk in bowl. Coat chicken with flour; dip in egg mixture. Roll in bread crumbs. Sauté chicken in oil in skillet until brown on all sides. Transfer to baking sheet. Bake at 400 degrees for 8 to 10 minutes or until chicken is tender. Serve with Dill Butter Sauce.

Approx Per Serving: Cal 1293; Prot 67 g; Carbo 54 g;
    Fiber 3 g; T Fat 88 g; 61% Calories from Fat;
    Chol 464 mg; Sod 1956 mg.
    Nutritional information includes Dill Butter Sauce.

Dill Butter Sauce

2 tablespoons finely
    chopped shallots
1/2 cup dry white wine
1 1/2 tablespoons lemon juice
3/4 cup whipping cream
1 tablespoon dillweed
1 teaspoon salt
1/2 teaspoon hot pepper
    sauce
1 cup unsalted butter, cut
    into pieces

Yield: 4 servings

Combine shallots, white wine and lemon juice in saucepan. Simmer over medium heat until liquid is reduced to 2 tablespoons, stirring constantly. Stir in whipping cream. Cook until liquid is reduced to 1/2 cup, stirring constantly. Add dillweed, salt and hot pepper sauce; mix well. Whisk in butter just before serving. Cook just until heated through, stirring constantly. Do not boil. Serve with Chicken Alouette. May also serve over seafood and assorted vegetables.

Lora James

Cold Lemon Chicken

3 whole chicken breasts,
  split, skinned
1 cup water
1/2 cup white wine
1/2 cup lemon juice
1/4 cup mayonnaise
2 teaspoons lemon juice
2 teaspoons grated lemon
  rind
4 teaspoons chopped seeded
  cucumber
1/4 teaspoon salt
1/4 teaspoon pepper
6 lemon slices

Yield: 6 servings

Rinse chicken. Bring water, white wine and 1/2 cup lemon juice to a boil in large saucepan. Add chicken. Cook over medium-low heat for 20 to 25 minutes or until chicken is tender; drain. Arrange chicken in dish. Spread with mixture of mayonnaise, 2 teaspoons lemon juice, lemon rind, cucumber, salt and pepper. Top with lemon slices. Chill, covered, until serving time.

Approx Per Serving: Cal 228; Prot 27 g; Carbo 3 g;
    Fiber <1 g; T Fat 10 g; 41% Calories from Fat;
    Chol 78 mg; Sod 205 mg.

Molly Kirkland

Chicken in Sour Cream

4 boneless chicken breasts
2 tablespoons rosemary
1/4 cup butter
4 chicken bouillon cubes
2 cups sour cream

Yield: 4 servings

Rinse chicken and pat dry. Sauté rosemary in butter in skillet until crisp. Add bouillon cubes. Cook until dissolved, stirring constantly. Add chicken. Sauté until partially cooked. Transfer chicken to baking pan. Add sour cream to skillet; mix well. Pour sour cream mixture over chicken. Bake at 350 degrees for 25 minutes. Serve over egg noodles.

Approx Per Serving: Cal 502; Prot 31 g; Carbo 7 g;
    Fiber 1 g; T Fat 39 g; 70% Calories from Fat;
    Chol 155 mg; Sod 1394 mg.

Patty Valentine

Succulent Chicken Breasts

4 chicken breast filets
1/4 cup (about) buttermilk
1/2 cup flour
Oil for frying
Salt and pepper to taste

Yield: 4 servings

Rinse chicken and pat dry. Dip filets in buttermilk; coat with flour. Fry in 1/4-inch deep oil in skillet until golden brown. Season with salt and pepper. May substitute grated Parmesan cheese for flour.

Approx Per Serving: Cal 199; Prot 29 g; Carbo 13 g; Fiber <1 g; T Fat 12 g; 45% Calories from Fat; Chol 72 mg; Sod 65 mg.
Nutritional information does not include oil for frying.

B. L. Cosey

Wine-Baked Chicken Breasts

4 chicken breasts
Juice of 1 lemon
Salt and pepper to taste
1 large onion, grated
1 teaspoon dry mustard
4 teaspoons chopped parsley
1/2 cup butter
Paprika to taste
1/2 cup white wine

Yield: 4 servings

Rinse chicken and pat dry. Arrange in baking pan. Sprinkle with lemon juice, salt, pepper, onion, dry mustard and parsley. Dot with butter. Sprinkle with paprika. Bake at 350 degrees for 1 hour or until chicken is tender. Add white wine just before chicken is done. Serve with hot cooked rice.

Approx Per Serving: Cal 384; Prot 27 g; Carbo 5 g; Fiber 1 g; T Fat 26 g; 62% Calories from Fat; Chol 134 mg; Sod 301 mg.

Mildred R. Tucker

Little St. George Island

Accessed only by boat, this ten-mile-long state-owned island is wonderfully preserved. A 78-foot lighthouse still operates at Cape St. George. Once 400 yards inland, today it is beachside. Old camp buildings still exist at Government Dock on the bay side and old turpentine roads make for great hiking explorations. There are willow swamps, dune ridges, savannahs and upland woods. Loggerhead turtles nest in the summer. Many people anchor off the shoreline and wade in, but the safest way is to dock at Government Dock and walk across the Island...a beautiful 45-minute nature walk.

White Chili

2 cups dried navy beans
1   48-ounce can chicken
    broth
12 chicken breast filets, cut
    into bite-sized pieces
6 medium onions, chopped
1 clove of garlic, finely
    chopped
3 tablespoons oil
1 1/2 teaspoons salt
3   4-ounce cans chopped
    green chilies
2 tablespoons cumin
1 1/2 teaspoons red pepper
2 tablespoons oregano
1 teaspoon ground cloves
1 cup shredded Monterey
    Jack cheese

Yield: 10 servings

Sort beans; rinse. Soak beans in enough water to cover in stockpot overnight; drain. Add chicken broth to beans. Simmer for 2 to 3 hours or until beans are tender. Chill, covered, for 24 hours. Sauté chopped chicken, onions and garlic in oil in skillet until onions are tender. Stir in salt, green chilies, cumin, red pepper, oregano and cloves. Cook until combined, stirring constantly. Add mixture to cooked navy beans; mix well. Simmer for 20 to 30 minutes or until heated through, stirring frequently. Add additional water for desired consistency. Serve with Monterey Jack cheese. May add one 10-ounce can cream of chicken soup.

Approx Per Serving: Cal 474; Prot 51 g; Carbo 37 g; Fiber 10 g; T Fat 14 g; 26% Calories from Fat; Chol 98 mg; Sod 1716 mg.

Rose Drye

Chicken Delite

2 cups chopped cooked
    chicken
1/3 cup shredded Cheddar
    cheese
1   8-count can crescent rolls
1   10-ounce can cream of
    chicken soup
1 cup milk
2/3 cup shredded Cheddar
    cheese

Yield: 8 servings

Combine chicken and 1/3 cup cheese in bowl; mix well. Unroll crescent roll dough. Separate into rectangles. Spread with chicken mixture. Roll to enclose filling, sealing edge. Combine soup, milk and 1/3 cup cheese in saucepan; mix well. Cook until cheese melts, stirring constantly. Pour 1/2 of the cheese sauce in baking dish. Arrange chicken rolls over sauce. Top with remaining cheese sauce. Bake at 350 degrees for 25 minutes. Sprinkle with remaining 1/3 cup cheese. Bake for 5 minutes or until cheese melts. May add cooked shrimp with chicken.

Approx Per Serving: Cal 262; Prot 17 g; Carbo 17 g; Fiber <1 g; T Fat 14 g; 47% Calories from Fat; Chol 56 mg; Sod 682 mg.

Edna Rudasill

Pennsylvania Dutch Potpie

1 medium potato, cut into
  1/4-inch slices
2 chicken breasts
3 quarts water
Salt to taste
2 chicken bouillon cubes
1/2 teaspoon celery salt
1 teaspoon celery flakes
1 cup flour
Salt and pepper to taste
1 egg, beaten
1 1/2 tablespoons water

Yield: 4 servings

Soak potato slices in cold water in bowl; set aside. Rinse chicken. Combine chicken, 3 quarts water and salt in stockpot. Boil until chicken is tender. Remove chicken to plate, reserving broth. Cool. Chop chicken, discarding skin and bones. Add bouillon cubes, celery salt and celery flakes to broth; mix well. Combine flour, salt and pepper in bowl; mix well. Stir in mixture of egg and 1 1/2 tablespoons water. Mix until ball forms; mixture should be moist. Divide into 2 portions. Roll dough into thin rectangle on lightly floured surface; cut into 2-inch strips. Cut strips into 2 to 3-inch pieces. Drop into boiling broth. Add drained potato. Cook until potato and dumplings are tender. Stir in chicken. May substitute beef for chicken.

Approx Per Serving: Cal 235; Prot 19 g; Carbo 31 g;
    Fiber 1 g; T Fat 3 g; 13% Calories from Fat;
    Chol 90 mg; Sod 813 mg.

Tom Gross

Chicken and Rice Casserole Supreme

1 onion, chopped
1/2 cup butter
3 tablespoons flour
2 10-ounce cans cream of
   mushroom soup
1 12-ounce can evaporated
   milk
5 pounds chopped cooked
   chicken breast filets
2 cups cooked rice
1 6-ounce can mushrooms,
   drained
16 ounces sharp Cheddar
   cheese, shredded

Yield: 20 servings

Sauté chopped onion in butter in skillet until tender. Stir in flour, soup and evaporated milk, stirring until combined. Combine soup mixture, chicken, rice and mushrooms in bowl; mix well. Spoon into large baking dish. Sprinkle with Cheddar cheese. Bake at 350 degrees for 45 minutes.

Approx Per Serving: Cal 407; Prot 43 g; Carbo 12 g;
    Fiber <1 g; T Fat 20 g; 45% Calories from Fat;
    Chol 138 mg; Sod 573 mg.

Jim and Rhonda Lambert

Mexican Chicken

12 corn tortillas, finely
   sliced
4 or 5 chicken breast filets,
   cooked, cut into
   bite-sized pieces
1 cup milk
1 16-ounce can chili
   without beans
1 4-ounce can chopped
   green chilies
1 10-ounce can cream of
   mushroom soup
1 medium onion, chopped

Yield: 12 servings

Line bottom of greased baking dish with tortillas. Sprinkle with chicken. Pour mixture of milk, chili, chilies, soup and onion over chicken. Bake at 350 degrees for 35 to 45 minutes or until bubbly.

Approx Per Serving: Cal 214; Prot 18 g; Carbo 20 g;
    Fiber 2 g; T Fat 7 g; 30% Calories from Fat;
    Chol 45 mg; Sod 595 mg.

Helen Marsh

Stir-Fry Chicken

4 chicken breast filets
1 tablespoon dry sherry
1 egg white, slightly beaten
1/2 teaspoon sesame oil
2 tablespoons cornstarch
6 tablespoons oil
3 celery stalks, thinly sliced
6 or 8 large mushrooms,
   sliced
3 tablespoons chicken stock
1 10-ounce package frozen
   snow peas, thawed
1/4 teaspoon salt
1/2 teaspoon sugar
1/4 cup cornstarch
3 tablespoons chicken stock
1/2 cup slivered almonds

Yield: 4 servings

Rinse chicken and pat dry; cut into bite-sized pieces. Combine chicken with mixture of sherry, egg white, sesame oil and 2 tablespoons cornstarch in bowl; mix well. Let stand for 10 minutes; drain. Stir-fry chicken in 4 tablespoons oil in heavy skillet or wok until chicken is firm. Remove chicken to colander to drain. Wipe skillet with paper towel. Heat 2 tablespoons oil in skillet or wok. Add celery and mushrooms. Stir-fry for 2 minutes. Add 3 tablespoons stock; mix well. Steam, covered, for 2 minutes. Add snow peas, chicken, salt and sugar; mix well. Stir in mixture of 1/4 cup cornstarch and 3 tablespoons chicken stock. Cook for 30 seconds or until thickened. Stir in almonds. Serve immediately. May season with soy sauce. May substitute 1 pound peeled shrimp for chicken.

Approx Per Serving: Cal 526; Prot 34 g; Carbo 23 g;
    Fiber 5 g; T Fat 33 g; 57% Calories from Fat;
    Chol 72 mg; Sod 316 mg.

Pat Morrison

Tennessee Chicken Casserole

1　3-pound chicken
1/4 cup margarine
1　5-ounce package egg
　　noodles
1　2-ounce jar sliced black
　　olives
1　4-ounce can sliced
　　mushrooms
1　10-ounce can cream of
　　mushroom soup
Salt and pepper to taste
1 cup chopped celery
1 cup chopped onion
1 cup chopped green bell
　　pepper
2 tablespoons margarine
1　6-ounce can French-fried
　　onions

Yield: 8 servings

Rinse chicken. Combine chicken and enough water to cover in stockpot. Cook over medium heat until chicken is tender. Drain, reserving chicken stock. Chop chicken, discarding skin and bones. Add 1/4 cup margarine to reserved chicken stock. Cook noodles in stock using package directions; drain. Combine noodles, olives, mushrooms, soup, salt, pepper and chicken in bowl; mix well. Sauté celery, onion and green pepper in 2 tablespoons margarine in skillet until tender. Stir into chicken mixture. Spoon into large baking pan. Bake at 350 degrees for 25 to 35 minutes or until bubbly. Sprinkle with French-fried onions. Bake for 5 minutes. May freeze uncooked casserole for future use.

Approx Per Serving: Cal 434; Prot 30 g; Carbo 28 g;
　　Fiber 1 g; T Fat 29 g; 53% Calories from Fat;
　　Chol 107 mg; Sod 744 mg.

Bernice Holmes

Chicken and Dumplings

10 pounds chicken leg
　　quarters
Salt and pepper to taste
3 pounds self-rising flour
3 1/2 to 4 cups water

Yield: 25 servings

Rinse chicken pieces. Combine chicken, salt, pepper and enough water to cover in stockpot. Cook over medium heat until tender. Remove chicken, reserving chicken stock. Chop chicken, discarding skin and bones. Return to stock; simmer. Combine flour with water in bowl, stirring until of consistency of biscuit dough. Drop by tablespoonfuls into simmering stock. Cook until broth thickens and dumplings are tender.

Approx Per Serving: Cal 379; Prot 30 g; Carbo 40 g;
　　Fiber 1 g; T Fat 9 g; 23% Calories from Fat;
　　Chol 84 mg; Sod 775 mg.

John Henry and Nelle Spratt

Easy Chicken 'n Dumplings

4 pieces of chicken
6 flour tortillas
1/4 cup flour
5 to 6 cups chicken broth
1   5-ounce can evaporated
    milk
Salt and pepper to taste

Yield: 6 servings

Rinse chicken. Combine chicken and enough water to cover in saucepan. Cook over medium heat until tender; drain. Chop chicken, discarding skin and bones. Dust tortillas with flour. Make 4 cuts horizontally and vertically in tortillas in checkerboard pattern. Heat chicken broth in stockpot. Drop tortilla pieces 1 at a time into hot broth. Simmer for 20 minutes. Stir in chicken, evaporated milk, salt and pepper. Simmer for 15 minutes.

Approx Per Serving: Cal 320; Prot 28 g; Carbo 27 g;
    Fiber 1 g; T Fat 10 g; 30% Calories from Fat;
    Chol 61 mg; Sod 1022 mg.

Dana Troutman Keith

Hot Turkey Salad

2 cups chopped turkey
2 cups chopped celery
1 cup mayonnaise
2 tablespoons lemon juice
1/2 cup slivered almonds
1/2 teaspoon salt
2 teaspoons finely chopped
    onion
1 cup crushed potato chips
1/2 cup shredded medium
    Cheddar cheese

Yield: 6 servings

Combine turkey, celery, mayonnaise, lemon juice, almonds, salt and onion in bowl; mix well. Spoon into 8x8-inch baking pan. Top with potato chips; sprinkle with cheese. Bake at 450 degrees for 10 minutes or until cheese melts. May change the amounts of ingredients to suit your taste.

Approx Per Serving: Cal 506; Prot 20 g; Carbo 10 g;
    Fiber 2 g; T Fat 44 g; 77% Calories from Fat;
    Chol 67 mg; Sod 570 mg.

Sharen Clark

Grilled Wild Duck Breasts

2 wild duck breasts,
  skinned, deboned
Salt to taste
1 cup lime juice
1/2 cup melted butter

Yield: 2 servings

Rinse duck and pat dry; sprinkle lightly with salt. Marinate duck in enough lime juice to cover in bowl for 30 to 45 minutes; drain. Brush duck with melted butter. Grill over very hot coals for 2 minutes per side for small breasts and 3 minutes per side for large breasts, basting with butter frequently. Remove to serving platter; brush with melted butter. Let stand for 5 minutes. Cut duck into thin slices; baste with juices.

Approx Per Serving: Cal 644; Prot 34 g; Carbo 11 g; Fiber <1 g; T Fat 53 g; 73% Calories from Fat; Chol 252 mg; Sod 565 mg.

Roy Hoffman, Jr.

My Quail

2 quail
1/4 cup flour
Salt and pepper to taste
1/2 cup margarine
1/4 cup cream sherry
1/4 cup water

Yield: 2 servings

Rinse quail and pat dry inside and out. Coat with flour; season with salt and pepper. Cook quail in margarine in cast-iron skillet until brown on all sides. Transfer quail to heavy baking pan. Pour pan drippings over quail. Top with mixture of sherry and water. Bake at 250 degrees for 3 hours or until tender, basting with pan drippings occasionally. May add additional sherry and water if quail become too dry. May adjust ingredients for larger crowds.

Approx Per Serving: Cal 711; Prot 22 g; Carbo 26 g; Fiber <1 g; T Fat 50 g; 63% Calories from Fat; Chol 64 mg; Sod 585 mg.

Katherine Autrey

Seafood Entrées

The Oysterman
by Karen Dingler

The Apalachicola Basin:
A Natural Paradise

Apalachicola River is the terminal segment of a three-river basin that also includes the Chattahoochee and Flint rivers. Collectively, they drain 19,800 square miles. Eighty-eight percent of the drainage basin is in Georgia and Alabama. Based on average flow, 84 percent of the fresh water that feeds Apalachicola Bay originates outside of Florida.

On a production-per-acre basis, Apalachicola Bay is one of the most productive estuaries in the Northern Hemisphere. Over 90 percent of all the oysters harvested in Florida and over 10 percent of the national harvest come from our bay. Three species of shrimp (white, pink and brown) are harvested from local waters. We also have an active blue crab and finfish industry. At the consumer level, our seafood industry is estimated to be worth 70 to 80 million dollars per year. Even though impressive, this economic value does not come close to depicting the worth of Apalachicola Bay. In the Gulf of Mexico, 95 percent of all species harvested commercially must spend a portion of their life cycle in an estuary. Blue crabs, for example, migrate as far as 300 miles to spawn in Apalachicola Bay. They spend their larval and juvenile stages in our marshes, then scatter all over the Gulf. So do the shrimp and finfish. They are harvested and landed elsewhere and are reflected in someone else's economic value. However, that product would not be available except for the productivity of Apalachicola Bay.

In addition to the natural resources that make money, the Apalachicola Basin has many other bragging rights. More than 1,300 different plant species have been identified within the basin and 107 of them are listed as threatened or endangered. A new species, the Apalachicola Daisy was recently discovered. Our basin contains more than 40 species of amphibians and 80 species of reptiles. This is the highest diversity of these animal groups in North America north of Mexico.

Mammals also abound in our system. Fifty-seven species, including the threatened Florida black bear and the endangered West Indian manatee, may be found. Our area is among the most important bird habitats in the southeastern United States. We boast 315 species of birds found locally. Over 180 species of fish have been documented from the river and bay.

Because we choose to live here, we have a great responsibility for proper stewardship of an incredible array of natural resources.

Cashew-Romano Fish Fillets

3 tablespoons butter
3 tablespoons oil
6 4-ounce firm white fish
   fillets
1 egg, beaten
3/4 cup grated Romano
   cheese
2 tablespoons flour
1/2 cup chopped cashews

Yield: 6 servings

Melt butter in shallow baking pan in 425-degree oven. Remove pan from oven. Add oil; swirl in pan. Dip fillets in egg; roll in mixture of cheese and flour. Place in prepared pan. Sprinkle with cashews. Bake for 10 minutes. Garnish with lemon wedges. May substitute margarine for butter.

Approx Per Serving: Cal 394; Prot 29 g; Carbo 5 g;
   Fiber 1 g; T Fat 28 g; 65% Calories from Fat;
   Chol 134 mg; Sod 279 mg.

Pam Vest

Hobson's Mexican Fish

12 corn tortillas
1 16-ounce jar mild or hot
   salsa
8 fish fillets
1/2 cup cornmeal
Salt and pepper to taste
12 ounces sharp Cheddar
   cheese, shredded
2 cups guacamole

Yield: 8 servings

Line bottom of greased 9x13-inch glass baking dish with corn tortillas. Spread with thin layer of salsa. Roll fillets in mixture of cornmeal, salt and pepper. Sauté in skillet or broil on rack until fish flakes. Arrange over salsa layer. Top with remaining salsa; sprinkle with cheese. Bake at 400 degrees until cheese melts and salsa is bubbly. Spread with guacamole before serving.

Approx Per Serving: Cal 489; Prot 37 g; Carbo 36 g;
   Fiber 4 g; T Fat 24 g; 42% Calories from Fat;
   Chol 75 mg; Sod 1591 mg.

Hobson Fulmer, DVM

Oven-Fried White Fish Fillets

4 white fish fillets
Salt and pepper to taste
1/2 cup mayonnaise
2 cups crushed cornflakes

Yield: 4 servings

Line baking sheet with foil; spray with nonstick cooking spray. Season fillets with salt and pepper. Coat both sides with mayonnaise; roll in cornflakes. Arrange in prepared pan. Bake at 400 degrees for 20 minutes or until golden brown.

Approx Per Serving: Cal 499; Prot 26 g; Carbo 33 g; Fiber 2 g; T Fat 29 g; 53% Calories from Fat; Chol 86 mg; Sod 598 mg.

Nancy Watts-Bloom

Apalachicola River Catfish Stew

5 pounds river catfish
8 slices bacon
2 large onions, chopped
6 medium potatoes, coarsely chopped
2 teaspoons salt
1   10-ounce can tomato soup
Pepper to taste

Yield: 12 servings

Combine catfish and enough water to cover in large stockpot. Cook until catfish flakes easily. Drain, reserving stock. Discard skin and bones, reserving catfish. Fry bacon in skillet until crisp. Drain, reserving bacon drippings. Cook onions and potatoes in reserved bacon drippings in skillet until tender, stirring frequently. Add mixture to reserved fish stock. Bring to a boil; reduce heat. Stir in salt, reserved catfish and tomato soup. Simmer for 5 minutes or until potatoes are tender. Season with pepper. May add crushed saltine crackers for thicker consistency.

Approx Per Serving: Cal 326; Prot 38 g; Carbo 19 g; Fiber 1 g; T Fat 11 g; 30% Calories from Fat; Chol 113 mg; Sod 710 mg.

Bo Suber

Flounder En Papillote

1/4 cup butter, softened
1/2 cup chopped shallots
1 teaspoon salt
1/8 teaspoon white pepper
12 mushroom caps, sliced
12 3-ounce flounder fillets
12 mushroom caps
12 carrot slices
6 1/2 ounces or 1 split dry
    white champagne
1 cup skimmed canned
    chicken broth
1 tablespoon butter,
    softened
1/2 cup flour
1/2 cup butter, softened
1/4 cup whipping cream
2 tablespoons lemon juice
2 tablespoons chopped
    fresh parsley
1 egg white, slightly beaten
2 teaspoons water
Lemon wedges

Yield: 6 servings

Spread 1/4 cup butter in baking pan; sprinkle with shallots, salt and white pepper. Place sliced mushroom caps in center of each fillet. Fold to enclose filling. Place seam side down in prepared pan. Arrange 12 mushroom caps and carrot slices around fish. Pour in champagne and chicken broth; cover with foil. Bring to a boil over medium heat. Transfer to 350-degree oven. Bake for 20 minutes. Cut 14x20-inch and 15x21-inch ovals from butcher paper. Spread 1 tablespoon butter on the smaller oval to within 1-inch of edge; place on baking sheet. Transfer the fillets, mushrooms and carrots with a slotted spoon to a plate, reserving fish stock. Cover with foil to keep warm. Pour the fish stock into a saucepan. Add mixture of flour and 1/2 cup butter gradually. Whisk over medium heat until smooth and slightly thickened, adding more or less of butter mixture. Stir in cream. Add lemon juice; mix well. Arrange drained fillets on buttered baking parchment. Make slits in mushroom caps; place carrot slice in each slit. Garnish each fillet with mushroom and carrot. Spoon 1 cup sauce over fillets; sprinkle with parsley. Brush edges of parchment with mixture of egg white and water. Place remaining parchment oval over fish. Roll the bottom edge over the top edge, crimping to form tight seal. Brush the edges and top with remaining egg white mixture. Bake at 400 degrees for 10 minutes or until parchment crisps and puffs up. Serve with lemon wedges and remaining sauce. This dish looks and tastes very elegant. Use a delicate fish and a sauce made from champagne and tiny mushrooms; wrap in parchment. When the paper is torn open with a flourish a gastronomic feast is revealed and the most exquisite flavor is released.

Approx Per Serving: Cal 510; Prot 37 g; Carbo 15 g;
    Fiber 1 g; T Fat 31 g; 55% Calories from Fat;
    Chol 173 mg; Sod 829 mg.

Pamela Amato

Grouper Florentine

6 ounces grouper, cut into
  3/4-inch pieces
2 teaspoons lemon juice
1/2 cup milk
1 tablespoon butter
1 tablespoon flour
1/2 cup chopped cooked
  spinach, drained
Garlic powder, salt and
  pepper to taste
8 butter crackers, crushed
3 tablespoons grated
  Parmesan cheese
1 tablespoon melted butter

Yield: 2 servings

Place grouper in 2 shell baking dishes. Sprinkle with lemon juice. Scald milk in saucepan. Whisk in 1 tablespoon butter and flour. Simmer for 3 to 5 minutes or until thickened, stirring constantly. Remove from heat. Stir in spinach, garlic powder, salt and pepper. Spoon sauce over grouper. Sprinkle with mixture of crushed butter crackers and Parmesan cheese. Drizzle with 1 tablespoon melted butter.

Approx Per Serving: Cal 348; Prot 26 g; Carbo 16 g;
  Fiber 1 g; T Fat 20 g; 53% Calories from Fat;
  Chol 79 mg; Sod 491 mg.

Sandra Thaxton

Grouper à la Carol

1   4-ounce can tiny shrimp
6   4-ounce grouper fillets
6 large mushrooms, sliced
2 tablespoons chopped
  fresh chives
1 cup lemon yogurt
1 1/2 teaspoons
  confectioners' sugar
2 teaspoons cornstarch
1/3 cup grated Parmesan
  cheese
1/3 cup fine bread crumbs
1/4 cup melted butter
1 tablespoon parsley flakes
1 tablespoon pepper

Yield: 6 servings

Rinse shrimp in cold water; pat dry with paper towel. Arrange fillets in buttered baking dish. Sprinkle with mushrooms and chives. Top with shrimp. Spoon mixture of lemon yogurt, confectioners' sugar and cornstarch over shrimp. Sprinkle with Parmesan cheese and bread crumbs. Drizzle with mixture of melted butter, parsley and pepper. Bake at 325 degrees for 15 to 20 minutes or until fish flakes easily. Serve over brown rice pilaf or wild rice.

Approx Per Serving: Cal 297; Prot 32 g; Carbo 12 g;
  Fiber 1 g; T Fat 13 g; 39% Calories from Fat;
  Chol 104 mg; Sod 337 mg.

Carol Haberkern

Island-Style Fish Casserole

2¹/₂ to 3 pounds grouper,
   cut into 2 to 3-inch pieces
1 cup olive oil
1 envelope onion soup mix
1   10-ounce can Cheddar
   cheese soup
1   10-ounce can cream of
   mushroom soup
1   6-ounce can light tuna
¹/₂ cup milk
1 pound shrimp, shelled,
   deveined
2 tablespoons lemon herb
   seasoning
1 cup flour
¹/₄ cup bread crumbs

Yield: 12 servings

Combine grouper and olive oil in bowl. Marinate, covered, for 30 minutes; drain. Combine soup mix, soups, undrained tuna and milk in saucepan; mix well. Cook over low heat until blended, stirring constantly. Add shrimp; mix well. Cook over low heat for 5 minutes or until shrimp test done, stirring occasionally. Spoon enough of the shrimp sauce into a baking dish to cover the bottom. Sprinkle grouper with lemon herb seasoning; coat with flour. Arrange in prepared baking dish. Pour remaining shrimp sauce over fish; sprinkle with bread crumbs. Bake at 325 degrees for 30 minutes. May substitute snapper or amberjack white meat for grouper and cooking wine for olive oil.

Approx Per Serving: Cal 421; Prot 35 g; Carbo 14 g;
   Fiber 1 g; T Fat 24 g; 53% Calories from Fat;
   Chol 107 mg; Sod 633 mg.

Bill Short

Baked King Mackerel

1 cup sliced mushrooms
1 medium onion, sliced
2 tablespoons chopped
   green bell pepper
2 tablespoons lemon juice
2 tablespoons olive oil
Salt and pepper to taste
¹/₂ teaspoon dillseed
4 mackerel steaks
4 bay leaves
4 thick tomato slices

Yield: 4 servings

Cut 4 large squares of foil. Combine mushrooms, onion, green pepper, lemon juice, olive oil, salt, pepper and dillseed in bowl; mix well. Place ¹/₂ of the vegetable mixture on foil squares; top with mackerel steaks. Season with salt and pepper. Place 1 bay leaf and 1 tomato slice on each steak; top with remaining vegetable mixture. Wrap tightly in foil. Place on baking sheet. Bake at 425 degrees for 45 to 60 minutes or until fish flakes. Discard bay leaves before serving.

Approx Per Serving: Cal 320; Prot 23 g; Carbo 5 g;
   Fiber 1 g; T Fat 23 g; 65% Calories from Fat;
   Chol 68 mg; Sod 79 mg.

Carol Mitchell

Mullet-Cheese Bake

4 mullet fillets
Garlic powder, salt and
    pepper to taste
1 cup shredded Cheddar
    cheese
1/2 green bell pepper,
    chopped
1/2 red bell pepper, chopped
1 onion, chopped
1/2 cup grated Parmesan
    cheese
1/4 cup margarine

Yield: 4 servings

Season fillets with garlic powder, salt and pepper. Arrange in shallow baking dish. Sprinkle with Cheddar cheese, green and red peppers and onion. Top with Parmesan cheese; dot with margarine. Bake at 350 degrees for 20 minutes or until fish flakes easily and cheese is bubbly. May substitute Monterey Jack cheese for Cheddar cheese.

Approx Per Serving: Cal 427; Prot 36 g; Carbo 5 g;
    Fiber 1 g; T Fat 29 g; 62% Calories from Fat;
    Chol 98 mg; Sod 609 mg.

Kathy Morton

Salsa Fish

1 pound 1/2-inch thick cod
    fillets
1 cup chopped tomato
1/2 cup chopped green bell
    pepper
1/4 cup chopped onion
2 tablespoons chopped
    parsley
1/4 teaspoon salt
1/4 cup dry white wine

Yield: 4 servings

Spray 10-inch nonstick skillet with nonstick cooking spray. Heat skillet over medium heat. Arrange fillets in single layer in skillet. Cook for 4 to 6 minutes or until fish flakes easily, turning once. Remove to warm platter. Combine tomato, green pepper, onion, parsley, and salt in skillet. Cook for 3 to 5 minutes or until green pepper and onion are tender-crisp, stirring frequently. Stir in wine. Cook until heated through, stirring constantly. Spoon mixture over cod fillets. May substitute orange roughy or other medium-fat fish for cod. May substitute chicken broth for wine.

Approx Per Serving: Cal 122; Prot 22 g; Carbo 4 g;
    Fiber 1 g; T Fat 1 g; 7% Calories from Fat;
    Chol 43 mg; Sod 222 mg.

Phyllis Vitale-Lewis

Orange Roughy with Bell Peppers

1 teaspoon olive oil
1 small onion, cut into thin
   slices
2 red or green bell peppers,
   cut into strips
1/2 teaspoon dried thyme
1/8 teaspoon pepper
1 pound orange roughy
   fillets
1/2 teaspoon dried thyme
1/8 teaspoon pepper

Yield: 4 servings

Heat olive oil in 10-inch nonstick skillet. Layer onion and red or green peppers in skillet; sprinkle with 1/2 teaspoon thyme and 1/8 teaspoon pepper. Arrange fillets over vegetables; sprinkle with 1/2 teaspoon thyme and 1/8 teaspoon pepper. Cook, covered, over low heat for 15 minutes. Cook, uncovered, for 10 to 15 minutes or until fish flakes easily. May substitute vegetable oil for olive oil.

Approx Per Serving: Cal 107; Prot 18 g; Carbo 4 g;
   Fiber 1 g; T Fat 2 g; 18% Calories from Fat;
   Chol 24 mg; Sod 75 mg.

Phyllis Vitale-Lewis

Grilled Salmon Steaks

1/2 cup melted margarine
1 tablespoon parsley flakes
2 tablespoons lemon juice
1 tablespoon soy sauce
1 teaspoon garlic powder
1 teaspoon dillweed
1 teaspoon seasoned salt
1/4 teaspoon lemon pepper
   seasoning
6 1-inch thick salmon
   steaks

Yield: 6 servings

Combine margarine, parsley, lemon juice, soy sauce, garlic powder, dillweed, seasoned salt and lemon pepper in bowl; mix well. Let stand for 15 to 20 minutes. Brush salmon steaks with sauce. Spray grill with nonstick cooking spray. Grill over hot coals for 3 to 4 minutes on 1 side, basting once. Turn steaks over. Grill for 3 to 4 minutes or until fish flakes easily, basting once. May substitute tuna for salmon.

Approx Per Serving: Cal 336; Prot 25 g; Carbo 1 g;
   Fiber <1 g; T Fat 25 g; 68% Calories from Fat;
   Chol 79 mg; Sod 660 mg.

Ann Sharp

Judi Little makes **Dijon Mustard Sauce** to serve with salmon. Blend 1/4 cup Dijon mustard, 1 tablespoon white wine, 1 tablespoon lemon juice, 2 tablespoons honey and cayenne pepper to taste in bowl; mix well. Stir in enough mayonnaise to make desired consistency.

Stuffed Snapper

2 pounds snapper fillets
1/2 pound crab meat
8 slices bread, cut into cubes
1/4 cup finely chopped celery
1/2 cup finely chopped onion
1/2 cup melted butter
Salt and pepper to taste
Garlic salt to taste

Yield: 8 servings

Layer 1/2 of the fillets skin side down in foil-lined baking pan. Combine remaining ingredients in skillet. Sauté until celery and onion are tender. Spread mixture over fillets. Arrange remaining fillets skin side up over mixture. Cook, covered with foil, at 350 degrees for 25 minutes. Remove foil. Broil for 5 minutes.

Approx Per Serving: Cal 327; Prot 32 g; Carbo 15 g;
    Fiber 1 g; T Fat 15 g; 41% Calories from Fat;
    Chol 103 mg; Sod 395 mg.

Jane Pitts

Seafood Marinade for Grilling

2 tablespoons soy sauce
1/4 cup dry red wine
1/4 cup oil
2 tablespoons red wine
    vinegar
2 cloves of garlic, finely
    chopped
1 tablespoon tiger sauce
2 tablespoons corn syrup

Yield: 1 cup

Combine soy sauce, red wine, oil, wine vinegar, garlic, tiger sauce and corn syrup in bowl; mix well. Marinate tuna, amberjack or any seafood for 2 hours before grilling. May substitute honey for corn syrup.

Approx Per Cup: Cal 672; Prot 2 g; Carbo 39 g;
    Fiber <1 g; T Fat 55 g; 71% Calories from Fat;
    Chol 0 mg; Sod 2108 mg.

Diane Hunt

Caper Sauce

1 cup mayonnaise
3 tablespoons drained
    capers

Yield: 1 cup

Combine mayonnaise and capers in bowl; mix well. Serve with fish.

Approx Per Cup: Cal 1582; Prot 2 g; Carbo 6 g;
    Fiber 0 g; T Fat 176 g; 98% Calories from Fat;
    Chol 130 mg; Sod 1254 mg.

Judi Little

New Orleans Tartar Sauce

1 cup homemade
   mayonnaise
1 teaspoon dry mustard
1 teaspoon grated onion
2 tablespoons minced
   parsley
1/2 clove of garlic, mashed
1/8 teaspoon red pepper
2 tablespoons chopped dill
   pickle
2 tablespoons capers,
   drained, chopped
1 tablespoon finely chopped
   green onion tops

Yield: 1 1/2 cups

Combine mayonnaise, dry mustard, onion, parsley, garlic, red pepper, dill pickle, capers and green onions in bowl; mix well. Serve with assorted seafood.

Approx Per Recipe: Cal 1624; Prot 4 g; Carbo 13 g;
   Fiber 2 g; T Fat 177 g; 96% Calories from Fat;
   Chol 130 mg; Sod 2490 mg.

John B. Spohrer, Jr.

Baked Clams

1 small onion, chopped
2 or 3 cloves of garlic,
   chopped
1/2 cup melted butter
3 7-ounce cans minced
   clams
1/4 cup grated Parmesan
   cheese
1 cup shredded mozzarella
   cheese
1 cup seasoned bread
   crumbs
1/2 teaspoon oregano
Salt and pepper to taste
Paprika to taste

Yield: 8 servings

Sauté onion and garlic in butter in saucepan until tender. Combine with clams, Parmesan cheese, mozzarella cheese, bread crumbs, oregano, salt and pepper in bowl; mix well. Spoon into clam shells; sprinkle with paprika. Place on baking sheet. Bake at 400 degrees for 20 minutes or until done to taste. This can be frozen before baking.

Approx Per Serving: Cal 269; Prot 16 g; Carbo 13 g;
   Fiber 1 g; T Fat 17 g; 57% Calories from Fat;
   Chol 71 mg; Sod 455 mg.

Edna Bono

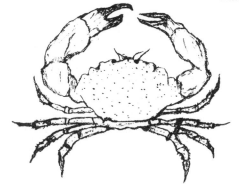

Linguine with Clam Sauce

5 tablespoons butter
2 7-ounce cans minced
   clams
1 clove of garlic, minced
5 tablespoons olive oil
2 tablespoons chopped
   parsley
1/4 teaspoon oregano
1/2 teaspoon basil
3/4 teaspoon salt
Pepper to taste
1 8-ounce package
   linguine, cooked

Yield: 4 servings

Melt butter in saucepan. Add undrained clams, garlic, olive oil, parsley, oregano, basil, salt and pepper; mix well. Simmer for 10 minutes. Serve over linguine. May substitute margarine for butter.

Approx Per Serving: Cal 567; Prot 21 g; Carbo 46 g; Fiber 1 g; T Fat 33 g; 53% Calories from Fat; Chol 74 mg; Sod 710 mg.

Anna Johnson Riedel

Light White Clam Sauce

3 cloves of garlic, chopped
1 teaspoon oregano
1 teaspoon basil
1/4 teaspoon red pepper
   flakes
1/2 cup olive oil
36 fresh clams, steamed,
   chopped
11/2 cups fresh or canned
   clam juice
1/2 cup dry vermouth
1/4 cup chopped parsley

Yield: 4 servings

Sauté garlic, oregano, basil and red pepper flakes in olive oil in saucepan for 3 minutes. Add clams. Sauté for 5 minutes. Add clam juice, wine and parsley. Simmer for 30 minutes. Serve over pasta. May substitute 3 cans of clams for the fresh clams.

Approx Per Serving: Cal 531; Prot 44 g; Carbo 11 g; Fiber <1 g; T Fat 30 g; 52% Calories from Fat; Chol 116 mg; Sod 389 mg.
Nutritional information for this recipe does not include the pasta.

Edna Bono

Crab and Broccoli Rolls

1 cup crab meat
1 cup cooked chopped
  broccoli
1/4 cup mayonnaise
1/2 cup shredded Swiss
  cheese
1   8-count can crescent rolls

Yield: 8 servings

Combine crab meat, broccoli, mayonnaise and cheese in bowl; mix well. Separate roll dough. Spread with crab mixture. Roll to enclose filling; place in greased baking pan. Bake at 375 degrees for 20 minutes.

Approx Per Serving: Cal 180; Prot 7 g; Carbo 14 g;
      Fiber 1 g; T Fat 11 g; 53% Calories from Fat;
      Chol 28 mg; Sod 353 mg.

Patty Valentine

Crab Cakes

1 small green bell pepper,
  chopped
1 small onion, chopped
1/4 cup butter
1 pound crab meat
1 egg, slightly beaten
2 tablespoons mayonnaise
2 tablespoons mustard
12 crackers, coarsely
  crushed
Garlic salt and celery salt to
  taste
Paprika to taste

Yield: 4 servings

Sauté green pepper and onion in butter in saucepan. Cool to room temperature. Combine with crab meat, egg, mayonnaise, mustard, cracker crumbs, garlic salt and celery salt in bowl; mix well. Shape into cakes; sprinkle with paprika. Place in baking pan. Bake at 400 degrees for 15 to 20 minutes or until cooked through. May spoon mixture into greased crab shells and bake if preferred. May substitute margarine for butter.

Approx Per Serving: Cal 339; Prot 26 g; Carbo 10 g;
      Fiber 1 g; T Fat 22 g; 58% Calories from Fat;
      Chol 202 mg; Sod 704 mg.

Cathy Buzzett

Tred Avon River Crab Cakes

2 pounds backfin crab meat
2 tablespoons chopped
   parsley
2 teaspoons Dijon mustard
2 eggs, beaten
1/4 cup mayonnaise
20 saltines, crushed
1 teaspoon (about)
   Worcestershire sauce
2 teaspoons Old Bay
   seasoning
2 tablespoons butter

Yield: 8 servings

Combine crab meat, parsley, mustard, eggs, mayonnaise, cracker crumbs, Worcestershire sauce and Old Bay seasoning in a bowl; mix well. Shape into medium cakes. Sauté in butter in skillet until golden brown and cooked through.

Approx Per Serving: Cal 243; Prot 25 g; Carbo 6 g;
   Fiber <1 g; T Fat 13 g; 48% Calories from Fat;
   Chol 178 mg; Sod 539 mg.
   Nutritional information does not include Old Bay seasoning.

Vicki Sayle

Crab Casserole

1 pound cooked crab meat
3/4 cup chopped celery
3/4 cup chopped onion
1/2 cup chopped green bell
   pepper
1 1/2 cups cracker crumbs
1 egg
1/2 cup melted margarine

Yield: 4 servings

Combine crab meat, celery, onion, green pepper, cracker crumbs, egg and margarine in bowl; mix well. Spoon into baking dish. Bake at 375 degrees for 30 minutes or until heated through. May add Worcestershire sauce if desired.

Approx Per Serving: Cal 492; Prot 28 g; Carbo 27 g;
   Fiber 2 g; T Fat 30 g; 55% Calories from Fat;
   Chol 166 mg; Sod 1030 mg.

Fred Lawhon

Delicious Crab Casserole

1 onion, chopped
1/2 cup chopped green bell
   pepper
1 cup chopped celery
3 to 4 tablespoons olive oil
2 tablespoons flour
3/4 cup milk
1 tablespoon lemon juice
1 teaspoon mustard
1 teaspoon Worcestershire
   sauce
3 drops of hot sauce
Salt and pepper to taste
1 egg, beaten
1 pound crab meat
1 tablespoon parsley flakes
1 cup bread crumbs

Yield: 4 servings

Sauté onion, green pepper and celery in olive oil in skillet. Stir in flour. Add milk gradually. Cook until thickened, stirring constantly. Add lemon juice, mustard, Worcestershire sauce, hot sauce, salt and pepper; mix well. Stir a small amount of hot mixture into egg; stir egg into hot mixture. Stir in crab meat and parsley flakes. Spoon into greased baking dish. Sprinkle with bread crumbs. Bake at 350 degrees for 25 minutes. Garnish with lemon slices.

Approx Per Serving: Cal 415; Prot 30 g; Carbo 28 g;
   Fiber 2 g; T Fat 20 g; 43% Calories from Fat;
   Chol 173 mg; Sod 628 mg.

Phyllis Stanley Stephens

Creamed Lump Crab

4 medium mushrooms,
   sliced
1/4 cup unsalted butter
1 tablespoon chopped
   shallots
2 tomatoes, peeled, chopped
1 pound fresh backfin crab
   meat
Salt and pepper to taste
1 cup whipping cream
1 teaspoon chopped mixed
   herbs, such as chives,
   chervil and parsley
2 tablespoons brandy

Yield: 5 servings

Sauté mushrooms in butter in skillet for 3 minutes. Add shallots and tomatoes. Cook for 3 minutes. Add crab meat, salt and pepper; cook until heated through. Stir in cream gently. Cook for 1 minute. Add herbs and brandy. Serve immediately.

Approx Per Serving: Cal 365; Prot 20 g; Carbo 5 g;
   Fiber 1 g; T Fat 29 g; 70% Calories from Fat;
   Chol 181 mg; Sod 277 mg.

Katherine Autrey

Deviled Crab

1 pound crab meat
1/2 large green bell pepper,
  chopped
3 saltines, crushed
1 egg
1/2 cup melted butter
1 tablespoon
  Worcestershire sauce
1 tablespoon lemon juice

Yield: 4 servings

Combine crab meat, green pepper, cracker crumbs, egg, butter, Worcestershire sauce and lemon juice in bowl; mix well. Spoon into baking dish. Bake at 350 degrees for 30 minutes. May use mixture to stuff flounder if desired.

Approx Per Serving: Cal 352; Prot 25 g; Carbo 3 g; Fiber <1 g; T Fat 27 g; 68% Calories from Fat; Chol 229 mg; Sod 638 mg.

Linda Arnold

Nanny's Deviled Crab

40 saltines, crushed
1 pound crab meat
1/4 cup chopped onion
2 eggs
1/3 cup milk
1 tablespoon
  Worcestershire sauce
Garlic powder to taste
1/8 teaspoon chili powder
1/2 cup butter

Yield: 4 servings

Reserve 1/4 cup cracker crumbs. Combine remaining cracker crumbs with crab meat, onion, eggs, milk, Worcestershire sauce, garlic powder and chili powder in bowl; mix well. Spoon into baking dish. Sprinkle with reserved crumbs; dot with butter. Bake at 350 degrees until golden brown.

Approx Per Serving: Cal 504; Prot 30 g; Carbo 24 g; Fiber 1 g; T Fat 32 g; 57% Calories from Fat; Chol 284 mg; Sod 1024 mg.

Jayne Bamburg

St. George Island

Glistening sands and whispering winds
zircons floating on the sea.
Meringue-tipped waves on seas
sugar in the sun.
Seagulls standing guarding the surf
racing, scampering sandpipers.
Candy clouds marshmallow white
toasted by the wind.
St. George Island.

—Frances Reiter 1991

Shrimp and Crab Divine

1 pound crab meat
1 pound cooked shrimp
1 tablespoon chopped green
   bell pepper
1/2 cup chopped onion
1 tablespoon
   Worcestershire sauce
3 cups cooked rice
1 cup chopped celery
1 4-ounce can mushrooms,
   drained
1 cup mayonnaise
3/4 cup light cream
Tabasco sauce to taste
1 teaspoon salt
1/2 teaspoon pepper
1 cup bread crumbs
2 tablespoons melted butter
Paprika to taste

Yield: 8 servings

Combine crab meat, shrimp, green pepper, onion, Worcestershire sauce, cooked rice, celery, mushrooms, mayonnaise, light cream, Tabasco sauce, salt and pepper in bowl; mix well. Spoon into large baking dish. Top with mixture of bread crumbs and melted butter; sprinkle with paprika. Bake at 350 degrees for 35 minutes. May add 1 small package frozen green peas and 1/3 cup chopped parsley or bake in individual ramekins if desired.

Approx Per Serving: Cal 527; Prot 28 g; Carbo 35 g;
   Fiber 2 g; T Fat 30 g; 52% Calories from Fat;
   Chol 200 mg; Sod 950 mg.

Alice Bell

Crab Meat Gumbo

4 large mushrooms, sliced
2 tablespoons butter
2 teaspoons grated mild
   onion
2 tomatoes, peeled, chopped
1 pound crab meat
Salt and cayenne pepper to
   taste
1 1/4 cups whipping cream
2 teaspoons minced parsley
1 teaspoon finely chopped
   chives
1 1/2 ounces brandy

Yield: 4 servings

Sauté mushrooms in butter in saucepan for 5 minutes. Add onion and tomatoes. Sauté for 5 minutes. Stir in crab meat, salt and cayenne pepper. Stir in cream. Boil for 1 minute. Add parsley, chives and brandy. Ladle over a spoonful of rice in shallow bowls. Make this in an earthenware or flameproof shallow dish and serve from the dish for a festive occasion.

Approx Per Serving: Cal 465; Prot 25 g; Carbo 6 g;
   Fiber 1 g; T Fat 36 g; 68% Calories from Fat;
   Chol 231 mg; Sod 410 mg.
   Nutritional information for this recipe does not
   include rice.

Sally Lonbom

Crab Meat Stew

1/3 cup chopped onion
1/3 cup chopped green bell
    pepper
1/3 cup chopped celery
1/2 cup butter
2 tablespoons cornstarch
4 cups milk
1 pound crab meat
1/2 cup sherry
1 teaspoon Worcestershire
    sauce
Tabasco sauce to taste
Salt and pepper to taste

Yield: 6 servings

Sauté onion, green pepper and celery in butter in saucepan. Blend cornstarch with 1 cup of the milk. Add to saucepan with remaining milk. Cook until thickened and heated through, stirring constantly. Add crab meat, wine, Worcestershire sauce, Tabasco sauce, salt and pepper. Heat just until heated through; do not boil. Garnish servings with nutmeg. May substitute dry white wine for sherry.

Approx Per Serving: Cal 342; Prot 21 g; Carbo 12 g;
    Fiber <1 g; T Fat 22 g; 58% Calories from Fat;
    Chol 139 mg; Sod 464 mg.

Tomie Jean Blanton

Crawfish Cardinale

2 onions, chopped
1/4 cup butter
1 pound crawfish tails
3 tablespoons flour
1/2 cup melted butter
2 cups milk
1/2 teaspoon garlic salt
Salt and pepper to taste
1/2 cup white wine
6 baked puff pastry shells

Yield: 6 servings

Sauté onions in 1/4 cup butter in skillet. Add crawfish tails. Cook for 2 minutes. Blend flour into 1/2 cup melted butter in saucepan. Add milk, garlic salt, salt and pepper. Cook until thickened, stirring constantly. Stir in crawfish mixture and wine. Spoon into baking dish. Bake at 350 degrees until bubbly. Serve in puff pastry shells. May substitute shrimp or lobster for crawfish tails.

Approx Per Serving: Cal 571; Prot 20 g; Carbo 26 g;
    Fiber 1 g; T Fat 42 g; 66% Calories from Fat;
    Chol 174 mg; Sod 698 mg.

Lora James

Italian Oysters

24 fresh oysters on the half
  shell
Oregano, garlic powder, salt
  and pepper to taste
1 1/2 cups shredded
  mozzarella cheese
1/2 cup grated Parmesan
  cheese
6 tablespoons butter

Yield: 4 servings

Place oysters in baking pan. Sprinkle with oregano, garlic powder, salt and pepper. Top each with 1 tablespoon mozzarella cheese. Sprinkle with Parmesan cheese and dot with butter. Bake at 400 degrees until bubbly and cooked through. Serve with garlic bread.

Approx Per Serving: Cal 386; Prot 20 g; Carbo 5 g;
    Fiber 0 g; T Fat 32 g; 75% Calories from Fat;
    Chol 134 mg; Sod 742 mg.

Diane Hunt

Oyster Cove Restaurant Oyster Loaf

1 loaf French bread
Butter
1 egg
Worcestershire sauce and
  Tabasco sauce to taste
Creole seasonings, salt and
  pepper to taste
1/2 cup cream or evaporated
  milk
Several dozen oysters
1/2 cup flour
1/2 cup cornmeal or flour
Shortening for frying
Lemon juice
Mayonnaise
Catsup
Shredded lettuce
Chopped tomatoes
Pickles

Yield: variable

Slice top third from loaf; scoop out center portion of bread, reserving shell and top. Toast bread shell and top lightly. Spread with butter; keep warm. Combine egg, Worcestershire sauce, Tabasco sauce, Creole seasonings, salt and pepper in bowl; mix well. Add cream; beat until smooth. Pat oysters dry. Dip oysters into the cream mixture; coat with a mixture of flour and cornmeal. Fry in shortening in skillet until golden brown; drain well. Drizzle with lemon juice. Place oysters in bread shell. Dollop with mayonnaise and catsup; top with lettuce, tomatoes and pickles. Replace top of bread; place on baking sheet. Bake until heated to taste.

Nutritional information for this recipe is not available.

John B. Spohrer, Jr.

Pelican Oysters

12 fresh oysters on the half
  shell
Rock salt
12 small mushrooms, finely
  chopped
1 small green bell pepper,
  finely chopped
1/2 medium onion, finely
  chopped
6 tablespoons melted butter
1 cup bread crumbs
3/4 cup shredded Cheddar
  cheese
1/2 cup grated Parmesan
  cheese

Yield: 2 servings

Arrange oysters in shells on rock salt in 10x15-inch baking pan. Sauté mushrooms, green pepper and onion in butter in skillet. Spoon onto oysters; sprinkle with bread crumbs and cheeses. Bake at 375 degrees until the cheeses melt. We prepared this dish for diners at the Happy Pelican about 10 years ago. It was devised by one of the waitresses and has been enjoyed by many people since then.

Approx Per Serving: Cal 882; Prot 36 g; Carbo 49 g;
  Fiber 4 g; T Fat 61 g; 62% Calories from Fat;
  Chol 202 mg; Sod 1692 mg.

Linda Arnold

Oyster Rockefella Casserole

18 medium oysters
1 medium onion, finely
  chopped
3 tablespoons finely
  chopped parsley
2 tablespoons finely
  chopped celery
1/4 cup olive oil
1   10-ounce package frozen
  spinach, thawed, drained
2 tablespoons Louisiana hot
  sauce
1 teaspoon salt
1 cup seasoned bread
  crumbs

Yield: 4 servings

Drain oysters, reserving liquid. Sauté onion, parsley and celery in olive oil in skillet until tender. Add spinach, hot sauce and salt. Cook for 5 minutes. Stir in half the bread crumbs. Spread in greased baking dish. Place oysters over top; drizzle with reserved liquid. Sprinkle with remaining bread crumbs. Bake at 400 degrees for 20 minutes.

Approx Per Serving: Cal 284; Prot 11 g; Carbo 26 g;
  Fiber 2 g; T Fat 16 g; 50% Calories from Fat;
  Chol 34 mg; Sod 1437 mg.

Howard Gann

Scalloped Oysters

6 tablespoons chopped
    onion
1/2 cup butter
2 cups fresh white bread
    crumbs
Salt and pepper to taste
6 tablespoons chopped
    parsley
24 oysters

Yield: 4 servings

Sauté onion in butter in skillet. Stir in bread crumbs, coating well. Cook for several minutes. Season with salt and pepper; stir in parsley. Layer half the bread crumb mixture, oysters and remaining bread crumbs in baking dish. Bake at 450 degrees for 8 to 10 minutes or until bubbly and cooked through. Serve immediately.

Approx Per Serving: Cal 329; Prot 8 g; Carbo 16 g;
    Fiber 1 g; T Fat 26 g; 70% Calories from Fat;
    Chol 107 mg; Sod 529 mg.

Peggy Juppé

Ritzy Scalloped Oysters

2 cups crushed butter
    crackers
1/2 cup melted butter
Salt and pepper to taste
2 cups oysters
1 cup milk
1/4 teaspoon Worcestershire
    sauce

Yield: 4 servings

Mix cracker crumbs, melted butter, salt and pepper in bowl. Reserve 1/3 of the crumbs. Layer remaining crumbs and oysters 1/2 at a time in greased baking dish. Pour mixture of milk and Worcestershire sauce over layers. Top with reserved crumbs. Bake at 350 degrees for 30 minutes.

Approx Per Serving: Cal 560; Prot 19 g; Carbo 33 g;
    Fiber 1 g; T Fat 39 g; 63% Calories from Fat;
    Chol 176 mg; Sod 996 mg.

Jane Pitts

Oystering...Apalachicola Bay Style

Driving across the causeway it is enchanting to see hundreds of oyster boats, or Lolly boats as they are sometimes called, dotting the Bay. Oystermen typically go out early in the morning. Besides the oyster tongs, other essentials are a culling iron, culling board and a drag anchor. As the oysters are brought up, they are deposited on the culling board which extends across the boat. After the culling board is full, the tonger, using the iron, breaks off the extraneous material and small oysters and then the culled matter is returned to the water. Tongs are long, doubled-handled rakes. The oysterman reaches nine or more feet into the water, scrapes shells from the beds, and brings the oysters to the surface. Tonging is laborious but remains an art.

Yankee Oyster Stew

2 pints oysters
1 small onion, finely
  chopped
1 tablespoon
  Worcestershire sauce
1/2 teaspoon chopped parsley
1 cup margarine
2 cups half and half
1/2 to 2/3 gallon 2% milk
Salt and pepper to taste

Yield: 8 servings

Drain 1 pint of oysters. Combine with undrained oysters, chopped onion, Worcestershire sauce and parsley in heavy saucepan. Cook over high heat until oysters curl. Add margarine, half and half, milk, salt and pepper. Bring to a simmer. Simmer over low heat for 15 to 20 minutes; do not boil. Ladle into soup bowls. Garnish servings with green onion tops. Serve with crackers. May substitute 2% milk for half and half to reduce fat content.

Approx Per Serving: Cal 586; Prot 27 g; Carbo 27 g; Fiber <1 g; T Fat 41 g; 63% Calories from Fat; Chol 152 mg; Sod 899 mg.

Shirley Gelch

Coquilles Saint Jacques

1 pound fresh bay scallops
1 small onion, finely
  chopped
1/2 cup dry white wine
8 ounces fresh mushrooms,
  sliced
1/2 cup (or less) water
Juice of 1 lemon
2 tablespoons flour
2 tablespoons melted butter
2/3 cup whipping cream
1 cup fine bread crumbs
1/2 cup grated Parmesan
  cheese

Yield: 6 servings

Cook scallops and onion in wine in saucepan for 5 minutes. Drain, reserving cooking liquid. Cook mushrooms in water and lemon juice in small saucepan until tender. Drain, reserving cooking liquid. Blend flour into melted butter in saucepan. Cook for several minutes. Stir in cream and reserved cooking liquids. Cook until thickened and smooth, stirring constantly. Add scallops and mushrooms. Spoon into scallop shells or individual baking ramekins; sprinkle with bread crumbs and Parmesan cheese. Bake at 400 degrees until topping is light brown. May serve as an appetizer or substitute Swiss cheese for Parmesan cheese.

Approx Per Serving: Cal 332; Prot 17 g; Carbo 20 g; Fiber 1 g; T Fat 19 g; 52% Calories from Fat; Chol 72 mg; Sod 462 mg.

Jane and Sue Booth

Scallops in White Wine

1 pound bay scallops
2 tablespoons butter
Salt and pepper to taste
2 tablespoons finely
 chopped shallots
1/2 clove of garlic, finely
 minced
4 mushrooms, sliced
1/4 cup dry white wine
1 cup whipping cream
1 tablespoon chopped
 parsley

Yield: 4 servings

Sauté scallops in butter in skillet. Sprinkle with salt and pepper. Add shallots, garlic and mushrooms. Cook for 1 minute. Spoon into warm dish. Add wine to skillet, stirring to deglaze. Cook over high heat for 1 minute. Add cream. Cook for 2 minutes. Add scallops; sprinkle with parsley. Cook just until heated through. Serve over noodles or rice. May substitute white sauce made with skim milk for cream.

Approx Per Serving: Cal 372; Prot 17 g; Carbo 6 g;
 Fiber <1 g; T Fat 31 g; 74% Calories from Fat;
 Chol 126 mg; Sod 251 mg.

Marilyn Bean

Barbecued Shrimp

2 1/2 pounds fresh large
 shrimp in shells
1 cup butter
1/2 cup Worcestershire sauce
3/4 cup fresh lemon juice
2 teaspoons hot sauce
3 cloves of garlic, chopped
1 teaspoon dried rosemary
1 tablespoon salt
1 tablespoon pepper
1 medium onion, sliced into
 rings
1 lemon, sliced

Yield: 6 servings

Place shrimp in 9x13-inch baking dish. Melt butter in saucepan. Stir in Worcestershire sauce, lemon juice, hot sauce, garlic, rosemary, salt and pepper. Pour over shrimp, stirring to coat well. Arrange onion rings and lemon slices over shrimp. Bake at 400 degrees for 20 minutes. Serve with French bread for dipping.

Approx Per Serving: Cal 440; Prot 29 g; Carbo 10 g;
 Fiber 1 g; T Fat 32 g; 65% Calories from Fat;
 Chol 346 mg; Sod 1916 mg.

Vicki Sayle

Shrimp Baked with Feta

2 pounds fresh shrimp,
  peeled, deveined
2 tablespoons lemon juice
3/4 cup chopped onion
2 stalks celery, chopped
2 tablespoons chopped
  parsley
2 cloves of garlic, finely
  chopped
6 tablespoons olive oil
1   24-ounce can tomatoes
1/4 cup sugar
1 teaspoon oregano
Salt and pepper to taste
1   4-ounce can shrimp,
  drained
2 tablespoons margarine
3 tablespoons Metaxa
  Cognac
3 tablespoons ouzo
3/4 cup feta cheese

Yield: 4 servings

Sprinkle fresh shrimp with lemon juice in bowl. Sauté onion, celery, parsley and garlic in olive oil in skillet. Drain tomatoes. Reserve 1 whole tomato; chop remaining tomatoes and add to skillet. Add sugar, oregano, salt and pepper. Cook until reduced to desired consistency. Stir in canned shrimp. Spread in small baking dish; place reserved tomato in center. Sauté fresh shrimp in margarine in skillet over medium-high heat just until pink. Add Cognac and ouzo. Arrange around tomato in prepared dish; sprinkle with cheese. Bake at 400° F. for 15 minutes or until cheese melts. Serve with rice and crisp green salad.

Approx Per Serving: Cal 696; Prot 49 g; Carbo 27 g;
    Fiber 3 g; T Fat 39 g; 50% Calories from Fat;
    Chol 406 mg; Sod 1288 mg.

Jane M. Burke

Shrimp Boats

1 pound shrimp, cooked,
  peeled, cut into 1/2-inch
  pieces
1 green bell pepper, chopped
1 onion, chopped
1 stalk celery, chopped
1   7-ounce can water
  chestnuts, drained,
  chopped
Juice of 1/2 lemon or lime
Dillweed, salt and pepper to
  taste
1/2 cup (about) mayonnaise
4 pita rounds
1/4 cup ranch salad dressing
1/2 cup alfalfa sprouts
4 slices havarti cheese

Yield: 4 servings

Combine shrimp, green pepper, onion, celery and water chestnuts in bowl. Add lemon juice, dillweed, salt, pepper and enough mayonnaise to moisten; mix gently. Split the tops of the pita rounds; fill with the shrimp mixture. Stand the pockets up in a baking dish. Spoon ranch dressing and sprouts into each pocket; top with cheese. Bake in moderate oven or microwave just until cheese melts. Serve with lettuce and tomato. May omit water chestnuts and alfalfa sprouts if preferred. May substitute 3 green onions for onion.

Approx Per Serving: Cal 647; Prot 31 g; Carbo 46 g;
    Fiber 3 g; T Fat 38 g; 52% Calories from Fat;
    Chol 207 mg; Sod 897 mg.

Diane Hunt

Deviled Shrimp Casserole

6 hard-boiled eggs
1 tablespoon Dijon mustard
2 tablespoons mayonnaise
Onion powder, salt and
   pepper to taste
1 8-ounce can sliced
   mushrooms, drained
1 pound shrimp, peeled
2 cups shredded sharp
   American cheese
1/4 cup flour
1/4 cup melted margarine
2 cups milk
1 teaspoon Worcestershire
   sauce

Yield: 6 servings

Slice eggs lengthwise; remove yolks to bowl and mash. Add mustard, mayonnaise, onion powder, salt and pepper; mix well. Spoon into egg whites; arrange in baking dish. Spread mushrooms and shrimp over eggs; sprinkle with cheese. Blend flour into melted margarine in saucepan. Cook for several minutes. Stir in milk, Worcestershire sauce, salt and pepper. Cook until thickened, stirring constantly. Spoon over casserole. Bake at 350 degrees for 20 minutes. May use liquid from mushrooms in white sauce if desired.

Approx Per Serving: Cal 455; Prot 30 g; Carbo 11 g; Fiber 1 g; T Fat 32 g; 64% Calories from Fat; Chol 367 mg; Sod 1115 mg.

Katherine Autrey

Shrimp Casserole

8 slices bread, cubed
1/2 cup chopped green bell
   pepper
1 cup chopped celery
1 small onion, chopped
1/4 cup butter
2 cups cooked small shrimp
   or chopped large shrimp
1/2 cup mayonnaise
4 eggs
3 cups milk
1 10-ounce can cream of
   celery soup
1 cup shredded Cheddar
   cheese

Yield: 8 servings

Spread bread cubes in large baking dish. Sauté green pepper, celery and onion in butter in skillet; remove from heat. Add shrimp and mayonnaise. Spread over bread cubes. Beat eggs in bowl. Add milk; beat until smooth. Pour over layers. Chill for 3 hours to overnight. Spread soup over top; sprinkle with cheese. Bake at 325 degrees for 50 to 60 minutes or until set and golden brown.

Approx Per Serving: Cal 451; Prot 22 g; Carbo 24 g; Fiber 1 g; T Fat 30 g; 60% Calories from Fat; Chol 241 mg; Sod 836 mg.

Betty Day

Sweet and Sour Shrimp Casserole

3 tablespoons oil
1 medium onion, sliced, cut
   into strips
1 green bell pepper, cut into
   strips
1 1/2 pounds shrimp, peeled,
   deveined
1   16-ounce can pineapple
   chunks
3 tablespoons cornstarch
1/3 cup packed brown sugar
1/4 cup soy sauce
1/4 cup vinegar
1/4 teaspoon ginger
1/4 teaspoon pepper
1   5-ounce can sliced water
   chestnuts, drained

Yield: 6 servings

Combine oil, onion and green pepper in 1-quart microwave-safe dish. Microwave, covered, for 4 minutes. Stir in shrimp. Microwave for 1 minute. Drain pineapple, reserving 1/2 cup juice. Combine reserved juice with cornstarch, brown sugar, soy sauce, vinegar, ginger and pepper in microwave-safe dish; mix well. Microwave for 4 to 5 minutes or until blended, stirring 2 times. Stir into shrimp mixture. Add pineapple and water chestnuts; mix well. Microwave for 4 to 5 minutes or until heated through. Serve over hot cooked rice. May substitute chicken for shrimp.

Approx Per Serving: Cal 282; Prot 18 g; Carbo 36 g;
    Fiber 2 g; T Fat 8 g; 25% Calories from Fat;
    Chol 158 mg; Sod 874 mg.

Gladys Scudder

Zesty Shrimp Casserole

8 slices white bread
1 cup chopped celery
1/2 cup chopped green bell
   pepper
1 onion, chopped
1/2 cup margarine
1 tablespoon olive oil
3 1/2 cups peeled, deveined,
   cooked shrimp
1/2 cup mayonnaise
1 tablespoon each
   Worcestershire sauce,
   lemon juice and red wine
   vinegar
4 eggs
3 cups milk
1   10-ounce can cream of
   mushroom soup
1 cup shredded mild
   Cheddar cheese
1 cup bread crumbs

Yield: 8 servings

Crumble bread; sprinkle over bottom of 3-quart baking dish sprayed with nonstick cooking spray. Sauté celery, green pepper and onion in margarine and olive oil in skillet until soft. Add shrimp; mix well. Stir in mixture of mayonnaise, Worcestershire sauce, lemon juice and wine vinegar. Spoon over crumbled bread. Beat eggs, milk and soup in bowl until smooth. Pour over shrimp mixture. Sprinkle with shredded cheese and bread crumbs. Let stand for 1 hour. Bake, covered, at 325 degrees for 50 minutes.

Approx Per Serving: Cal 612; Prot 30 g; Carbo 34 g;
    Fiber 2 g; T Fat 40 g; 58% Calories from Fat;
    Chol 281 mg; Sod 1129 mg.

Phyllis Stanley Stephens

Shrimp and Crab Meat Casserole

1/2 cup butter
1/2 cup flour
2 cups half and half
5 slices bacon
2 cups chopped celery
1 medium onion, chopped
1 green bell pepper, chopped
1 clove of garlic, finely
  chopped
1   8-ounce jar Cheez Whiz
Salt and pepper to taste
5 pounds shrimp, cooked,
  peeled, deveined
1 pound lump or select crab
  meat
1 cup shredded Cheddar
  cheese
1 tablespoon bread crumbs

Yield: 20 servings

Melt butter in 4 or 5-quart saucepan. Add flour; mix well. Cook over medium heat until of roux consistency, stirring constantly. Stir in half and half until blended. Fry bacon in skillet until crisp; drain, reserving drippings. Crumble bacon; set aside. Sauté celery, onion, green pepper and garlic in reserved drippings in skillet until vegetables are tender. Stir mixture into prepared cream sauce. Add Cheez Whiz; mix well. Cook over medium heat until combined, stirring constantly. Season with salt and pepper. Add shrimp; mix well. Stir in crumbled bacon. Fold in crab meat. Spoon into large baking dish or individual baking dishes. Sprinkle with cheese and bread crumbs. Bake at 350 degrees for 20 minutes or until bubbly. Add 1/2 cup chicken broth or white wine for moister casserole.

Approx Per Serving: Cal 258; Prot 27 g; Carbo 6 g;
    Fiber <1 g; T Fat 14 g; 49% Calories from Fat;
    Chol 216 mg; Sod 527 mg.

Bo Suber

Shrimp and Wild Rice Casserole

1/2 cup thinly sliced onion
1/4 cup thinly sliced green
  bell pepper
8 ounces mushrooms, sliced
1/2 cup margarine
1 tablespoon
  Worcestershire sauce
4 drops of Tabasco sauce
1   6-ounce package wild
  rice and herbs, cooked
1 1/2 pounds shrimp, cooked,
  peeled, deveined
2 tablespoons margarine
2 tablespoons flour
2 cups chicken broth

Yield: 6 servings

Sauté onion, green pepper and mushrooms in 1/2 cup margarine in saucepan until tender. Stir in Worcestershire sauce and Tabasco sauce. Add rice and shrimp; mix well. Melt 2 tablespoons margarine in skillet. Stir in flour until blended. Add chicken broth; mix well. Cook until thickened, stirring constantly. Stir into shrimp mixture. Spoon into baking dish. Bake at 300 degrees for 30 to 45 minutes or until bubbly.

Approx Per Serving: Cal 389; Prot 24 g; Carbo 27 g;
    Fiber 1 g; T Fat 21 g; 48% Calories from Fat;
    Chol 158 mg; Sod 695 mg.

Virginia Pendleton

Crab Stuffed Shrimp Bundles

1 pound crab meat, drained
45 saltines, crushed
1/2 cup mayonnaise
1/2 cup catsup
1/4 cup melted butter
2 tablespoons prepared
  mustard
1 egg, beaten
1 teaspoon Worcestershire
  sauce
Hot sauce to taste
30 to 40 jumbo shrimp,
  peeled, deveined
10 slices bacon

Yield: 5 servings

Combine crab meat, crackers, mayonnaise, catsup, melted butter, mustard, egg, Worcestershire sauce and hot sauce in bowl; mix well. Lay 2 shrimp side by side in center of each bacon slice. Spoon 3 tablespoons crab meat mixture over shrimp. Fold ends of bacon over filling; secure with wooden pick. Arrange in 9x13-inch baking dish. Bake at 350 degrees for 40 minutes. Broil for 1 to 2 minutes or until brown.

Approx Per Serving: Cal 614; Prot 37 g; Carbo 27 g;
  Fiber 1 g; T Fat 40 g; 58% Calories from Fat;
  Chol 275 mg; Sod 1525 mg.

Marilyn Bean

Easy Shrimp Creole

1 cup chopped celery
1/4 cup chopped green bell
  pepper
1 clove of garlic, finely
  chopped *more*
1 cup sliced onion
1/2 cup margarine
1 tablespoon chili powder
2 tablespoons flour
1 teaspoon salt
1 teaspoon sugar
1/2 cup water
2 1/2 cups stewed tomatoes *canned chopped*
1 tablespoon vinegar
2 cups peeled cooked shrimp

Yield: 4 servings

Sauté celery, green pepper, garlic and onion in margarine in skillet until vegetables are tender. Stir in chili powder, flour, salt, sugar and water. Simmer for 15 minutes, stirring occasionally. Add tomatoes, vinegar and shrimp; mix well. Cook just until heated through, stirring occasionally. Serve over hot cooked rice.

Approx Per Serving: Cal 369; Prot 20 g; Carbo 20 g;
  Fiber 4 g; T Fat 24 g; 58% Calories from Fat;
  Chol 158 mg; Sod 1434 mg.

H. Lee Simmons

Shrimp Creole

1 cup finely chopped onion
1/3 cup oil
1 1/2 cups catsup
1/2 cup water
1/2 cup plus 2 tablespoons
   lemon juice
1/4 cup sugar
2 1/2 teaspoons salt
1/4 cup Worcestershire sauce
1/2 teaspoon pepper
4 drops of Tabasco sauce
1/2 cup chopped green bell
   pepper
1/2 cup chopped celery
1 tablespoon oil
1 pound shrimp, cooked,
   peeled, deveined

Yield: 4 servings

Sauté onion in oil in saucepan until tender and brown. Stir in catsup, water, lemon juice, sugar, salt, Worcestershire sauce, pepper and Tabasco sauce. Simmer for 15 minutes, stirring occasionally. Cool. Sauté green pepper and celery in oil in saucepan until tender. Stir in shrimp and red sauce. Cook just until heated through, stirring frequently. Serve over hot cooked rice.

Approx Per Serving: Cal 627; Prot 20 g; Carbo 72 g; Fiber 4 g; T Fat 32 g; 46% Calories from Fat; Chol 158 mg; Sod 4078 mg.

Alice Powell

Curried Shrimp

1 small onion, chopped
1/2 teaspoon curry powder
1 tablespoon butter
1   10-ounce can cream of
   mushroom soup
1/3 soup can water
1 pound shrimp, cooked,
   peeled, deveined

Yield: 4 servings

Sauté onion with curry powder in butter in skillet until onion is tender. Stir in soup and water. Add shrimp; mix well. Simmer just until heated through, stirring constantly. Serve over hot cooked rice.

Approx Per Serving: Cal 192; Prot 18 g; Carbo 7 g; Fiber 1 g; T Fat 10 g; 46% Calories from Fat; Chol 166 mg; Sod 829 mg.

Ann Robuck

Shrimp Dijon

8 ounces mushrooms, sliced
2 tablespoons butter
2 pounds shrimp, peeled,
  deveined
2 tablespoons butter
1/2 cup chopped green
  onions with tops
1/2 cup chopped parsley
1/4 cup Dijon mustard
1/2 cup whipping cream
2 tablespoons dry white
  wine
Salt and pepper to taste
9 ounces fresh linguine,
  cooked
1/4 cup grated Parmesan
  cheese

Yield: 6 servings

Sauté mushrooms in 2 tablespoons butter in skillet until tender; remove to platter. Sauté shrimp in 2 tablespoons butter in skillet for 1 to 2 minutes or until shrimp turn pink; remove to platter. Add green onions and parsley to skillet. Cook for 1 to 2 minutes or until green onions are tender. Stir in mustard, cream, wine, salt and pepper. Return mushrooms and shrimp to skillet; mix well. Simmer for 5 minutes, stirring frequently. Spoon over hot cooked linguine; sprinkle with Parmesan cheese. Serve with tossed green salad, French bread and dry white wine.

Approx Per Serving: Cal 454; Prot 32 g; Carbo 36 g; Fiber 2 g; T Fat 20 g; 39% Calories from Fat; Chol 262 mg; Sod 681 mg.

Liz Hoffman

Jambalaya

12 ounces smoked sausage
2 ounces pepperoni, thinly
  sliced
3/4 cup chopped green bell
  pepper
1/2 cup chopped onion
2 1/2 cups water
1 1/2 cups peeled shrimp
1 medium tomato, chopped
2 chicken bouillon cubes
1 1/2 cups uncooked rice
1 tablespoon
  Worcestershire sauce
1 teaspoon salt
1/2 teaspoon thyme
1/4 teaspoon pepper
1/8 teaspoon garlic powder

Yield: 6 servings

Sauté sausage, pepperoni, green pepper and onion in saucepan until vegetables are tender-crisp. Add water, shrimp, tomato and bouillon cubes; mix well. Bring to a boil; reduce heat. Stir in rice, Worcestershire sauce, salt, thyme, pepper and garlic powder. Cook, covered, for 30 minutes or until rice is tender and all liquids have been absorbed.

Approx Per Serving: Cal 377; Prot 20 g; Carbo 41 g; Fiber 1 g; T Fat 14 g; 33% Calories from Fat; Chol 105 mg; Sod 1455 mg.

Alice D. Collins

Shrimp de Jonghe

5 to 6 cups peeled cooked
   shrimp
1 cup melted butter
2 cloves of garlic, finely
   chopped
1/3 cup chopped parsley
1/2 teaspoon paprika
Cayenne pepper to taste
2/3 cup sherry
2 cups soft bread crumbs
Chopped parsley to taste

Yield: 8 servings

Arrange shrimp in 7x11-inch baking dish. Combine butter, garlic, 1/3 cup parsley, paprika, cayenne pepper and sherry in bowl. Add bread crumbs, tossing to coat. Spoon over shrimp. Bake at 325 degrees for 20 to 25 minutes or until brown. Sprinkle with chopped parsley.

Approx Per Serving: Cal 370; Prot 27 g; Carbo 6 g;
   Fiber <1 g; T Fat 25 g; 60% Calories from Fat;
   Chol 299 mg; Sod 566 mg.

Jeanne Crozier

Lighthouse Shrimp

1/2 cup butter
1 1/2 tablespoons blackened
   fish seasoning
1 1/2 tablespoons cajun
   seasoning
2 tablespoons shrimp
   seasoning
2 1/2 tablespoons lemon herb
   seasoning
1 teaspoon parsley flakes
2 pounds medium shrimp,
   peeled, deveined

Yield: 8 servings

Melt butter in skillet over medium-low heat. Stir in blackened fish seasoning, cajun seasoning, shrimp seasoning, lemon herb seasoning and parsley flakes. Add shrimp; mix well. Cook until shrimp turn pink, stirring occasionally. Serve with noodles or rice pilaf and French bread. May substitute margarine or olive oil for butter.

Approx Per Serving: Cal 182; Prot 17 g; Carbo <1 g;
   Fiber 0 g; T Fat 12 g; 62% Calories from Fat;
   Chol 189 mg; Sod 299 mg.

Bill Short

Microwave Steamed Shrimp

1 to 2 pounds unpeeled
   shrimp
Seasoned salt to taste

Yield: 6 servings

Place shrimp in a 1-gallon sealable plastic bag. Sprinkle heavily with seasoned salt; seal bag. Microwave on High for 3 minutes. Turn bag over. Microwave on High for 3 minutes longer. Remove shrimp from bag; peel.

Approx Per Serving: Cal 107; Prot 23 g; Carbo 0 g;
   Fiber 0 g; T Fat 1 g; 10% Calories from Fat;
   Chol 211 mg; Sod 242 mg.

Kathy Morton

Shrimp Newburg

3 tablespoons margarine
3 tablespoons flour
1 cup half and half
1/2 cup catsup
Salt and pepper to taste
Cajun Sunshine to taste
1 1/2 cups peeled boiled or
   steamed shrimp

Yield: 4 servings

Melt margarine in saucepan. Stir in flour until blended. Add half and half; mix well. Cook until thickened, stirring constantly. Stir in catsup, salt, pepper and shrimp. Cook just until heated through, stirring constantly. Serve over hot cooked rice. May substitute lobster meat or crab meat for shrimp.

Approx Per Serving: Cal 269; Prot 16 g; Carbo 16 g;
   Fiber 1 g; T Fat 16 g; 54% Calories from Fat;
   Chol 141 mg; Sod 624 mg.

Virginia Norris

John B. Spohrer, Jr. makes **Creole Seafood Cocktail Sauce** to serve with oysters, shrimp or crawfish by combining 1 cup catsup, 1 tablespoon horseradish, 1 tablespoon Worcestershire sauce, 1 teaspoon hot sauce, 1/2 cup minced celery and salt to taste.

Oriental Shrimp

1 pound shrimp, peeled,
   deveined
3 tablespoons oil
1/2 cup chicken broth
1 8-ounce can water
   chestnuts, drained, thinly
   sliced
2 cups snow peas
1 cup sliced onion
2 cups celery sliced 1/4 inch
   diagonally
1 tablespoon cornstarch
1 teaspoon sugar
2 tablespoons soy sauce
2 tablespoons water
1 teaspoon salt
1/4 teaspoon pepper

Yield: 6 servings

Split shrimp lengthwise. Cook in oil in wok or skillet for 1 minute or until shrimp turn pink. Add broth, water chestnuts, snow peas, onion and celery. Cook, covered, for 1 1/2 minutes; stir. Stir in mixture of cornstarch, sugar, soy sauce, water, salt and pepper. Cook until slightly thickened, stirring constantly. Serve over hot cooked rice.

Approx Per Serving: Cal 181; Prot 14 g; Carbo 14 g;
   Fiber 3 g; T Fat 8 g; 38% Calories from Fat;
   Chol 105 mg; Sod 924 mg.

Jean Lively

Shrimp Ramekins

1 1/2 pounds peeled and
   deveined shrimp
1/3 cup butter
8 ounces mushrooms, sliced
1 1/2 cups sour cream
Salt and pepper to taste
2 teaspoons soy sauce
Paprika to taste
1/2 cup grated Parmesan
   cheese

Yield: 6 servings

Sauté shrimp in butter in skillet for 1 to 2 minutes or until shrimp turn pink. Add sliced mushrooms. Cook for 8 to 10 minutes or until mushrooms are tender, stirring frequently. Heat sour cream to boiling point in saucepan. Season with salt, pepper and soy sauce. Stir in enough paprika to tint mixture pink. Stir into shrimp mixture. Cook until thickened, stirring constantly. Spoon into 6 buttered ramekins; sprinkle with Parmesan cheese. Broil until brown and bubbly. Serve with white rice.

Approx Per Serving: Cal 352; Prot 25 g; Carbo 5 g;
   Fiber <1 g; T Fat 26 g; 66% Calories from Fat;
   Chol 237 mg; Sod 609 mg.

Irene LaSlavic

Sautéed Shrimp with Tomato-Basil Vinaigrette

1 pound ripe plum
   tomatoes, peeled, seeded,
   chopped
2 medium shallots, finely
   chopped
2 cloves of garlic, blanched,
   julienned
3 tablespoons chopped
   fresh basil
1 tablespoon chopped fresh
   parsley
Salt and freshly ground
   pepper to taste
1 tablespoon wine vinegar
1 tablespoon lime juice
1/2 cup plus 2 tablespoons
   extra-virgin olive oil
16 large peeled shrimp with
   tails
4 sprigs of basil

Yield: 4 servings

Combine tomatoes, shallots, garlic, chopped basil and parsley in bowl; mix well. Season with salt and pepper. Stir in vinegar, lime juice and 1/2 cup olive oil. Season shrimp with salt and pepper. Heat remaining 2 tablespoons olive oil in 10-inch skillet. Cook shrimp in small batches over medium-high heat for 30 seconds per side; drain. Spoon tomato-basil vinaigrette onto 4 plates. Top each with 4 shrimp; garnish with basil sprigs. Serve immediately. May prepare vinaigrette ahead of time.

Approx Per Serving: Cal 379; Prot 7 g; Carbo 13 g;
   Fiber 2 g; T Fat 35 g; 79% Calories from Fat;
   Chol 47 mg; Sod 70 mg.

Conrad Gleber and Gail Rubini

Sautéed Shrimp

1/4 cup butter
1 envelope reduced-calorie
   Italian salad dressing mix
2 pounds shrimp, peeled,
   deveined

Yield: 4 servings

Melt butter in skillet. Stir in dressing mix. Add shrimp; mix well. Cook over medium heat until shrimp turn pink, stirring constantly. May serve over rice. May substitute margarine for butter.

Approx Per Serving: Cal 262; Prot 34 g; Carbo <1 g;
   Fiber 0 g; T Fat 13 g; 47% Calories from Fat;
   Chol 347 mg; Sod 480 mg.

Tomie Jean Blanton

Shrimp Alfredo

2 pounds shrimp, peeled,
  deveined
1 cup chopped onion
1 cup chopped green bell
  pepper
Salt and pepper to taste
1 recipe Alfredo sauce

Yield: 6 servings

Sauté shrimp, onion and green pepper in nonstick skillet. Season with salt and pepper. Stir in Alfredo sauce. Cook until heated through, stirring constantly. Serve over fettucini or rice. May substitute scallops, clams, oysters or lobster for shrimp.

Approx Per Serving: Cal 301; Prot 30 g; Carbo 5 g;
  Fiber <1 g; T Fat 17 g; 53% Calories from Fat;
  Chol 211 mg; Sod 682 mg.

Beverly Troutman

Shrimp Fettucini

1   16-ounce package
  fettucini
1 cup shredded Swiss cheese
1/2 cup grated Parmesan
  cheese
8 ounces cooked peeled
  shrimp
1/4 cup melted butter
2 cups half and half
1 envelope onion-mushroom
  soup mix
Fresh chopped parsley

Yield: 6 servings

Cook fettucini using package directions; drain, rinse and drain well. Keep warm. Combine fettucini, Swiss cheese, Parmesan cheese and shrimp in bowl; toss to mix. Blend butter, half and half and soup mix in skillet. Cook over low heat until consistency of thick gravy, stirring constantly. Stir into shrimp mixture. Top with parsley. Serve immediately. May substitute margarine for butter and whipping cream for half and half.

Approx Per Serving: Cal 599; Prot 29 g; Carbo 62 g;
  Fiber 2 g; T Fat 26 g; 39% Calories from Fat;
  Chol 147 mg; Sod 509 mg.

Ellen Whitlock

Shrimp and Basil with Linguine

2 pounds shrimp, peeled,
  deveined
2 tablespoons olive oil
2 green onions with tops,
  finely chopped
3 or 4 tomatoes, seeded,
  chopped
1 to 1¹/₂ cups evaporated
  skim milk
8 ounces mushrooms, sliced
Chopped fresh basil to taste
Salt and freshly ground
  pepper to taste
1 16-ounce package
  linguine, cooked

Yield: 6 servings

Sauté shrimp in olive oil in skillet until shrimp turn pink. Remove shrimp to plate. Add green onions to skillet. Cook until tender, stirring constantly. Stir in tomatoes. Cook until tender, stirring constantly; reduce heat. Stir in evaporated skim milk. Cook until slightly thickened, stirring constantly. Add mushrooms; mix well. Stir in shrimp, basil, salt and pepper; mix well. Cook until heated through, stirring constantly. Serve over hot cooked linguine. May substitute whipping cream for evaporated skim milk, scallops for shrimp and 1 chopped clove of garlic for green onions.

Approx Per Serving: Cal 505; Prot 39 g; Carbo 70 g;
    Fiber 3 g; T Fat 7 g; 13% Calories from Fat;
    Chol 213 mg; Sod 330 mg.

Susan Ficklen

Mock Lasagna

8 ounces cream cheese,
  softened
1 cup cottage cheese
¹/₂ cup sour cream
1 tablespoon poppy seeds
8 ounces lasagna noodles,
  cooked, drained
1 tablespoon chopped onion
1 tablespoon chopped green
  bell pepper
2 8-ounce cans tomato
  sauce
¹/₄ teaspoon basil
Salt and pepper to taste
1 pound shrimp, cooked,
  peeled

Yield: 4 servings

Combine cream cheese, cottage cheese, sour cream and poppy seeds in bowl; mix until blended. Add noodles; mix well. Sauté onion and green pepper in nonstick skillet until tender. Stir into noodle mixture. Spoon into baking dish. Make well in center of noodle mixture. Pour mixture of tomato sauce, basil, salt, pepper and shrimp into well. Bake at 350 degrees for 30 minutes or until bubbly. May substitute 1 pound chopped cooked beef for shrimp.

Approx Per Serving: Cal 645; Prot 37 g; Carbo 52 g;
    Fiber 5 g; T Fat 32 g; 44% Calories from Fat;
    Chol 213 mg; Sod 1219 mg.

Edna Bono

Garlic-Buttered Shrimp

1/2 cup margarine
1/2 cup olive oil
1/4 cup finely chopped fresh
   parsley
1 green onion, finely
   chopped
3 cloves of garlic, finely
   chopped
1/4 teaspoon coarsely
   ground pepper
2 pounds fresh peeled
   shrimp with tails
8 ounces linguine, cooked,
   drained

Yield: 6 servings

Place margarine in 9x13-inch microwave-safe dish. Microwave on High for 1 minute. Stir in olive oil, parsley, green onion, garlic and pepper. Arrange shrimp around outer edge of dish. Marinate, covered with plastic wrap, in refrigerator for 1 hour. Microwave, covered, on High for 7 1/2 minutes or until shrimp turn pink. Serve over hot cooked linguine.

Approx Per Serving: Cal 559; Prot 31 g; Carbo 29 g;
   Fiber 1 g; T Fat 35 g; 57% Calories from Fat;
   Chol 236 mg; Sod 454 mg.

Mary Lou Short

Shrimp St. George

1 small onion, chopped
4 ounces mushrooms, sliced
1 or 2 cloves of garlic,
   finely chopped
2 tablespoons butter
1 10-ounce package frozen
   spinach, thawed
1 cup crab meat, flaked
Salt and pepper to taste
1 teaspoon basil
6 ounces linguine, spaghetti
   or fettucini, cooked *al
   dente*, drained
1 to 1 1/2 pounds shrimp,
   cooked, peeled
8 ounces mozzarella cheese,
   shredded
2 tablespoons melted butter

Yield: 6 servings

Sauté onion, mushrooms and garlic in 2 tablespoons butter in skillet until onion is tender. Squeeze moisture from spinach. Add to onion mixture; mix well. Cook until heated through, stirring constantly. Stir in crab meat, salt, pepper and basil gently. Line greased baking dish with linguine. Arrange shrimp over pasta; top with spinach mixture. Sprinkle with cheese; drizzle with 2 tablespoons melted butter. Bake at 375 degrees until bubbly. Serve with Parmesan cheese. May substitute flaked fish for crab meat and provolone cheese for mozzarella. May substitute olive oil for melted butter and butter.

Approx Per Serving: Cal 401; Prot 34 g; Carbo 26 g;
   Fiber 2 g; T Fat 18 g; 40% Calories from Fat;
   Chol 228 mg; Sod 492 mg.

Diane Hunt

Shrimp and Green Noodles

1 8-ounce package spinach
   noodles, cooked, drained
2 pounds peeled and
   deveined shrimp
1/2 cup clarified butter
1 10-ounce can cream of
   mushroom soup
1 cup sour cream
1 cup mayonnaise
1 teaspoon chopped chives
1/2 teaspoon Dijon mustard
1/4 cup sherry
1/2 cup shredded sharp
   Cheddar cheese

Yield: 6 servings

Line baking dish with spinach noodles. Sauté shrimp in butter in skillet for 5 minutes or until shrimp turn pink. Spoon shrimp over noodles. Combine soup, sour cream, mayonnaise and chives in bowl; mix well. Stir in Dijon mustard and sherry. Spoon over shrimp; sprinkle with shredded cheese. Bake in moderate oven until bubbly.

Approx Per Serving: Cal 749; Prot 32 g; Carbo 16 g;
   Fiber 1 g; T Fat 62 g; 74% Calories from Fat;
   Chol 339 mg; Sod 1143 mg.

Jerry Plowden

Shrimp Stroganoff

1 cup sour cream
1 10-ounce can cream of
   mushroom soup
1 teaspoon dillweed
1/4 cup sliced green onions
1/4 cup sliced black olives
1/2 cup shredded Cheddar
   cheese
24 medium shrimp, cooked,
   shelled, deveined
1 8-ounce package
   noodles, cooked, drained
1/2 cup shredded Cheddar
   cheese

Yield: 6 servings

Combine sour cream, soup and dillweed in bowl; mix well. Stir in green onions, olives, 1/2 cup cheese and shrimp. Add noodles; mix well. Spoon into lightly greased 2-quart baking dish. Bake, covered, at 350 degrees for 30 minutes. Sprinkle with 1/2 cup cheese. Bake, uncovered, for 5 minutes.

Approx Per Serving: Cal 245; Prot 17 g; Carbo 33 g;
   Fiber <1 g; T Fat 21 g; 49% Calories from Fat;
   Chol 150 mg; Sod 655 mg.

Marilyn Bean

Frogmore Stew

1 gallon water
1/4 cup salt
Old Bay seafood seasoning
  to taste
4 ounces smoked link
  sausage, cut into 2-inch
  pieces
1 1/2 to 2 ears of corn, cut
  into 3-inch pieces
8 ounces small new potatoes
8 ounces peeled deveined
  shrimp

Yield: 1 serving

Bring water, salt and seafood seasoning to a boil in stockpot. Add sausage; mix well. Boil for 7 minutes. Add corn. Boil for 7 minutes. Add new potatoes. Boil for 7 minutes or until potatoes are tender. Stir in shrimp. Boil for 1 minute. Remove stockpot from heat. Let stand for 10 minutes; drain.

Approx Per Serving: Cal 801; Prot 60 g; Carbo 97 g; Fiber 12 g; T Fat 21 g; 23% Calories from Fat; Chol 390 mg; Sod 26826 mg.
Nutritional information includes entire amount of salt used in cooking.

Sandra Thaxton

Shrimp Stir-Fry

3 cups chopped broccoli
4 large cloves of garlic,
  finely chopped
2 red bell peppers, cut into
  julienne strips
1 large onion, thinly sliced
1 tablespoon oil
2 tablespoons pine nuts
1 tablespoon raisins
8 ounces cooked peeled
  shrimp

Yield: 4 servings

Steam broccoli in saucepan until tender-crisp; drain. Sauté garlic, red peppers and onion in oil in skillet until vegetables are tender. Stir in broccoli, pine nuts, raisins and shrimp. Cook just until heated through, stirring frequently. Serve over rice.

Approx Per Serving: Cal 163; Prot 16 g; Carbo 13 g; Fiber 4 g; T Fat 7 g; 34% Calories from Fat; Chol 111 mg; Sod 148 mg.

Peggy Juppé

Lemon-Pepper Shrimp and Zucchini

2 medium zucchini
2 tablespoons olive oil
1 pound peeled deveined
  large shrimp
1 1/2 teaspoons lemon pepper
1/2 teaspoon salt

Yield: 4 servings

Cut zucchini diagonally into 1/2-inch slices. Sauté zucchini in olive oil in skillet over medium-high heat until tender-crisp and brown. Remove to plate. Add shrimp, lemon pepper and salt to skillet. Cook over high heat until shrimp turn pink. Stir in zucchini. Cook until heated through, stirring constantly.

Approx Per Serving: Cal 170; Prot 21 g; Carbo 4 g;
    Fiber 2 g; T Fat 8 g; 42% Calories from Fat;
    Chol 177 mg; Sod 777 mg.

Diana Prickett

Seafood Casserole

1/2 cup chopped green bell
  pepper
1/2 cup chopped onion
1/2 cup chopped celery
1/2 cup margarine
2/3 cup flour
1/2 teaspoon crushed garlic
1/2 teaspoon salt
1/4 teaspoon paprika
Red pepper to taste
1   10-ounce can cream of
  shrimp soup
2 cups milk
7 to 8 ounces crab meat,
  flaked
12 to 18 ounces cooked,
  peeled, deveined shrimp
1   8-ounce can sliced water
  chestnuts, drained
1   4-ounce can sliced
  mushrooms, drained
2 tablespoons butter,
  softened
1/2 cup shredded Cheddar
  cheese
1/2 cup bread crumbs

Yield: 6 servings

Sauté green pepper, onion and celery in margarine in skillet until vegetables are tender. Stir in flour. Cook for 1 minute, stirring constantly. Add garlic, salt, paprika, red pepper, soup and milk; mix well. Cook until thickened, stirring constantly. Combine crab meat, shrimp, water chestnuts and mushrooms in bowl; mix well. Spoon mixture into buttered 2-quart baking dish. Top with sauce. Sprinkle with mixture of butter, cheese and bread crumbs. Bake at 350 degrees for 30 to 35 minutes or until bubbly.

Approx Per Serving: Cal 533; Prot 35 g; Carbo 32 g;
    Fiber 2 g; T Fat 29 g; 50% Calories from Fat;
    Chol 242 mg; Sod 1349 mg.

Lora James

Creamed Seafood with Rice

1 small onion, chopped
1 clove of garlic, finely
  chopped
4 ounces mushrooms, cut
  into quarters
2 tablespoons butter
2¹/₂ tablespoons flour
1 cup light cream
³/₄ cup white wine
³/₄ teaspoon salt
¹/₈ teaspoon pepper
1 tablespoon Cognac
12 ounces shelled oysters
8 ounces cooked, peeled,
  deveined shrimp
1   5-ounce can lobster meat
3 to 4 cups cooked rice

Yield: 6 servings

Sauté onion, garlic and mushrooms in butter in skillet until brown. Stir in flour. Add cream and wine gradually, stirring until blended. Bring to a boil. Cook until thickened, stirring constantly. Stir in salt, pepper, Cognac, oysters, shrimp and lobster meat. Cook just until heated through, stirring frequently. Serve over hot cooked rice.

Approx Per Serving: Cal 498; Prot 25 g; Carbo 48 g;
    Fiber 1 g; T Fat 19 g; 36% Calories from Fat;
    Chol 193 mg; Sod 689 mg.

Jane and Sue Booth

St. George Seafood Pasta

3 cloves of garlic, finely
  chopped
1 cup sliced mushrooms
1 tablespoon finely chopped
  parsley
¹/₂ cup butter
4 ounces small scallops
4 ounces crab meat
4 ounces small shrimp,
  peeled, deveined
1   15-ounce can tomato
  sauce
4 cups cooked shell pasta
Seasoned salt to taste
White pepper to taste
¹/₄ cup grated Parmesan
  cheese
Chopped fresh parsley

Yield: 4 servings

Sauté garlic, mushrooms and 1 tablespoon parsley in butter in skillet until mushrooms are tender. Stir in scallops, crab meat and shrimp. Cook for 3 to 5 minutes or until shrimp turn pink, stirring frequently. Add tomato sauce and pasta; mix well. Cook until heated through. Season with seasoned salt and white pepper. Spoon mixture onto 4 plates; sprinkle with Parmesan cheese and chopped parsley.

Approx Per Serving: Cal 542; Prot 25 g; Carbo 50 g;
    Fiber 5 g; T Fat 28 g; 45% Calories from Fat;
    Chol 142 mg; Sod 1163 mg.

Helene Wagner

Seafood Lasagna

1 1-pound grouper fillet
1 pound scallops
1 pound shrimp, peeled
2 cups water
1 onion, sliced
8 ounces mushrooms, sliced
2 tablespoons butter
2 tablespoons olive oil
1 or 2 cloves of garlic, minced
1/4 cup flour
Salt and pepper to taste
1 teaspoon oregano
1 teaspoon basil
2 bay leaves
2 cups milk
1 16-ounce package
   lasagna noodles
2 cups low-fat cottage cheese
16 ounces mozzarella
   cheese, shredded
1/4 cup grated Parmesan
   cheese

Yield: 8 servings

Cut grouper into bite-sized pieces. Boil scallops, shrimp and grouper separately in water in saucepan just until tender; drain, reserving liquid. Combine reserved liquid with enough water to measure 2 cups. Sauté onion and mushrooms in butter and olive oil in skillet until onion is tender. Add garlic; mix well. Stir in flour, salt and pepper. Add reserved liquid 1 cup at a time, stirring until blended. Add oregano, basil and bay leaves; mix well. Add milk; mix well. Cook until thickened, stirring constantly. Discard bay leaves. Cook lasagna noodles *al dente* using package directions. Spoon some of sauce in bottom of baking dish. Layer noodles, seafood, cottage cheese and mozzarella cheese over sauce. Top with remaining sauce; sprinkle with Parmesan cheese. Bake at 350 degrees until bubbly.

Approx Per Serving: Cal 680; Prot 57 g; Carbo 52 g;
    Fiber 3 g; T Fat 26 g; 35% Calories from Fat;
    Chol 183 mg; Sod 758 mg.

Diane Hunt

Hobson's Seafood Special

8 ounces thinly sliced
   bacon, cut into 4-inch
   strips
2 pounds peeled deveined
   shrimp
1 large onion, chopped
1 tablespoon crushed garlic
2 cups scallops
2 10-ounce cans cream of
   mushroom soup
1 cup sour cream
Salt and pepper to taste

Yield: 8 servings

Fry bacon in skillet until partially cooked; drain, reserving 1 tablespoon drippings. Wrap each shrimp in 1 piece of bacon; secure with uncooked spaghetti. Place on rack in broiler pan. Broil until bacon is crisp; drain. Sauté onion in reserved bacon drippings in skillet until tender. Add garlic and scallops. Cook for 1 minute, stirring constantly; drain. Mix scallop mixture with soup and shrimp. Spoon into baking dish. Bake at 400 degrees until bubbly. Stir in sour cream, salt and pepper just before serving. Serve over hot cooked rice or pasta.

Approx Per Serving: Cal 336; Prot 29 g; Carbo 10 g;
    Fiber 1 g; T Fat 20 g; 53% Calories from Fat;
    Chol 209 mg; Sod 1037 mg.

Hobson Fulmer, DVM

Vegetables and Side Dishes

First Baptist Church of St. George Island
by Linda Holzhausen

St. George Island United Methodist Church
by Karen Dingler

Churches of
St. George Island

First Baptist Church

The First Baptist Church of St. George Island, Florida was started as a mission from the First Baptist Church, Apalachicola, Florida in 1978. The church operated as a mission under the direction of the Missions Committee: Mr. George Kirvin, Chairman, Mr. Adolph Maddox, Mr. E.E. "Red" Sizemore, Mr. James Bloodworth, Mrs. Elizabeth Stewart, and Mrs. Myrtle Kerr, with Rev. J. B. Grey serving as bi-vocational pastor until November, 1981. At this time the church constituted into a Southern Baptist church with Rev. Phillip Kelly serving as bi-vocational pastor. The church continued to operate in this manner until September, 1985 when Rev. Roy B. Bateman, Sr. was called as its first full-time pastor. The church currently has a membership of 96 and celebrated its 13th anniversary on Sunday, November 14, 1993.

United Methodist Church

Each summer, from 1971 to 1980, the First United Methodist Church of Apalachicola maintained a preaching mission on St. George Island utilizing seminarians. They met under an arbor of palm fronds. This preaching mission was eventually dropped, but the dream for a United Methodist Church on St. George Island continued. On November 19, 1984, the pastor of the First United Methodist Church in Apalachicola, the Reverend Don McMillan, began a home Bible study group on the island, and on February 1, 1987, the group began to worship as a mission of the Apalachicola Church in a temporary facility prepared by the new congregation at the home of Ken and Marcie Collins on St. George Island. The Reverend Don McMillan served as first pastor. The mission was later transferred to the First United Methodist Church of Eastpoint on February 14, 1988, with Rev. David Day serving as the new pastor. From the small beginning of 16 members, the congregation has grown to the current membership of 44 in five short years. The original facility, which was located in a private residence, has been replaced by a sanctuary and Sunday school building on church property located on East Gulf Beach Drive. The present pastor is the Reverend Jim Thomas. The church was chartered on May 26, 1992.

Asparagus Casserole

pound asparagus, cooked
4-ounce cans chopped
  green chilies, drained
1/2 cups sour cream
eggs, beaten
cup shredded Cheddar
  cheese
Chopped parsley

Yield: 5 servings

Arrange asparagus in baking dish; sprinkle with chilies. Spread sour cream over chilies. Pour beaten eggs over mixture. Sprinkle with cheese and parsley. Bake at 350 degrees for 20 to 30 minutes or until bubbly. May substitute canned asparagus for fresh asparagus and fat-free sour cream for sour cream. May substitute broccoli for asparagus and egg substitute for eggs.

Approx Per Serving: Cal 297; Prot 13 g; Carbo 10 g;
    Fiber 2 g; T Fat 24 g; 70% Calories from Fat;
    Chol 129 mg; Sod 732 mg.

Helen Solomon

Island Black Beans

1 1-pound package dried
    black beans
2 medium onions, chopped
2 cloves of garlic, minced
1 28-ounce can tomatoes,
    chopped
1/4 teaspoon thyme
3/4 teaspoon oregano
1/2 teaspoon coriander
2 bay leaves
1 envelope ham flavoring

Yield: 6 servings

Sort beans; rinse. Bring beans and enough water to cover to a boil in stockpot. Remove from heat. Let stand for 1 hour. Add onions, garlic, tomatoes, thyme, oregano, coriander, bay leaves and ham flavoring; mix well. Bring to a boil; reduce heat. Cook over medium heat for 2 hours or until beans are tender. Remove bay leaves. Serve over rice; top with chopped onion.

Approx Per Serving: Cal 297; Prot 19 g; Carbo 55 g;
    Fiber 19 g; T Fat 1 g; 3% Calories from Fat;
    Chol 0 mg; Sod 226 mg.
    Nutritional information does not include ham
    flavoring.

Richard and Shelia Lawrence

Green Bean Stroganoff

1/2 large onion, coarsely
  chopped
2 tablespoons margarine
8 ounces mushrooms,
  coarsely chopped
2 tablespoons margarine
1/2 large eggplant, chopped
1 teaspoon salt
Pepper to taste
1 pound fresh green beans,
  cut into bite-sized pieces,
  steamed
2 cups plain yogurt

Yield: 6 servings

Sauté onion in 2 tablespoons margarine in skillet until tender. Add mushrooms, 2 tablespoons margarine and eggplant. Cook until vegetables are tender, stirring frequently. Season with salt and pepper. Add hot green beans; mix well. Stir in yogurt just before serving. Cook until heated through, stirring constantly. Do not boil.

Approx Per Serving: Cal 168; Prot 6 g; Carbo 15 g;
    Fiber 4 g; T Fat 11 g; 54% Calories from Fat;
    Chol 10 mg; Sod 490 mg.

Cass Stark

Louisiana Red Beans and Rice

1 12-ounce package dried
  red beans
4 cups water
Salt to taste
1 pound ham hocks
1/2 green bell pepper,
  chopped
1 large onion, chopped
1 clove of garlic, minced
2 bay leaves
1 stalk celery, chopped
Cumin to taste
Cayenne pepper to taste

Yield: 4 servings

Sort beans; rinse. Combine beans, water and salt in stockpot. Let stand overnight. Sauté ham hocks, bell pepper, onion, garlic, bay leaves and chopped celery in skillet until onion is tender. Stir mixture into beans. Add cumin, cayenne pepper and additional salt if desired; mix well. Cook over low heat for 4 hours or until of desired consistency. Remove bay leaves; mash beans slightly. Serve over rice with corn bread and green salad. May substitute ham bone or ham scraps for ham hocks.

Approx Per Serving: Cal 349; Prot 24 g; Carbo 56 g;
    Fiber 19 g; T Fat 4 g; 10% Calories from Fat;
    Chol 11 mg; Sod 228 mg.
Nutritional information does not include rice.

John B. Spohrer, Jr.

Red Cabbage

1 large red cabbage, finely
  shredded
2 tablespoons bacon
  drippings
4 apples, chopped
1 onion, chopped
1 teaspoon sugar
Cloves to taste
1/2 cup red wine

Yield: 6 servings

Combine shredded cabbage, bacon drippings, apples, onion, sugar, cloves and enough water to prevent scorching in saucepan; mix well. Simmer for 2 hours, stirring occasionally. Stir in wine. Cook until liquid is absorbed. May substitute vinegar for water. May substitute margarine for bacon drippings.

Approx Per Serving: Cal 155; Prot 2 g; Carbo 25 g;
    Fiber 6 g; T Fat 5 g; 29% Calories from Fat;
    Chol 5 mg; Sod 44 mg.

Marta Thompson

Carrot Casserole

2 cups sliced carrots
1 medium onion, chopped
1/4 cup butter
Salt, pepper and garlic
  powder to taste
3 tablespoons flour
1 1/2 cups milk
1 cup shredded Cheddar
  cheese
2 cups cornflakes
2 tablespoons melted butter

Yield: 4 servings

Sauté carrots and onion in nonstick skillet until tender, stirring frequently. Arrange in 2-quart baking dish. Melt 1/4 cup butter in saucepan. Stir in salt, pepper and garlic. Add flour gradually; mix well. Cook until blended, stirring constantly. Add milk; mix well. Cook until thickened, stirring constantly. Pour over vegetables; sprinkle with cheese. Top with mixture of cornflakes and 2 tablespoons melted butter. Bake at 350 degrees for 20 minutes.

Approx Per Serving: Cal 417; Prot 13 g; Carbo 26 g;
    Fiber 2 g; T Fat 30 g; 64% Calories from Fat;
    Chol 89 mg; Sod 537 mg.

Patty Durham

Shoe Peg Corn Casserole

1/2 cup margarine
8 ounces cream cheese
3 11-ounce cans Shoe Peg
  corn
1 4-ounce can green chilies
1 cup plain bread crumbs

Yield: 10 servings

Combine margarine and cream cheese in saucepan. Cook over medium heat until blended, stirring constantly. Add corn and chilies; mix well. Spoon into nonstick baking pan; sprinkle with bread crumbs. Bake at 350 degrees until bubbly. May omit green chilies.

Approx Per Serving: Cal 260; Prot 5 g; Carbo 23 g;
    Fiber 2 g; T Fat 18 g; 60% Calories from Fat;
    Chol 25 mg; Sod 629 mg.

Neil Sherman

Corn Casserole

1/2 cup melted margarine
2 eggs, beaten
1 16-ounce can whole
  kernel corn
1 17-ounce can cream-style
  corn
1 cup sour cream
1 7-ounce package corn
  muffin mix

Yield: 6 servings

Combine margarine, eggs, whole kernel corn, cream-style corn, sour cream and muffin mix in bowl; mix well. Spoon into greased 1 1/2-quart baking dish. Bake at 350 degrees for 35 minutes.

Approx Per Serving: Cal 409; Prot 7 g; Carbo 40 g;
    Fiber 2 g; T Fat 27 g; 57% Calories from Fat;
    Chol 79 mg; Sod 785 mg.

Mary Rodgers

Scalloped Corn Casserole

1 17-ounce can cream-style
   corn
2 eggs, beaten
1/2 cup crushed saltine
   crackers
1/4 cup evaporated skim milk
1/4 cup shredded carrots
1/4 cup chopped green bell
   pepper
1/2 cup chopped celery
1/2 cup chopped onion
6 drops (or more) Tabasco
   sauce
1/2 teaspoon sugar
1/2 teaspoon salt
1/2 cup shredded low-fat
   Cheddar cheese
Paprika to taste

Yield: 4 servings

Combine corn, eggs, crushed crackers, evaporated skim milk, carrots, green pepper, celery, onion, Tabasco sauce, sugar and salt in bowl; mix well. Spoon into baking dish sprayed with nonstick cooking spray. Top with cheese; sprinkle with paprika. Bake at 350 degrees for 30 minutes or until bubbly. May substitute 4 egg whites or egg substitute for eggs.

Approx Per Serving: Cal 229; Prot 12 g; Carbo 36 g;
     Fiber 3 g; T Fat 6 g; 22% Calories from Fat;
     Chol 102 mg; Sod 919 mg.

Doris Barrett

Greek Eggplant

1 eggplant, peeled, cut into
   1/2-inch slices
Salt to taste
2 tablespoons olive oil
4 ounces feta cheese,
   crumbled
2 tomatoes, sliced
1 cup shredded sharp
   Cheddar cheese

Yield: 4 servings

Sprinkle eggplant with salt. Sauté in olive oil in skillet until tender, stirring frequently. Layer eggplant, feta cheese, sliced tomatoes and Cheddar cheese in order listed in greased baking dish. Bake at 350 degrees for 30 to 40 minutes or until bubbly.

Approx Per Serving: Cal 298; Prot 13 g; Carbo 13 g;
     Fiber 5 g; T Fat 23 g; 66% Calories from Fat;
     Chol 55 mg; Sod 500 mg.

Jean Lively

Maui Onion Deep Dish

1 cup plus 2 tablespoons
 rice
1/2 cup butter
31/3 pounds Maui or yellow
 onions, coarsely chopped
1 cup plus 2 tablespoons
 shredded Swiss cheese
1 cup whipping cream
2 tablespoons chopped
 parsley
Salt and pepper to taste
Paprika to taste

Yield: 12 servings

Cook rice in water in covered saucepan for 5 minutes; drain. Melt butter in large saucepan. Add onions; mix well. Cook for 30 minutes or until golden brown, stirring frequently. Stir in rice, cheese, cream, parsley, salt and pepper. Spoon into buttered 9x13-inch baking dish. Sprinkle with paprika. Bake at 350 degrees for 1 hour or until brown. I prefer to use Italian arborio rice in this dish.

Approx Per Serving: Cal 285; Prot 6 g; Carbo 26 g;
 Fiber 2 g; T Fat 18 g; 56% Calories from Fat;
 Chol 57 mg; Sod 117 mg.

Dot Crozier

Onion Pies

1/4 cup butter, softened
1 cup crushed butter
 crackers
2 cups chopped Vidalia
 onions
2 tablespoons butter
2 eggs
3/4 cup milk
3/4 teaspoon salt
Pepper to taste
1/4 cup shredded Cheddar
 cheese
Paprika to taste

Yield: 12 servings

Cut 1/4 cup butter into crushed crackers in bowl until crumbly. Press evenly over bottoms and sides of two 8-inch pie plates. Sauté onions in 2 tablespoons butter in skillet until tender, stirring frequently. Spread over prepared layer. Beat eggs, milk, salt and pepper in bowl until blended. Pour over onions. Sprinkle with cheese and paprika. Bake at 350 degrees for 30 minutes. May substitute margarine for butter.

Approx Per Serving: Cal 121; Prot 3 g; Carbo 7 g;
 Fiber 1 g; T Fat 9 g; 69% Calories from Fat;
 Chol 51 mg; Sod 275 mg.

Frankie Hodgson

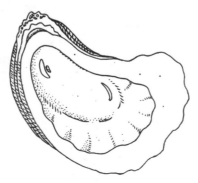

Herbed Peas

2 10-ounce packages
　frozen green peas,
　cooked, drained
2 tablespoons chopped
　chives
1/4 teaspoon paprika
2 tablespoons melted butter
1/2 teaspoon basil

Yield: 6 servings

Combine peas, chives, paprika, butter and basil in bowl; mix well. Spoon into center of rice ring.

Approx Per Serving: Cal 107; Prot 5 g; Carbo 13 g; Fiber 5 g; T Fat 4 g; 34% Calories from Fat; Chol 10 mg; Sod 145 mg.

Pat Morrison

Lettuce and Peas

18 ounces lettuce
Salt to taste
2 tablespoons butter
3 tablespoons flour
Nutmeg to taste
1 cup milk
1 small onion, chopped
1 10-ounce package frozen
　peas, cooked, drained

Yield: 4 servings

Cut lettuce into 1/8-inch shreds. Cook lettuce in salted water in saucepan for 5 minutes; drain. Melt butter in saucepan. Stir in flour, nutmeg and salt. Add milk and onion; mix well. Cook until thickened, stirring constantly. Stir in lettuce and peas.

Approx Per Serving: Cal 187; Prot 8 g; Carbo 21 g; Fiber 5 g; T Fat 8 g; 39% Calories from Fat; Chol 24 mg; Sod 180 mg.

Irene LaSlavic

Scottsdale Potatoes

1 2-pound package frozen
　hashed brown potatoes
2 1/2 cups shredded Cheddar
　cheese
2 cups sour cream
1 10-ounce can cream of
　chicken soup
1/2 cup chopped onion
1/4 cup melted butter
Salt and pepper to taste
2 cups crushed cornflakes
1/2 cup melted butter

Yield: 10 servings

Thaw potatoes. Combine potatoes, cheese, sour cream, soup, onion, 1/4 cup butter, salt and pepper in bowl; mix well. Spoon into buttered 9x13-inch baking dish. Top with mixture of cornflakes and 1/2 cup melted butter. Bake at 350 degrees for 45 minutes or until brown.

Approx Per Serving: Cal 497; Prot 13 g; Carbo 34 g; Fiber 1 g; T Fat 35 g; 63% Calories from Fat; Chol 90 mg; Sod 753 mg.

Sue Reitinger

Spinach Olé

4 green onions with tops,
  chopped
1 onion, chopped
3 stalks celery, chopped
1/4 cup butter
3 cups tomato purée
1/4 cup lemon juice
2 cloves of garlic, crushed
2 tablespoons chili powder
1 teaspoon cumin
1 teaspoon salt
1/4 teaspoon pepper
2   10-ounce packages
  frozen chopped spinach,
  cooked, drained
1 cup shredded Monterey
  Jack cheese

Yield: 8 servings

Sauté chopped green onions, onion and celery in butter in skillet until tender, stirring frequently. Add tomato purée, lemon juice, garlic, chili powder, cumin, salt and pepper; mix well. Simmer for 5 minutes, stirring frequently. Stir in spinach. Spoon into buttered baking dish; sprinkle with cheese. Bake at 350 degrees for 20 minutes.

Approx Per Serving: Cal 178; Prot 8 g; Carbo 17 g;
    Fiber 5 g; T Fat 11 g; 50% Calories from Fat;
    Chol 28 mg; Sod 861 mg.

Claire Dews

Green and Yellow Squash

1 Vidalia onion, chopped
1 tablespoon margarine
6 to 7 medium yellow
  squash, sliced
3 to 4 medium zucchini
  squash, sliced
Salt and pepper to taste
Fresh chopped basil to taste
Chopped parsley to taste

Yield: 6 servings

Combine onion and margarine in microwave-safe dish. Microwave on High until tender. Microwave yellow squash and zucchini squash in several batches in microwave-safe dish for 3 minutes or until tender. Stir in onion. Microwave just until heated through. Season with salt, pepper, basil and parsley.

Approx Per Serving: Cal 109; Prot 6 g; Carbo 20 g;
    Fiber 6 g; T Fat 3 g; 20% Calories from Fat;
    Chol 0 mg; Sod 34 mg.

Helen Marsh

Yellow Squash Casserole

6 cups thinly sliced yellow
  squash
1 cup sliced onions
1 cup shredded carrots
1 cup sour cream
1 10-ounce can cream of
  chicken soup
1 cup melted margarine
1 8-ounce package stuffing
  mix

Yield: 10 servings

Combine squash, onions and enough water to cover in saucepan. Boil for 5 minutes; drain. Combine carrots, sour cream and soup in bowl; mix well. Stir into squash mixture. Mix melted margarine and stuffing mix in bowl. Spoon 1/2 of stuffing mixture into 9x13-inch baking pan. Spread squash mixture over prepared layer. Top with remaining stuffing mixture. Bake, covered, at 350 degrees for 20 minutes. Bake, uncovered, for 15 minutes longer. May substitute zucchini squash for yellow squash.

Approx Per Serving: Cal 353; Prot 5 g; Carbo 26 g;
    Fiber 2 g; T Fat 26 g; 65% Calories from Fat;
    Chol 13 mg; Sod 833 mg.

John and Joan Ackerly

Sweet Potato-Berry Bake

2 16-ounce cans sweet
  potatoes
1 cup fresh or frozen whole
  cranberries
1/4 cup chopped pecans
1/2 cup orange marmalade

Yield: 8 servings

Drain sweet potatoes, reserving half the liquid. Slice sweet potatoes into bite-sized pieces. Arrange in 9x13-inch baking dish. Pour reserved liquid over potatoes. Sprinkle with cranberries and pecans; dot with marmalade. Bake at 350 degrees for 30 minutes.

Approx Per Serving: Cal 181; Prot 2 g; Carbo 39 g;
    Fiber 3 g; T Fat 3 g; 13% Calories from Fat;
    Chol 0 mg; Sod 61 mg.

Kristen Shelby

Sweet Potato Soufflé

1 20-ounce can sweet
     potatoes, drained, mashed
1 cup sugar
6 eggs, beaten
1/2 cup butter
1 cup shredded coconut
1 tablespoon vanilla extract
1 teaspoon salt
1 cup packed brown sugar
1/2 cup flour
1/2 cup butter, softened
1 cup chopped pecans

Yield: 6 servings

Combine sweet potatoes, sugar, eggs, 1/2 cup butter, shredded coconut, vanilla and salt in bowl; mix well. Spoon into nonstick baking pan. Bake at 350 degrees for 30 minutes. Sprinkle with mixture of brown sugar, flour, 1/2 cup butter and pecans. Bake at 300 degrees for 15 minutes. May substitute margarine for butter. May omit coconut.

Approx Per Serving: Cal 936; Prot 10 g; Carbo 107 g;
     Fiber 5 g; T Fat 54 g; 51% Calories from Fat;
     Chol 270 mg; Sod 813 mg.

Marti Fraker

Curried Tomatoes

8 ripe tomatoes, peeled,
     cored
1 cup tomato sauce
2 teaspoons curry powder
2 tablespoons currant jelly
3 tablespoons fresh bread
     crumbs
1/4 cup shredded Cheddar
     cheese
8 slices crisp-fried bacon,
     crumbled

Yield: 8 servings

Arrange tomatoes in baking dish. Combine tomato sauce, curry powder and jelly in saucepan; mix well. Cook for 5 minutes, stirring constantly. Spoon over tomatoes. Sprinkle with bread crumbs and cheese. Bake at 425 degrees for 15 minutes. Sprinkle with bacon.

Approx Per Serving: Cal 102; Prot 4 g; Carbo 12 g;
     Fiber 2 g; T Fat 5 g; 40% Calories from Fat;
     Chol 9 mg; Sod 326 mg.

Jeanne Crozier

Stuffed Tomatoes

4 large tomatoes
1 cup dry bread crumbs
1/4 cup chopped onion,
    sautéed
1 cup crumbled cooked
    sausage
3 tablespoons chopped
    fresh parsley

Yield: 4 servings

Cut tops from tomatoes. Scoop out pulp to form shells, reserving pulp. Arrange tomatoes in greased baking dish. Combine reserved tomato pulp, bread crumbs, onion, sausage and parsley in bowl; mix well. Spoon sausage mixture into tomatoes. Bake at 350 degrees until heated through. Garnish with shredded cheese.

Approx Per Serving: Cal 234; Prot 10 g; Carbo 28 g;
    Fiber 4 g; T Fat 10 g; 37% Calories from Fat;
    Chol 21 mg; Sod 557 mg.

Martha Gherardi

Zucchini Casserole

4 slices bacon, cut into
    pieces
4 medium zucchini, sliced
3 medium tomatoes,
    chopped
1 medium onion, chopped
Salt and pepper to taste
1 cup shredded Cheddar
    cheese

Yield: 8 servings

Fry bacon in skillet until light brown. Add zucchini, tomatoes, onion, salt and pepper. Cook, covered, over medium heat for 15 minutes, stirring occasionally. Remove cover. Cook until thickened and squash is tender-crisp, stirring frequently. Spoon into baking dish. Sprinkle with cheese. Broil until cheese melts.

Approx Per Serving: Cal 108; Prot 7 g; Carbo 7 g;
    Fiber 2 g; T Fat 7 g; 52% Calories from Fat;
    Chol 18 mg; Sod 147 mg.

Margaret Lawhon

Hot Pineapple Casserole

2 20-ounce cans pineapple
    chunks, drained
1 cup sugar
5 tablespoons flour
1½ cups shredded Cheddar
    cheese
1 cup crushed butter
    crackers
¼ cup melted butter

Yield: 8 servings

Arrange pineapple chunks in baking dish. Sprinkle with mixture of sugar and flour. Spread cheese over mixture. Sprinkle with crushed crackers; drizzle with melted butter. Bake at 350 degrees for 15 to 20 minutes or until bubbly.

Approx Per Serving: Cal 369; Prot 7 g; Carbo 54 g;
    Fiber 1 g; T Fat 15 g; 36% Calories from Fat;
    Chol 38 mg; Sod 268 mg.

Betty Day

Corn Bread Dressing

½ cup finely chopped onion
½ cup finely chopped green
    bell pepper
½ cup finely chopped celery
⅔ cup butter
8 cups corn bread crumbs
6 hard-boiled eggs, chopped
½ cup chopped pimentos
Salt and black pepper to
    taste
½ teaspoon red pepper
    flakes
1 to 1½ cups chicken stock
1 cup buttermilk

Yield: 16 servings

Sauté onion, green pepper and celery in butter in large saucepan until tender. Add corn bread crumbs, eggs and pimentos; mix well. Season with salt, pepper and red pepper flakes. Stir in just enough chicken stock to moisten. Stir in buttermilk. Spoon into buttered baking pan. Bake at 350 degrees until brown.

Approx Per Serving: Cal 253; Prot 7 g; Carbo 24 g;
    Fiber 2 g; T Fat 15 g; 52% Calories from Fat;
    Chol 128 mg; Sod 545 mg.

Claire Dews

Sausage and Rice Dressing

1 6-ounce package long
  grain and wild rice mix
1 pound mild or hot pork
  sausage
1 cup chopped onion
1 cup chopped celery
1/4 cup butter
1 6-ounce package stuffing
  mix
1 2-ounce can mushroom
  pieces and stems, drained
2 eggs, beaten
3 cups chicken broth
1/2 cup chopped pecans,
  toasted
1/4 teaspoon seasoned
  pepper
Poultry seasoning to taste

Yield: 10 servings

Prepare rice mix using package directions. Brown sausage in skillet, stirring until crumbly; drain. Sauté onion and celery in butter in skillet until tender. Combine rice, sausage, onion mixture, stuffing mix, mushrooms, eggs, chicken broth, pecans, seasoned pepper and poultry seasoning in bowl; mix well. Spoon into greased 9x13-inch baking pan. Bake at 350 degrees for 45 minutes. May substitute margarine for butter and walnuts for pecans. May stuff a 12-pound turkey with this recipe.

Approx Per Serving: Cal 349; Prot 11 g; Carbo 32 g;
    Fiber 1 g; T Fat 20 g; 51% Calories from Fat;
    Chol 68 mg; Sod 1214 mg.
    Nutritional information does not include seasoned
    pepper.

Alice D. Collins

Baked Garlic-Cheese Grits

1 cup quick-cooking grits
2 cups shredded Cheddar
  cheese
1 teaspoon finely chopped
  garlic
1/2 cup butter
1/2 cup chopped green
  onions with tops
2 eggs, beaten
3/4 cup milk

Yield: 4 servings

Prepare grits using package directions. Stir in cheese, garlic, butter and green onions. Spoon into buttered 2-quart baking dish. Cool completely. Pour mixture of eggs and milk over grits. Bake at 375 degrees for 1 hour or until set.

Approx Per Serving: Cal 641; Prot 22 g; Carbo 36 g;
    Fiber 5 g; T Fat 46 g; 64% Calories from Fat;
    Chol 221 mg; Sod 638 mg.

Jane E. Davis

Pasta-Cheese Crunch

4 ounces pasta
1¼ cups shredded Cheddar
 cheese
1 medium onion, finely
 chopped
½ red pepper, finely
 chopped
2 eggs, beaten
1 cup milk
Salt and pepper to taste
¼ cup melted butter
½ cup crushed cornflakes

Yield: 4 servings

Prepare pasta using package directions; drain. Combine pasta, cheese, onion, red pepper, eggs and milk in bowl; mix well. Season with salt and pepper. Spoon into shallow baking dish. Sprinkle with mixture of melted butter and cornflakes. Bake at 375 degrees for 40 minutes or until set. May substitute stuffing mix for crushed cornflakes.

Approx Per Serving: Cal 468; Prot 18 g; Carbo 36 g;
 Fiber 2 g; T Fat 28 g; 54% Calories from Fat;
 Chol 170 mg; Sod 492 mg.

Movitia Toomey

Confetti Rice Mold

1 cup rice, rinsed
1½ cups boiling water
1 teaspoon salt
½ cup butter
3 eggs, beaten
1   20-ounce can bean
 sprouts, drained
1 cup chopped green onions
 with tops
⅓ cup pimento strips
1 teaspoon salt
⅛ teaspoon pepper

Yield: 4 servings

Combine rice, boiling water and 1 teaspoon salt in saucepan. Cook, covered, over low heat until tender. Melt butter in large skillet. Stir in eggs. Cook until set, stirring constantly. Add rice, bean sprouts, green onions, pimento strips, 1 teaspoon salt and pepper; mix well. Cook, covered, for 10 minutes. Spoon into a heated and greased 6-cup ring mold. Serve with Herbed Peas on page 139.

Approx Per Serving: Cal 450; Prot 10 g; Carbo 43 g;
 Fiber 4 g; T Fat 27 g; 53% Calories from Fat;
 Chol 202 mg; Sod 1549 mg.

Pat Morrison

Dominic's Tomato Sauce

1 4-ounce pork chop, cut
  into bite-sized pieces
Salt and pepper to taste
3 cloves of garlic, chopped
1 cup chicken broth
2 16-ounce cans tomato
  sauce
3 tablespoons parsley
1 tablespoon basil
1 tablespoon sugar

Yield: 10 servings

Season pork with salt and pepper. Brown in skillet with garlic, stirring constantly. Stir in chicken broth. Boil for 5 minutes. Add tomato sauce, parsley, basil and sugar; mix well. Simmer for 30 to 45 minutes or until of desired consistency, stirring frequently.

Approx Per Serving: Cal 54; Prot 4 g; Carbo 8 g;
    Fiber 2 g; T Fat 1 g; 16% Calories from Fat;
    Chol 7 mg; Sod 633 mg.

Dominic Baragona

Marinara Sauce

2 cloves of garlic, sliced
1/4 cup olive oil
1 29-ounce can tomatoes
  with basil
1 1/4 teaspoons salt
1 teaspoon oregano
1/4 teaspoon parsley flakes
1/8 teaspoon pepper
1 to 2 tablespoons tomato
  paste

Yield: 12 servings

Sauté garlic in olive oil in skillet until brown, stirring constantly. Add tomatoes, salt, oregano, parsley, pepper and tomato paste gradually, stirring constantly. Cook over medium heat for 15 minutes or until thickened, stirring occasionally. Add 1/4 to 1/2 cup water if too thick. Serve with shrimp or over your favorite pasta.

Approx Per Serving: Cal 57; Prot 1 g; Carbo 4 g;
    Fiber 1 g; T Fat 5 g; 70% Calories from Fat;
    Chol 0 mg; Sod 355 mg.

Susan Ficklen

Mamma Gherardi's Tomato Sauce

3¹/2 to 4 pounds fresh
   tomatoes, peeled, cut into
   quarters
1 carrot, cut into 1-inch
   pieces
1 stalk celery, cut into
   1-inch pieces
1 medium onion, chopped
2 cloves of garlic, chopped
¹/3 cup chopped fresh
   parsley
¹/4 cup chopped fresh basil
1 tablespoon sugar
Salt to taste

Yield: 12 servings

Combine tomatoes, carrot, celery, onion, garlic, parsley, basil, sugar and salt in stockpot; mix well. Cook over low heat until vegetables are tender, stirring occasionally. Cool. Process in food processor until smooth. Serve over spaghetti or use as a base for soups and casseroles. May freeze for future use.

Approx Per Serving: Cal 44; Prot 2 g; Carbo 10 g;
   Fiber 2 g; T Fat 1 g; 10% Calories from Fat;
   Chol 0 mg; Sod 20 mg.

Martha Gherardi

Tomato and Garlic Sauce

1¹/2 pints cherry tomatoes,
   cut into halves
6 cloves of garlic, crushed
1 tablespoon rosemary
1 teaspoon salt
¹/4 teaspoon pepper
2 tablespoons olive oil
1   1-pound package
   linguine, cooked
1 clove of garlic, crushed
2 tablespoons bleu cheese,
   crumbled
¹/2 cup chopped parsley

Yield: 6 servings

Cook tomatoes, 6 cloves of garlic, rosemary, salt and pepper in olive oil in skillet for 3 minutes or until tomatoes are tender, stirring frequently. Combine linguine with 1 clove of garlic in bowl; mix well. Add tomato mixture, bleu cheese and chopped parsley, tossing to coat.

Approx Per Serving: Cal 356; Prot 11 g; Carbo 62 g;
   Fiber 3 g; T Fat 7 g; 17% Calories from Fat;
   Chol 2 mg; Sod 411 mg.

Patty Valentine

Breads

The Ferryboat Spica
by John Ficklen

Eastpoint to St. George Island by Ferry

Joe "Snooky" Barber of Apalachicola captained the St. George Island ferry when the bridge opened in 1965. Named for the brightest star in the heavens, the Sirius was designed to carry nine vehicles and was equipped with life jackets for 100 passengers.

The ferry made six round trips each day in the summer season from Cat Point on the mainland to the present Island boat basin. Toll for the 45 minute trip was one dollar per vehicle with driver, and 25 cents for each additional passenger. Toll was collected in both directions.

July 4th and Labor Day were the busiest, Barber recalls. One Labor Day a record 85 cars and 360 people used the ferry.

The Sirius was 65 feet long and 40 feet wide, with a propeller and rudder on each end and powered by twin 671 diesel engines.

The Sirius came to Franklin County from Long Island, where she was used on short 20 minute runs, never needing to turn around. The double prop/double rudder design made steering a challenge, Barber remembers, especially with the fog and high winds encountered in the Bay.

"We were good ambassadors for the Island," Barber says. He and engineer John Hathcock would go out of their way to make sure no one was stranded on the Island after the day's last run.

Visitors would bring the Captain and his crew bushel baskets of beans, peaches and field peas from up country.

Barber picked up the Island mail at the Eastpoint post office and each morning carried it across the Bay to the Island.

Once the bridge opened, Barber's last trip on the Sirius was to the Sherman Shipyard in Panama City where the ferry was overhauled and put to work by loggers hauling lumber and equipment.

Barber retired in 1987 as Captain of the Florida State University Marine Lab research vessel, Tursiops, which he skippered the seven seas over from its port at Turkey Point in eastern Franklin County.

The ferryboat Spica, which also ran across Apalachicola Bay to St. George Island, preceded the Sirius.

Easy Whole Wheat Angel Biscuits

2 packages dry yeast
2 teaspoons sugar
1/2 cup warm (105- to
    110-degree) water
3 cups whole wheat flour
2 cups all-purpose flour
1 cup butter, softened
1 tablespoon salt
1 teaspoon baking soda
1 teaspoon baking powder
13/4 cups buttermilk

Yield: 30 servings

Dissolve yeast and sugar in warm water. Combine whole wheat flour and all-purpose flour in bowl; mix well. Cut in butter with pastry blender until crumbly. Add salt, baking soda and baking powder; mix well. Stir in buttermilk and yeast mixture. Knead several times on lightly floured surface. Roll 1/2 inch thick; cut with biscuit cutter. Place on nonstick baking sheet. Bake at 400 degrees for 12 to 15 minutes or until brown. May store dough in oiled container in refrigerator for up to 1 week.

Approx Per Serving: Cal 134; Prot 3 g; Carbo 16 g;
    Fiber 2 g; T Fat 7 g; 43% Calories from Fat;
    Chol 17 mg; Sod 330 mg.

Judi Little

Butter Bits

1/3 cup butter
21/4 cups flour
1 tablespoon sugar
31/2 teaspoons baking
    powder
11/2 teaspoons salt
1 cup milk

Yield: 32 servings

Melt butter in 9x13-inch baking pan. Sift flour, sugar, baking powder and salt in bowl; mix well. Add milk, stirring with fork just until dough clings together. Knead on floured surface 10 times. Roll into 1/2-inch thick rectangle. Cut dough into halves lengthwise. Cut each portion crosswise into 16 strips. Dip both sides of the strips in melted butter. Arrange the strips in the prepared baking pan. Bake at 450 degrees for 15 to 20 minutes or until golden brown. May add 1/2 cup grated sharp Cheddar cheese to dry ingredients; or 1/2 clove of garlic, finely minced, to butter; or sprinkle paprika, celery seed or garlic salt over strips before baking; or add 1/4 cup minced chives or parsley to dry ingredients.

Approx Per Serving: Cal 56; Prot 1 g; Carbo 8 g;
    Fiber <1 g; T Fat 2 g; 37% Calories from Fat;
    Chol 6 mg; Sod 159 mg.

Ann Robuck

Sour Cream Biscuits

2 cups self-rising flour
1 cup melted margarine
2 cups sour cream

Yield: 12 servings

Combine self-rising flour, margarine and sour cream in bowl; mix well. Spoon into ungreased muffin cups immediately. Bake at 450 degrees for 15 to 20 minutes or until light brown.

Approx Per Serving: Cal 292; Prot 3 g; Carbo 17 g; Fiber 1 g; T Fat 24 g; 72% Calories from Fat; Chol 17 mg; Sod 463 mg.

Lora James

Anna's Corn Bread

1 tablespoon shortening
1 8-ounce can cream-style corn
1 cup self-rising cornmeal
1 cup sour cream
1/2 cup corn oil
2 eggs

Yield: 8 servings

Heat shortening in heavy cast-iron skillet in 425-degree oven until hot. Combine corn, cornmeal, sour cream, oil and eggs in bowl; mix well. Spoon batter into hot skillet. Bake for 20 minutes. May add chopped jalapeño peppers or okra to batter before baking. May double the recipe to serve a crowd and bake in 9x13-inch baking pan; cut into squares to serve.

Approx Per Serving: Cal 294; Prot 4 g; Carbo 19 g; Fiber 1 g; T Fat 23 g; 68% Calories from Fat; Chol 60 mg; Sod 342 mg.

Anna Johnson Riedel

Broccoli Corn Bread

1 10-ounce package frozen
   chopped broccoli
1/2 cup margarine, softened
1 teaspoon salt
6 to 8 ounces cottage cheese
4 eggs, beaten
1 medium or large onion,
   chopped
1 7-ounce package corn
   bread mix

Yield: 10 servings

Bring broccoli and enough water to cover to a boil in saucepan; drain. Combine broccoli, margarine, salt, cottage cheese, eggs, onion and corn bread mix in bowl; mix well. Spoon into nonstick 10-inch baking pan. Bake at 400 degrees for 30 minutes. May just thaw and drain broccoli before stirring into batter if desired. May add 1/2 cup cheese if desired.

Approx Per Serving: Cal 182; Prot 7 g; Carbo 11 g;
    Fiber 1 g; T Fat 13 g; 62% Calories from Fat;
    Chol 78 mg; Sod 541 mg.

Azilee Drake Foy and Sara Rodrigue

Mexican Corn Bread

1 1/2 pounds ground beef
1/2 onion, chopped
1 package taco seasoning
   mix
1 3/4 cups cornmeal
1/2 teaspoon baking soda
1 teaspoon salt
1 teaspoon baking powder
1 teaspoon picante sauce
2 eggs, beaten
1 cup buttermilk
1 17-ounce can cream-style
   corn
2 jalapeño peppers, chopped
1/3 cup oil
1 cup shredded sharp
   Cheddar cheese

Yield: 10 servings

Brown ground beef with chopped onion in skillet, stirring constantly until ground beef is crumbly; drain. Stir in taco seasoning mix. Combine cornmeal, baking soda, salt, baking powder, picante sauce, eggs and buttermilk in bowl; mix well. Stir in mixture of corn, jalapeño peppers and oil. Layer half the batter, ground beef mixture, cheese and remaining batter in greased cast-iron skillet. Bake at 400 degrees for 30 minutes or until golden brown.

Approx Per Serving: Cal 425; Prot 23 g; Carbo 33 g;
    Fiber 2 g; T Fat 22 g; 47% Calories from Fat;
    Chol 101 mg; Sod 920 mg.

Lora James

Corn Bread Muffins

1 cup (heaping) medium
    ground cornmeal
1 tablespoon (heaping) flour
1 teaspoon salt
1 teaspoon baking powder
1/2 teaspoon baking soda
1 1/2 cups buttermilk
1 egg, beaten
3 tablespoons bacon
    drippings

Yield: 12 servings

Combine cornmeal, flour, salt, baking powder and baking soda in bowl; mix well. Stir in buttermilk. Add egg; mix well. Mix in bacon drippings. Spoon into greased muffin cups. Bake at 400 degrees until golden brown. May substitute shortening for bacon drippings.

Approx Per Serving: Cal 93; Prot 2 g; Carbo 11 g;
    Fiber 1 g; T Fat 4 g; 42% Calories from Fat;
    Chol 18 mg; Sod 295 mg.

Bo Suber

Raisin Bran Muffins

1   15-ounce package Raisin
    Bran
1 cup raisins
5 cups flour
3 cups sugar
2 teaspoons salt
1 teaspoon cinnamon
1 teaspoon baking powder
5 teaspoons baking soda
4 eggs, beaten
4 cups buttermilk
1 cup oil

Yield: 36 servings

Combine cereal, raisins, flour, sugar, salt, cinnamon, baking powder and baking soda in bowl; mix well. Make well in center of dry ingredients. Add eggs, buttermilk and oil, stirring just until moistened. Spoon into greased muffin cups. Bake at 350 degrees for 20 minutes or until golden brown. May store batter, covered, in refrigerator for up to 5 weeks. To avoid danger of salmonella, use egg substitute instead of fresh eggs when planning to store batter in refrigerator.

Approx Per Serving: Cal 250; Prot 5 g; Carbo 44 g;
    Fiber 2 g; T Fat 7 g; 25% Calories from Fat;
    Chol 22 mg; Sod 343 mg.

Margaret Pfeifer

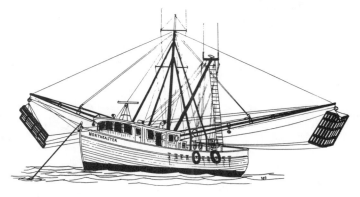

Easy Apple Bread

1/2 cup butter, softened
1 cup sugar
2 eggs
2 cups flour
1/2 teaspoon salt
1/2 teaspoon baking soda
1 teaspoon baking powder
2 tablespoons buttermilk
1 teaspoon vanilla extract
1 cup coarsely chopped
   unpeeled apples
1/2 cup chopped pecans

Yield: 12 servings

Cream butter and sugar in bowl. Beat in eggs. Add mixture of flour, salt, baking soda and baking powder. Blend in buttermilk and vanilla. Stir in apples and pecans. Spoon into greased and floured loaf pan. Bake at 350 degrees for 50 minutes or until bread tests done.

Approx Per Serving: Cal 262; Prot 4 g; Carbo 36 g;
    Fiber 1 g; T Fat 12 g; 41% Calories from Fat;
    Chol 52 mg; Sod 241 mg.

Chris Healy

Old-Fashioned Banana Bread

2 cups flour
1/2 cup sugar
1/2 cup shortening
3 ripe bananas, sliced
2 eggs
1 teaspoon baking soda

Yield: 12 servings

Beat all ingredients at medium speed in mixer bowl until combined. Spoon into greased 5x9-inch loaf pan. Bake at 350 degrees for 1 hour and 10 minutes.

Approx Per Serving: Cal 221; Prot 3 g; Carbo 31 g;
    Fiber 1 g; T Fat 10 g; 39% Calories from Fat;
    Chol 31 mg; Sod 78 mg.

Gwen Henkel

Pumpkin Bread

3 cups sugar
1 1/2 teaspoons salt
1 teaspoon cinnamon
1 teaspoon nutmeg
3 1/2 cups flour
1 1/2 teaspoons baking soda
1 cup oil
4 eggs, beaten
2/3 cup water
2 cups pumpkin
1 cup chopped walnuts

Yield: 36 servings

Combine sugar, salt, cinnamon, nutmeg, flour, baking soda, oil, eggs, water, pumpkin and walnuts in order listed in bowl; mix well. Spoon into 3 greased loaf pans. Bake at 350 degrees for 1 hour.

Approx Per Serving: Cal 196; Prot 2 g; Carbo 28 g;
    Fiber 1 g; T Fat 9 g; 40% Calories from Fat;
    Chol 21 mg; Sod 131 mg.

Vilma Baragona

Charlotte's Beer Bread

3 cups self-rising flour
3 tablespoons sugar
1 can beer, at room
  temperature
1/2 cup melted margarine

Yield: 12 servings

Mix flour, sugar and beer in bowl. Spoon into greased loaf pan. Bake at 350 degrees for 45 minutes. Drizzle with melted margarine. Bake for 15 minutes longer.

Approx Per Serving: Cal 202; Prot 3 g; Carbo 27 g; Fiber 1 g; T Fat 8 g; 35% Calories from Fat; Chol 0 mg; Sod 487 mg.

Charlotte James

Mark's Egg Bread

2 eggs, slightly beaten
2 cups buttermilk
1 teaspoon salt
1/2 teaspoon baking soda
1/4 cup canola oil
13/4 cups finely ground
  cornmeal

Yield: 8 servings

Combine eggs, buttermilk, salt, baking soda and canola oil in bowl; mix well. Stir in cornmeal. Spoon into greased baking pan. Bake at 375 degrees for 30 minutes.

Approx Per Serving: Cal 212; Prot 6 g; Carbo 27 g; Fiber 2 g; T Fat 9 g; 38% Calories from Fat; Chol 49 mg; Sod 397 mg.

Doris Barrett

Zucchini Bread

3 cups flour
1 teaspoon cinnamon
1 teaspoon salt
1 teaspoon baking soda
11/4 teaspoons baking powder
3 eggs, beaten
1 cup oil
21/4 cups sugar
2 cups grated zucchini
1 teaspoon vanilla extract
1 cup finely chopped pecans

Yield: 24 servings

Sift flour, cinnamon, salt, baking soda and baking powder together. Combine eggs, oil, sugar, zucchini, vanilla and dry ingredients in order listed in bowl; mix well. Stir in pecans. Spoon into 2 nonstick loaf pans. Bake at 350 degrees for 1 hour.

Approx Per Serving: Cal 255; Prot 3 g; Carbo 32 g; Fiber 1 g; T Fat 13 g; 46% Calories from Fat; Chol 23 mg; Sod 148 mg.

Vilma Baragona

Popovers

2 eggs
1 cup milk
1 cup flour
1/2 teaspoon salt

Yield: 10 servings

Combine eggs, milk, flour and salt in bowl; mix well. Spoon into greased muffin cups. Place in cold oven. Bake at 400 degrees for 30 minutes or until brown.

Approx Per Serving: Cal 74; Prot 3 g; Carbo 11 g; Fiber <1 g; T Fat 2 g; 23% Calories from Fat; Chol 41 mg; Sod 130 mg.

Kathy Gilbert

Broccoli and Sausage Bread

1 1/4 pounds Italian sausage
10 cloves of garlic, crushed
1   10-ounce package frozen chopped broccoli, thawed
1 pound package pizza dough
3 tablespoons olive oil

Yield: 12 servings

Brown sausage in skillet, stirring until crumbly; drain. Stir in garlic and broccoli; cool. Roll pizza dough into rectangle on lightly floured surface. Spread sausage mixture evenly over dough. Roll into a loaf, sealing edge and ends. Place seam side down in ungreased baking pan; brush with olive oil. Bake at 350 degrees for 45 to 60 minutes or until brown, basting with olive oil every 20 minutes.

Approx Per Serving: Cal 210; Prot 8 g; Carbo 19 g; Fiber 1 g; T Fat 11 g; 48% Calories from Fat; Chol 17 mg; Sod 456 mg.

Patty Valentine

A Happy Home Recipe

Take 4 cups of love and 2 cups loyalty; mix with 2 spoons of faith.
Blend it with 2 spoons of tenderness, 1 cup of friendship,
3 cups of forgiveness, 1 cup of understanding and 5 spoons of hope.
Sprinkle abundantly with 1 barrel of laughter.
Bake in sunshine. Serve daily in generous helpings.

—Beth Mosely

Sausage Bread

1   1-pound loaf frozen
    bread dough, thawed,
    risen
2 eggs, beaten
1¹/₂ pounds sausage,
    cooked, drained
12 ounces provolone
    cheese, shredded
8 ounces mozzarella cheese,
    shredded
1 cup grated Parmesan
    cheese

Yield: 12 servings

Roll bread dough on lightly floured surface into a thin square; cut into halves. Spread each portion with 1 beaten egg. Sprinkle the sausage and cheeses over the dough. Roll each portion into a loaf, sealing the edge and ends. Place on greased baking sheet. Let rise, covered, for 30 minutes. Bake at 375 degrees for 30 minutes. Cut into slices.

Approx Per Serving: Cal 401; Prot 24 g; Carbo 20 g;
    Fiber 1 g; T Fat 25 g; 56% Calories from Fat;
    Chol 94 mg; Sod 1003 mg.

Vilma Baragona

Potato Latkes

1 tablespoon dry yeast
1 cup lukewarm milk
1 egg, beaten
1 tablespoon oil
1 cup coarsely grated potato
1 teaspoon salt
¹/₂ cup whole wheat flour
¹/₄ cup wheat germ
1 tablespoon chopped
    onion, sautéed

Yield: 8 servings

Dissolve yeast in lukewarm milk in bowl; mix well. Stir in egg and oil. Add potato, salt, whole wheat flour, wheat germ and onion, stirring until combined. Let rise for 30 minutes; stir down. Spoon batter onto lightly greased griddle. Bake until brown on both sides, turning once. May omit sautéed onion.

Approx Per Serving: Cal 111; Prot 5 g; Carbo 16 g;
    Fiber 2 g; T Fat 4 g; 30% Calories from Fat;
    Chol 28 mg; Sod 292 mg.

Cass Stark

Desserts

Cape St. George Lighthouse
by Marilyn Bean

Cape St. George

In 1833, a lighthouse was constructed on what is now Little St. George Island. It served as a navigational aid but was moved to a more westerly site in 1848. A storm blew down the lighthouse, but it was rebuilt in 1853 and rebricked in 1948. Originally built approximately 400 yards inland, it is now at water's edge and in serious jeopardy. The keeper's house and other outbuildings are in ruins, but local citizens have mounted an effort to preserve the lighthouse and keeper's house.

The following excerpts were taken from "My Life Story," the memoirs of Pearl Porter Marshall, whose father was the lighthouse keeper on Little St. George until his death in 1913. "He was teaching us how to light the lantern, as it was difficult for him to climb the stairs up to the light. In those days the light used kerosene for fuel. I remember the lighthouse tender would anchor in the Gulf right by the lighthouse and they would have men with yokes on their shoulders and a five gallon can boxed in with wood, and a can on each side of the yoke, carrying it to the little birch oil house where it was stored." Recalling the keepers' houses: "There was a picket fence around the two houses, our house was a single story, with four big bedrooms that had a fireplace in the corner of each room connected to one central chimney. It had a porch all around and big kitchen and two pantries connected to the back porch." Today, all that remains of "Miss Pearl's" childhood home is the cedar shake roof and the central chimney.

Longtime Island resident Ollie Gunn recalls in an interview with the *Franklin County Chronicle*, "My father was assistant lighthouse keeper on Little St. George. There were two living on the Island and there were different shifts. The lamp was lit and a person was on duty all night with the light. In those days your beacons were lit by kerosene. You had a reflector that rolled around and reflected the beam across the shores and the Gulf."

Today, visitors to Cape St. George can still experience the beauty and serenity of the area. Your first sight of the lighthouse is breathtaking and the shell of the lighthouse keeper's house offers shelter from the noonday sun. Shells of every color are strewn about the beach around the lighthouse and as the breeze whispers in the pines...you can almost hear the voices...feel the history...go back in time.

Easy Cheesecake

1 recipe graham cracker
  crust mixture
48 ounces cream cheese,
  softened
10 eggs
1 cup sugar
1 teaspoon vanilla extract

Yield: 16 servings

Pat crumb mixture into greased springform pan. Combine cream cheese, eggs, sugar and vanilla in mixer bowl. Beat at high speed until smooth. Spoon over prepared layer. Bake at 350 degrees for 1 hour. Turn off oven. Let stand in oven with door closed for 1 hour.

Approx Per Serving: Cal 387; Prot 10 g; Carbo 15 g;
  Fiber 0 g; T Fat 32 g; 75% Calories from Fat;
  Chol 210 mg; Sod 286 mg.
  Nutritional information does not include graham cracker crust.

Libby Ringold

Chocolate Eclair Cake

1/2 cup margarine
1 cup sugar
1/2 cup baking cocoa
1/4 cup milk
1/2 teaspoon vanilla extract
1/8 teaspoon salt
2 4-ounce packages vanilla
  instant pudding mix
3 cups milk
8 ounces whipped topping
1 16-ounce package
  graham crackers

Yield: 15 servings

Melt margarine in saucepan. Stir in sugar, baking cocoa and 1/4 cup milk. Boil for 1 minute, stirring constantly. Remove from heat. Add vanilla and salt; mix well. Let stand to cool. Combine pudding mix and 3 cups milk in bowl; mix well. Fold in whipped topping. Line bottom of 9x13-inch glass dish with graham crackers. Spread 1/2 of the pudding mixture over graham crackers. Top with another layer of graham crackers and remaining pudding mixture. Layer graham crackers over top. Pour cooled cocoa mixture over graham crackers. Chill for 3 to 4 hours or until set. Cut into squares.

Approx Per Serving: Cal 370; Prot 5 g; Carbo 57 g;
  Fiber 2 g; T Fat 15 g; 36% Calories from Fat;
  Chol 7 mg; Sod 493 mg.

Betty Webb

Blender Mousse

2 cups semisweet chocolate
   chips
1/2 cup sugar
3 eggs
1 cup hot milk
2 to 4 tablespoons brandy

Yield: 8 servings

Combine chocolate chips, sugar, eggs, hot milk and brandy in blender container. Process on medium speed until smooth. Spoon into individual bowls. Chill for 1 hour. Garnish with whipped topping. May substitute orange juice for brandy. To avoid danger of salmonella, use egg substitute for fresh eggs.

Approx Per Serving: Cal 310; Prot 5 g; Carbo 41 g;
     Fiber 3 g; T Fat 15 g; 41% Calories from Fat;
     Chol 74 mg; Sod 41 mg.

Helene Wagner

Cobbler Madison

4 to 5 peaches, peeled,
   thinly sliced
3 to 4 Granny Smith apples,
   peeled, thinly sliced
4 plums, thinly sliced
1 cup blueberries
3 tablespoons margarine,
   cut into pieces
1/2 cup packed brown sugar
1 tablespoon cornstarch
Cinnamon to taste
1 frozen 9-inch pie shell,
   partially thawed
2 tablespoons sugar

Yield: 8 servings

Arrange 1/2 of the fruit in 8x10-inch baking pan sprayed with nonstick cooking spray. Dot with 1/2 of the margarine; sprinkle with half the brown sugar and cornstarch. Repeat the process. Sprinkle with cinnamon. Cut pie shell into 1/2-inch strips. Weave strips across top to form lattice. Sprinkle with sugar. Bake at 350 degrees for 45 minutes or until fruit is tender and pastry is light brown. Serve plain or with ice cream or ice milk.

Approx Per Serving: Cal 372; Prot 3 g; Carbo 54 g;
     Fiber 4 g; T Fat 17 g; 40% Calories from Fat;
     Chol 0 mg; Sod 242 mg.

Elaine Good

Dirt Cake

1 6-ounce package
 chocolate instant pudding
 mix
3½ cups milk
8 ounces cream cheese,
 softened
16 ounces whipped topping
1 16-ounce package
 chocolate sandwich
 cookies, crushed
1 12-ounce jar caramel ice
 cream topping
4 ounces chocolate candy
 bar, grated

Yield: 8 servings

Combine pudding mix and milk in bowl; mix well. Let stand until thickened. Fold in cream cheese and whipped topping. Layer crushed cookies, pudding mixture and caramel topping in a new clean flower pot until all ingredients are used, ending with crushed cookies. Sprinkle with grated candy bar. Chill in refrigerator. Garnish with gummy worms and artificial flowers. Serve with a trowel. May substitute French vanilla pudding for chocolate pudding. May omit ice cream topping.

Approx Per Serving: Cal 867; Prot 11 g; Carbo 114 g;
 Fiber 3 g; T Fat 44 g; 44% Calories from Fat;
 Chol 49 mg; Sod 957 mg.

Shirley Gelch and Clem and JoAnna Hallman

Sprite Plus Fruit Sherbet

1 20-ounce can crushed
 pineapple or pineapple
 tidbits
1 14-ounce can sweetened
 condensed milk
1 64-ounce bottle of Sprite
1 6-ounce can frozen
 limeade concentrate,
 thawed

Yield: 12 servings

Arrange pineapple in 4-quart ice cream freezer container. Place freezer dasher in container. Combine condensed milk with equal portion of Sprite in bowl; mix well. Pour mixture into container. Pour limeade concentrate into container. Add remaining Sprite; top with lid. Freeze using manufacturer's instructions. May substitute any fresh berries for pineapple.

Approx Per Serving: Cal 230; Prot 3 g; Carbo 50 g;
 Fiber <1 g; T Fat 3 g; 11% Calories from Fat;
 Chol 11 mg; Sod 59 mg.

Clarence Gissendanner

Frozen Cream

8 ounces cream cheese,
  softened
1 cup sifted confectioners'
  sugar
1 cup half and half
1/2 teaspoon vanilla extract
2 cups fresh or frozen
  strawberries

Yield: 8 servings

Beat cream cheese in small mixer bowl until light and fluffy. Add sifted confectioners' sugar, half and half and vanilla gradually, beating until smooth. Spoon into paper-lined muffin cups. Freeze for 2 hours or until firm. Remove paper liners; place on individual dessert plates. Let stand until slightly thawed. Spoon strawberries over top. May substitute evaporated skim milk for cream. May substitute raspberries, blueberries or peaches for strawberries.

Approx Per Serving: Cal 199; Prot 3 g; Carbo 17 g;
    Fiber 1 g; T Fat 14 g; 60% Calories from Fat;
    Chol 42 mg; Sod 96 mg.

Norma Hoopes

Orange Crush-Fruit Sherbet

1 11-ounce can mandarin
   oranges, drained
1 14-ounce can sweetened
   condensed milk
1 64-ounce bottle of
   Orange Crush
1 6-ounce can frozen
   orange juice concentrate,
   thawed

Yield: 12 servings

Arrange mandarin oranges in 4-quart ice cream freezer container. Place dasher in container. Combine condensed milk with equal portion of Orange Crush in bowl; mix well. Pour mixture into freezer container. Pour in orange juice concentrate. Add remaining Orange Crush; top with lid. Freeze using manufacturer's instructions.

Approx Per Serving: Cal 217; Prot 3 g; Carbo 46 g;
    Fiber <1 g; T Fat 3 g; 12% Calories from Fat;
    Chol 11 mg; Sod 62 mg.

Clarence Gissendanner

Linzer Torte

2 eggs
6 tablespoons butter,
    softened
6 tablespoons sugar
2 cups flour
Grated lemon rind to taste
2 ounces hazelnuts, ground
1 cup red currant jam

Yield: 8 servings

Cream eggs, butter and sugar in mixer bowl until light and fluffy. Add flour, lemon rind and hazelnuts; mix well. Knead the dough for 30 minutes. Roll ³/₄ of the dough into a 1-inch thick 9-inch circle on a lightly floured surface. Press 8-inch plate into dough to form indentation of about ¹/₂ inch. Fit into flan pan. Spread evenly with jam. Roll remaining dough on lightly floured surface; cut into thin strips. Weave strips across top to form lattice. Seal ends; flute edge. Bake at 375 degrees for 1 hour. May substitute raspberry jelly for red currant jam.

Approx Per Serving: Cal 396; Prot 6 g; Carbo 62 g;
    Fiber 2 g; T Fat 15 g; 32% Calories from Fat;
    Chol 70 mg; Sod 108 mg.

Marta Thompson

Punch Bowl Cake

1 2-layer package butter
    cake mix
1 6-ounce package vanilla
    instant pudding mix,
    prepared
1 20-ounce can crushed
    pineapple
1 6-ounce package frozen
    shredded coconut
1 21-ounce can cherry pie
    filling
16 ounces whipped topping
1 cup chopped pecans,
    toasted
1 4-ounce jar maraschino
    cherries, drained

Yield: 16 servings

Prepare and bake cake using package directions for a sheet cake. Remove to wire rack to cool; crumble. Layer crumbled cake, pudding, pineapple and coconut ¹/₃ at a time in large punch bowl. Spread with pie filling; top with whipped topping. Sprinkle with pecans and maraschino cherries. Chill until serving time.

Approx Per Serving: Cal 514; Prot 4 g; Carbo 70 g;
    Fiber 2 g; T Fat 26 g; 44% Calories from Fat;
    Chol 49 mg; Sod 410 mg.

Rachel L. Clague

Blackberry Jam Cake

3/4 cup butter, softened
1 cup sugar
Salt to taste
3 eggs
1 cup blackberry jam
Nutmeg and cinnamon to
    taste
2 cups flour
1 teaspoon baking soda
1/4 cup buttermilk
1 cup chopped pecans
1 cup raisins

Yield: 12 servings

Cream butter, sugar and salt in mixer bowl until light and fluffy. Add eggs 1 at a time, beating well after each addition. Add jam, nutmeg and cinnamon; mix well. Add a mixture of flour and baking soda alternately with buttermilk, mixing well after each addition. Spoon into 3 greased and floured cake pans. Bake at 350 degrees until cake tests done. Remove to wire rack to cool. Sprinkle pecans and raisins between layers. Frost with your favorite white icing.

Approx Per Serving: Cal 440; Prot 5 g; Carbo 64 g;
    Fiber 2 g; T Fat 20 g; 39% Calories from Fat;
    Chol 78 mg; Sod 210 mg.

Bo Suber

Blueberry Cake

1/2 cup butter, softened
1 cup sugar
1 egg
1/2 cup milk
2 cups cake flour
2 teaspoons baking powder
2 cups blueberries
2 tablespoons cornstarch
1/2 cup water
1/2 cup sugar
1 cup water
2 cups blueberries
Lemon juice to taste

Yield: 15 servings

Cream butter and 1 cup sugar in mixer bowl until light and fluffy. Add egg, milk, cake flour and baking powder; mix well. Fold in 2 cups blueberries. Spoon into greased 9x13-inch cake pan. Bake at 350 degrees for 45 minutes. Remove to wire rack to cool. Dissolve cornstarch in 1/2 cup water. Combine cornstarch, 1/2 cup sugar, 1 cup water, 2 cups blueberries and lemon juice in double boiler. Cook over hot water until thickened, stirring constantly. Serve cake with vanilla ice cream or whipped cream and blueberry sauce. May bake in tube pan for 1 hour.

Approx Per Serving: Cal 219; Prot 2 g; Carbo 35 g;
    Fiber 1 g; T Fat 9 g; 34% Calories from Fat;
    Chol 30 mg; Sod 164 mg.

Frannie Beman

Coconut Creole Cake

1/2 cup margarine, softened
2 cups sugar
4 eggs
1 cup buttermilk
1 1/2 cups shredded coconut
1 cup broken walnuts
16 ounces dates, chopped
3 1/2 cups flour
1 teaspoon baking soda
1 cup orange juice
2 cups confectioners' sugar
Grated rind of 1 orange

Yield: 16 servings

Beat margarine, sugar, eggs and buttermilk in mixer bowl until smooth. Stir in shredded coconut, walnuts, chopped dates, flour and baking soda. Spoon into non-stick tube pan. Bake at 325 degrees for 1 1/2 hours. Combine orange juice and confectioners' sugar in bowl, stirring until smooth. Add orange rind; mix well. Pierce hot cake with fork. Spoon orange juice mixture over cake. Remove to wire rack to cool. May freeze cake for future use.

Approx Per Serving: Cal 506; Prot 7 g; Carbo 90 g; Fiber 5 g; T Fat 15 g; 26% Calories from Fat; Chol 47 mg; Sod 174 mg.

Babs Ruhl

Chocolate Surprise Cake

1 2-layer package chocolate cake mix
1/2 cup semisweet chocolate chips
12 ounces cream cheese, softened
1/4 cup sugar
1 egg
1/2 teaspoon vanilla extract

Yield: 16 servings

Prepare cake mix using package directions. Fold in chocolate chips. Spoon into buttered and floured 12-cup bundt pan. Beat cream cheese and sugar in small mixer bowl until smooth. Add egg and vanilla; mix well. Spread over prepared layer. Bake at 350 degrees for 45 to 55 minutes or until cake tests done. Cool in pan. Invert onto serving platter. Sprinkle with confectioners' sugar.

Approx Per Serving: Cal 274; Prot 5 g; Carbo 33 g; Fiber 1 g; T Fat 15 g; 48% Calories from Fat; Chol 63 mg; Sod 361 mg.

Mary Lou Short

Milky Way Cake

6 2-ounce Milky Way
   candy bars
1/2 cup butter
2 cups sugar
1 cup shortening
4 eggs
2 1/2 cups flour
1 teaspoon salt
1 1/2 cups buttermilk
1/2 teaspoon baking soda
1 teaspoon vanilla extract

Yield: 12 servings

Combine candy bars and butter in saucepan. Cook over low heat until smooth, stirring constantly. Cream sugar and shortening in mixer bowl until light and fluffy. Add eggs, beating until smooth. Add mixture of flour and salt alternately with mixture of buttermilk and baking soda, mixing well after each addition. Stir in vanilla and candy bar mixture. Spoon batter into 3 greased and floured 9-inch cake pans. Bake at 350 degrees for 30 minutes or until layers test done. Remove to wire rack to cool. Frost cake with your favorite chocolate marshmallow icing.

Approx Per Serving: Cal 596; Prot 7 g; Carbo 75 g;
    Fiber 1 g; T Fat 31 g; 46% Calories from Fat;
    Chol 90 mg; Sod 409 mg.

Rachel L. Clague

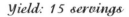

Snicker Bar Cake

1 2-layer package German
   chocolate cake mix
1 16-ounce package
   caramels
1/3 cup milk
1/2 cup margarine
3/4 cup chocolate chips
1 cup chopped pecans

Yield: 15 servings

Prepare cake mix using package directions. Spoon 1/2 of mixture into a greased 9x13-inch cake pan. Bake at 350 degrees for 20 minutes. Combine caramels, milk and margarine in saucepan. Cook over low heat until smooth, stirring constantly. Spread over baked layer; sprinkle with chocolate chips and pecans. Spoon remaining batter over top. Bake for 20 minutes. Reduce temperature to 325 degrees. Bake for 10 minutes.

Approx Per Serving: Cal 475; Prot 5 g; Carbo 59 g;
    Fiber 1 g; T Fat 26 g; 48% Calories from Fat;
    Chol 47 mg; Sod 485 mg.

Louise Dickerson

Cracker Cake

32 saltine crackers, crushed
1 cup chopped pecans
6 egg whites
1 1/2 cups sugar
1 teaspoon cream of tartar
1   21-ounce can cherry pie
     filling
1   20-ounce can pineapple
     in heavy syrup, drained
16 ounces whipped topping
1   7-ounce package
     shredded coconut

Yield: 15 servings

Combine crushed crackers and pecans in bowl; mix well. Beat egg whites, sugar and cream of tartar in mixer bowl until stiff peaks form. Stir egg white mixture into crackers and pecans. Spoon into nonstick 9x13-inch cake pan. Bake at 400 degrees for 20 minutes. Remove to wire rack to cool. Spread pie filling over baked layer. Spoon pineapple over pie filling. Top with whipped topping; sprinkle with coconut. Chill, covered, until set. The flavors are enhanced if the cake is prepared in advance. May substitute walnuts for pecans.

Approx Per Serving: Cal 394; Prot 4 g; Carbo 56 g;
    Fiber 3 g; T Fat 19 g; 42% Calories from Fat;
    Chol 0 mg; Sod 169 mg.

Nelle Spratt

Hummingbird Layer Cake

3 cups flour
2 cups sugar
1 teaspoon baking soda
1 teaspoon salt
1 teaspoon cinnamon
3 eggs, beaten
1 cup oil
1 1/2 teaspoons vanilla
     extract
1   8-ounce can crushed
     pineapple
1 cup chopped bananas
1 cup chopped pecans
8 ounces cream cheese,
     softened
1/2 cup butter, softened
1   1-pound package
     confectioners' sugar, sifted
1 teaspoon vanilla extract
1/2 cup chopped pecans

Yield: 12 servings

Combine flour, sugar, baking soda, salt and cinnamon in bowl; mix well. Add eggs and oil, stirring just until moistened. Stir in 1 1/2 teaspoons vanilla, pineapple, bananas and 1 cup pecans. Spoon batter into 3 greased and floured 9-inch round cake pans. Bake at 350 degrees for 25 to 30 minutes or until layers test done. Cool in pans for 10 minutes. Invert onto wire rack to cool completely. Beat cream cheese and butter in mixer bowl until smooth. Add confectioners' sugar and 1 teaspoon vanilla, beating until of spreading consistency. Stir in 1/2 cup pecans. Spread frosting between layers and over top and side of cake. May sprinkle pecans between layers instead of adding to frosting. May substitute margarine for butter.

Approx Per Serving: Cal 829; Prot 7 g; Carbo 105 g;
    Fiber 2 g; T Fat 44 g; 47% Calories from Fat;
    Chol 88 mg; Sod 396 mg.

Verna Dekle

Lemon Pudding Cake

3 tablespoons butter,
  softened
1 cup sugar
4 egg yolks
1/4 teaspoon salt
3 tablespoons flour
1/3 cup lemon juice
2 teaspoons grated lemon
  rind
1 cup milk
4 egg whites, stiffly beaten

Yield: 6 servings

Beat butter in mixer bowl until creamy. Add sugar gradually, beating until blended. Add egg yolks, beating until light and fluffy. Stir in salt, flour, lemon juice and lemon rind. Add milk gradually; mix well. Fold egg whites into batter. Spoon into 1-quart baking dish; set in pan of hot water. Bake at 345 degrees for 40 minutes.

Approx Per Serving: Cal 273; Prot 6 g; Carbo 40 g; Fiber <1 g; T Fat 11 g; 34% Calories from Fat; Chol 162 mg; Sod 209 mg.

Evelyn Stripling

Pineapple-Coconut Cake

2 cups cake flour
1 1/3 cups sugar
2 1/2 teaspoons baking
  powder
1 teaspoon salt
1/2 cup shortening
1 cup less 2 tablespoons
  milk
1 1/2 teaspoons vanilla
  extract
1 teaspoon butter extract
2 eggs
1   20-ounce can crushed
  pineapple
1/3 cup sugar
2 tablespoons cornstarch
2 egg whites
1 1/2 cups sugar
5 tablespoons cold water
1 teaspoon light corn syrup
1/8 teaspoon salt
1/2 teaspoon pineapple
  extract
1/2 teaspoon almond extract
1   3-ounce can flaked
  coconut

Yield: 12 servings

Combine cake flour, 1 1/3 cups sugar, baking powder, 1 teaspoon salt, shortening, milk, flavorings and eggs in mixer bowl. Beat at medium speed for 4 minutes, scraping bowl occasionally. Spoon batter into 3 greased and waxed paper-lined 8-inch round cake pans. Bake at 375 degrees for 20 to 30 minutes or until layers test done. Invert onto wire rack to cool. Combine undrained crushed pineapple, 1/3 cup sugar and cornstarch in saucepan. Cook over medium heat until thickened, stirring constantly. Cool. Spread between cake layers. Combine egg whites, 1 1/2 cups sugar, cold water, corn syrup, 1/8 teaspoon salt and flavorings in double boiler. Beat over boiling water for 7 minutes or until stiff peaks form. Spread over top and side of cake; sprinkle all over with coconut.

Approx Per Serving: Cal 449; Prot 3 g; Carbo 79 g; Fiber 1 g; T Fat 14 g; 28% Calories from Fat; Chol 34 mg; Sod 358 mg.

Jolene Armistead

Easy Pound Cake

2 cups flour
2 cups sugar
1 cup shortening
6 eggs
1 teaspoon vanilla extract

Yield: 12 servings

Combine flour, sugar, shortening, eggs and vanilla in mixer bowl. Beat at medium speed until smooth. Spoon into greased and floured loaf pan. Bake at 350 degrees for 45 minutes or until cake tests done.

Approx Per Serving: Cal 390; Prot 5 g; Carbo 50 g; Fiber 1 g; T Fat 20 g; 45% Calories from Fat; Chol 94 mg; Sod 29 mg.

Shirley Gunn

Hershey Bar Pound Cake

1 cup butter, softened
2 cups sugar
4 eggs
2¹/₂ cups sifted flour
¹/₄ teaspoon salt
¹/₂ teaspoon baking soda
1 cup buttermilk
³/₄ cup Hershey's chocolate syrup
4 2-ounce Hershey's chocolate candy bars
1 tablespoon vanilla extract
¹/₄ cup margarine, softened
2 cups confectioners' sugar, sifted
¹/₄ cup Hershey's chocolate syrup

Yield: 16 servings

Cream butter and sugar in mixer bowl until light and fluffy. Beat in 2 eggs until smooth. Add 2 eggs, beating until blended. Add mixture of flour, salt and baking soda alternately with buttermilk, mixing well after each addition. Combine 6 tablespoons chocolate syrup and candy bars in saucepan. Cook over low heat until well mixed, stirring constantly. Add chocolate mixture and 6 tablespoons chocolate syrup to cake batter; mix well. Stir in vanilla. Spoon into greased tube pan. Bake at 350 degrees for 1 hour and 10 minutes. Remove to wire rack to cool. Beat margarine in mixer bowl until creamy. Add confectioners' sugar and ¹/₄ cup chocolate syrup, beating until of spreading consistency. Frost cake with icing. Do not make icing until cake has cooled as icing has a tendency to harden quickly. May substitute margarine for butter.

Approx Per Serving: Cal 487; Prot 5 g; Carbo 74 g; Fiber 1 g; T Fat 20 g; 37% Calories from Fat; Chol 82 mg; Sod 270 mg.

Edna Rudasill

Peach Pound Cake

3 cups flour
1/4 teaspoon baking soda
3/4 teaspoon salt
1 cup butter, softened
3 cups sugar
6 eggs
1/2 cup sour cream
2 cups chopped peeled
   peaches
1 teaspoon vanilla extract
1 teaspoon almond extract

Yield: 16 servings

Mix flour, baking soda and salt together. Cream butter and sugar in mixer bowl until light and fluffy. Add eggs 1 at a time, beating well after each addition. Add dry ingredients alternately with mixture of sour cream and peaches, beginning and ending with dry ingredients and mixing well after each addition. Stir in flavorings. Spoon batter into greased and floured 10-inch tube pan. Bake at 350 degrees for 1 hour and 15 minutes to 1 hour and 20 minutes or until cake tests done. May substitute margarine for butter.

Approx Per Serving: Cal 383; Prot 5 g; Carbo 58 g;
      Fiber 1 g; T Fat 15 g; 35% Calories from Fat;
      Chol 104 mg; Sod 255 mg.

Paula Kemp

Sour Cream Pound Cake

1 cup butter, softened
3 cups sugar
6 eggs
1 cup sour cream
1/8 teaspoon baking soda
3 cups cake flour
1 to 2 teaspoons vanilla
   extract

Yield: 16 servings

Cream butter and sugar in mixer bowl until light and fluffy. Add eggs 1 at a time, beating well after each addition. Add mixture of sour cream and baking soda; mix well. Add cake flour gradually, mixing until blended. Stir in vanilla. Spoon mixture into nonstick bundt or tube pan. Bake at 325 degrees for 1 to 1 1/4 hours or until cake tests done. Invert onto wire rack to cool. May use egg substitute and light sour cream to lower cholesterol content of recipe.

Approx Per Serving: Cal 377; Prot 4 g; Carbo 50 g;
      Fiber <1 g; T Fat 19 g; 44% Calories from Fat;
      Chol 108 mg; Sod 219 mg.

Kathy Gunter

Three-Flavor Pound Cake

8 egg whites
2/3 cup sugar
1 cup butter, softened
1 cup shortening
2 cups sugar
8 egg yolks
1/2 cup milk
3 1/2 cups cake flour
1 tablespoon vanilla extract
1 tablespoon lemon extract
1 tablespoon butternut
    extract

Yield: 16 servings

*B*eat egg whites in mixer bowl until foamy. Add 2/3 cup sugar gradually, beating constantly until stiff peaks form. Place in refrigerator. Cream butter, shortening and 2 cups sugar in mixer bowl until light and fluffy. Add egg yolks, milk, cake flour and flavorings gradually, mixing well after each addition. Fold in beaten egg whites. Spoon into nonstick 10-inch tube pan. Bake at 300 degrees for 2 hours. Invert onto wire rack to cool.

Approx Per Serving: Cal 480; Prot 5 g; Carbo 48 g;
    Fiber <1 g; T Fat 30 g; 56% Calories from Fat;
    Chol 139 mg; Sod 230 mg.

Marcia Rentz

Sacher Torte

10 tablespoons butter,
    softened
10 tablespoons sugar
1 1/4 cups flour
5 egg yolks
5 ounces chocolate, grated
5 egg whites, stiffly beaten
2 tablespoons apricot jam

Yield: 12 servings

*C*ream butter and sugar in mixer bowl until light and fluffy. Add flour and egg yolks alternately, mixing well after each addition. Add chocolate; mix well. Fold in egg whites. Spoon batter into nonstick cake pan. Bake at 350 to 375 degrees until brown. Remove to wire rack to cool. Slice cake horizontally into two portions. Spread the bottom layer with apricot jam; top with remaining cake layer. Frost with your favorite chocolate icing. May spread whipped cream on top and sprinkle with coarsely ground nuts instead of frosting with chocolate icing.

Approx Per Serving: Cal 274; Prot 5 g; Carbo 30 g;
    Fiber 1 g; T Fat 16 g; 50% Calories from Fat;
    Chol 117 mg; Sod 134 mg.

Marta Thompson

Evelyn's Famous Tomato Soup Cake

2 cups flour
1 teaspoon cinnamon
1 teaspoon ground cloves
1 teaspoon nutmeg
1 teaspoon baking powder
1 teaspoon baking soda
1 cup sugar
3/4 cup shortening
1   10-ounce can tomato
    soup
2/3 cup evaporated milk
2 cups raisins

Yield: 12 servings

Sift flour, cinnamon, cloves, nutmeg, baking powder and baking soda together. Cream sugar and shortening in mixer bowl until light and fluffy. Add dry ingredients, beating until smooth. Add soup and evaporated milk; mix well. Stir in raisins. Spoon into nonstick cake pan. Bake at 350 degrees for 30 to 40 minutes or until edges pull from sides of pan. Frost with your favorite vanilla icing. May substitute eggnog for the evaporated milk and add green food coloring to the icing for a festive touch at Christmas.

Approx Per Serving: Cal 372; Prot 4 g; Carbo 59 g; Fiber 2 g; T Fat 15 g; 34% Calories from Fat; Chol 4 mg; Sod 291 mg.

Kathleen Whalen

Microwave Fudge

1   1-pound package
    confectioners' sugar
1/2 cup margarine
1/4 cup milk
1/3 cup baking cocoa
1/2 cup chopped pecans
1 teaspoon vanilla extract

Yield: 24 servings

Combine confectioners' sugar, margarine, milk and baking cocoa in microwave-safe dish. Microwave on High for 2 minutes or until margarine melts. Stir until blended. Stir in pecans and vanilla. Spoon into 8x8-inch dish. Chill for 30 minutes. Cut into squares. May omit pecans.

Approx Per Serving: Cal 129; Prot 1 g; Carbo 20 g; Fiber 1 g; T Fat 6 g; 39% Calories from Fat; Chol <1 mg; Sod 46 mg.

Susan Florin

Decadent Truffles

1¹/₃ cups whipping cream
¹/₄ cup packed brown sugar
¹/₄ teaspoon salt
2 teaspoons vanilla extract
16 ounces semisweet
  chocolate, chopped
16 ounces milk chocolate,
  chopped
1 cup finely chopped pecans

Yield: 72 servings

Combine whipping cream, brown sugar, salt and vanilla in saucepan. Cook over medium heat until sugar dissolves and mixture is hot, stirring constantly. Remove from heat. Add semisweet chocolate and milk chocolate, stirring until smooth. May return to heat to melt chocolate. Spoon into shallow dish. Chill, covered, for 1 to 2 hours or until firm. Shape into balls; roll in chopped pecans. Store truffles in refrigerator. May freeze for future use. May roll truffles in sprinkles or shredded coconut.

Approx Per Serving: Cal 91; Prot 1 g; Carbo 9 g;
    Fiber 1 g; T Fat 7 g; 60% Calories from Fat;
    Chol 7 mg; Sod 15 mg.

Karen C. Powers

Margaret Hoefer's Peanut Brittle

2 cups shelled raw peanuts
1 cup sugar
1 cup light corn syrup
1 tablespoon baking soda

Yield: 48 servings

Combine peanuts, sugar and corn syrup in large saucepan. Cook over medium-high heat to 300 to 310 degrees on candy thermometer, hard-crack stage, stirring constantly. Remove from heat. Beat in baking soda immediately. Pour mixture into 2 buttered 10x15-inch shallow dishes. Pull brittle as thin as possible with buttered fingers. Cool. Break into pieces.

Approx Per Serving: Cal 70; Prot 2 g; Carbo 10 g;
    Fiber <1 g; T Fat 3 g; 36% Calories from Fat;
    Chol 0 mg; Sod 61 mg.

Doris Barrett

Party Pecans

1 1/2 cups sugar
1/2 cup water
1 teaspoon light corn syrup
1/2 teaspoon nutmeg
1/2 teaspoon ground cloves
2 teaspoons cinnamon
3 1/2 to 4 cups pecan halves

Yield: 36 servings

Combine sugar, water, corn syrup, nutmeg, cloves and cinnamon in saucepan. Cook over medium heat to 280 degrees, soft-crack stage. Remove from heat. Stir in pecan halves; mix until of creamy appearance. Pour onto waxed paper; separate with fork. Cool. Store in airtight container.

Approx Per Serving: Cal 113; Prot 1 g; Carbo 11 g;
Fiber 1 g; T Fat 8 g; 61% Calories from Fat;
Chol 0 mg; Sod <1 mg.

Josie Davis

Aunt Eleanor's Quick Chip Bars

1 2-layer package white or yellow cake mix
3 egg whites
1/2 cup packed brown sugar
1/3 cup oil
2 cups chocolate chips
1/3 cup chopped pecans

Yield: 36 servings

Combine cake mix, egg whites, brown sugar and oil in bowl; mix well. Spoon into nonstick 9x13-inch baking pan. Press chocolate chips and pecans into batter. Bake at 350 degrees for 25 to 35 minutes or until edges pull from sides of pan. Cool. Cut into bars.

Approx Per Serving: Cal 142; Prot 1 g; Carbo 20 g;
Fiber 1 g; T Fat 7 g; 43% Calories from Fat;
Chol <1 mg; Sod 100 mg.

Bobbie Felice

Chocolate No-Bake Cookies

2 cups sugar
1/2 cup milk
1/2 cup margarine
5 tablespoons baking cocoa
1/2 cup peanut butter
3 cups rolled oats
1 teaspoon vanilla extract

Yield: 36 servings

Combine sugar, milk, margarine and baking cocoa in saucepan. Cook over medium heat to 234 to 240 degrees on candy thermometer, soft-ball stage, stirring constantly. Stir in peanut butter, oats and vanilla immediately. Drop by teaspoonfuls onto waxed paper. Cool completely.

Approx Per Serving: Cal 117; Prot 2 g; Carbo 17 g;
    Fiber 1 g; T Fat 5 g; 37% Calories from Fat;
    Chol <1 mg; Sod 49 mg.

Elaine Poindexter

Congo Squares

2/3 cup melted shortening
1 1-pound package brown
    sugar
3 eggs
2³/4 cups flour
2¹/2 teaspoons baking
    powder
1/2 teaspoon salt
1 cup chopped pecans
1 cup semisweet chocolate
    chips

Yield: 36 servings

Combine shortening and brown sugar in bowl, stirring until blended. Cool slightly. Add eggs 1 at a time, mixing well after each addition. Add mixture of flour, baking powder and salt; mix well. Stir in pecans and chocolate chips. Spoon into greased 9x13-inch baking pan. Bake at 350 degrees for 25 to 30 minutes or until edges pull from sides of pan. Cool. Cut into squares.

Approx Per Serving: Cal 166; Prot 2 g; Carbo 23 g;
    Fiber 1 g; T Fat 8 g; 41% Calories from Fat;
    Chol 16 mg; Sod 63 mg.

Linda Protsman

Cream Cheese Bars

1/2 cup packed brown sugar
1/4 cup butter, softened
1 cup baking mix
1/2 cup chopped walnuts
1/4 cup sugar
8 ounces cream cheese, softened
1 tablespoon lemon juice
2 teaspoons milk
1/2 teaspoon vanilla extract
1 egg

Yield: 16 servings

Beat brown sugar and butter in mixer bowl until light and fluffy. Stir in baking mix and walnuts until crumbly; reserve 1 cup. Press remaining crumb mixture into greased 8x8-inch baking pan. Bake at 350 degrees for 12 minutes. Cream sugar and cream cheese in mixer bowl until light and fluffy. Add lemon juice, milk, vanilla and egg, beating until smooth. Spread over baked layer; sprinkle with reserved crumb mixture. Bake for 25 minutes or until set. Cool completely. Cut into 2-inch bars. Store in refrigerator.

Approx Per Serving: Cal 168; Prot 3 g; Carbo 14 g; Fiber <1 g; T Fat 12 g; 61% Calories from Fat; Chol 35 mg; Sod 168 mg.

Martha Fulmer

Gingersnaps

2 cups flour
1 teaspoon baking soda
1/2 teaspoon ground cloves
2 teaspoons ginger
1/2 teaspoon cinnamon
3/4 cup margarine, softened
1 cup sugar
1 egg
1/4 cup molasses
1/4 cup sugar

Yield: 36 servings

Mix flour, baking soda, cloves, ginger and cinnamon together. Cream margarine, 1 cup sugar and egg in mixer bowl until light and fluffy. Add molasses; mix well. Add flour mixture, mixing until smooth. Shape into 1-inch balls; roll in 1/4 cup sugar. Place on nonstick cookie sheet; flatten slightly. Bake at 350 degrees for 12 to 15 minutes or until light brown. Remove to wire rack to cool. May substitute 1/3 cup chopped crystallized ginger coated in flour for ground ginger. May substitute butter for margarine.

Approx Per Serving: Cal 94; Prot 1 g; Carbo 14 g; Fiber <1 g; T Fat 4 g; 38% Calories from Fat; Chol 5 mg; Sod 70 mg.

Frannie Beman

Judi's Favorite Cookies

1 cup butter, softened
2/3 cup packed brown sugar
2/3 cup sugar
2 eggs
2 teaspoons vanilla extract
1 cup whole wheat flour
1 teaspoon salt
1 teaspoon baking soda
1 cup bran
1 1/2 cups rolled oats
1 cup unsalted sunflower
  seeds
1 cup chopped pecans
1 cup raisins
1 cup chocolate chips
1 cup carob chips

Yield: 48 servings

Cream butter, brown sugar and sugar in mixer bowl until light and fluffy. Beat in eggs. Add vanilla, whole wheat flour, salt and baking soda; mix well. Stir in bran, oats, sunflower seeds, pecans, raisins, chocolate chips and carob chips. Drop by heaping teaspoonfuls onto cookie sheet. Bake for 10 to 12 minutes or until brown. Remove to wire rack to cool. May substitute 1/2 cup margarine and 1/2 cup butter for 1 cup butter.

Approx Per Serving: Cal 157; Prot 2 g; Carbo 18 g; Fiber 2 g; T Fat 10 g; 51% Calories from Fat; Chol 18 mg; Sod 106 mg.

Judi Little

Fabulous Potato Chip Cookies

3/4 cup butter, softened
3/4 cup sugar
1 egg yolk
1 teaspoon vanilla extract
1 1/4 cups flour
3/4 cup finely crushed
  potato chips
3/4 cup finely chopped
  pecans
3 tablespoons sugar
30 pecan halves

Yield: 30 servings

Cream butter, 3/4 cup sugar, egg yolk and vanilla in mixer bowl until light and fluffy. Add flour, potato chips and chopped pecans; mix well. Shape into 1 1/2-inch balls. Place 3 inches apart on ungreased cookie sheet. Flatten balls with glass dipped in 3 tablespoons sugar; top with pecan halves. Bake at 375 degrees for 8 to 10 minutes. Cool in pan slightly. Remove to wire rack to cool completely. May substitute margarine for butter and walnuts for pecans.

Approx Per Serving: Cal 126; Prot 1 g; Carbo 12 g; Fiber 1 g; T Fat 9 g; 60% Calories from Fat; Chol 20 mg; Sod 56 mg.

Beth Krontz

Old-Fashioned Chess Pie

1/2 cup butter, softened
1 1/2 cups sugar
1 tablespoon flour
4 teaspoons cornmeal
3 eggs
1/2 cup half and half
1 tablespoon vinegar
1 teaspoon vanilla extract
1 unbaked 9-inch pie shell

Yield: 8 servings

Cream butter and sugar in mixer bowl until light and fluffy. Add flour and cornmeal; mix well. Beat in eggs, half and half, vinegar and vanilla until combined. Spoon into pie shell. Bake at 300 degrees until knife inserted in center comes out clean. May substitute margarine for butter and milk for half and half.

Approx Per Serving: Cal 489; Prot 5 g; Carbo 57 g; Fiber 1 g; T Fat 27 g; 50% Calories from Fat; Chol 107 mg; Sod 337 mg.

Nelle Spratt

Chocolate-Rum Pie

1 envelope unflavored
    gelatin
1/4 cup sugar
1/8 teaspoon salt
2 egg yolks, beaten
1 cup milk
1/4 cup rum
2 cups semisweet chocolate
    chips, melted
2 egg whites
1/2 cup sugar
1 cup whipping cream
1 tablespoon vanilla extract
1/4 cup sugar
1 baked 9-inch pie shell

Yield: 6 servings

Mix gelatin, 1/4 cup sugar and salt in double boiler. Combine egg yolks, milk and rum in bowl, stirring until smooth. Add to gelatin mixture. Cook over boiling water until slightly thickened, stirring constantly. Stir in melted chocolate chips. Let stand to cool. Beat egg whites in mixer bowl until foamy. Add 1/2 cup sugar gradually, beating constantly until stiff peaks form. Fold into chocolate mixture. Beat whipping cream, vanilla and 1/4 cup sugar in mixer bowl until stiff peaks form. Layer chocolate mixture and whipped cream 1/2 at a time in pie shell. Chill until set.

Approx Per Serving: Cal 777; Prot 10 g; Carbo 87 g; Fiber 4 g; T Fat 45 g; 50% Calories from Fat; Chol 131 mg; Sod 271 mg.

Marti Fraker

Dot's Fudge Pie

1/2 cup melted margarine
1/4 cup baking cocoa
2 eggs, beaten
1 cup sugar
1/4 cup sifted flour
1/2 teaspoon vanilla extract
1 cup chopped pecans
1 unbaked 10-inch pie shell

Yield: 8 servings

Combine margarine and baking cocoa in bowl; mix well. Stir in eggs, sugar, flour, vanilla and pecans. Spoon into pie shell. Bake at 350 degrees for 25 minutes. Cool on wire rack. Chill overnight. Serve with whipped topping or vanilla ice cream. May freeze for future use. May substitute butter for margarine.

Approx Per Serving: Cal 466; Prot 5 g; Carbo 44 g; Fiber 2 g; T Fat 32 g; 59% Calories from Fat; Chol 47 mg; Sod 284 mg.

Jane Pitts

Fruit Pies

1 16-ounce can sliced peaches, drained, chopped
1 8-ounce can pineapple chunks, drained, chopped
1 4-ounce jar maraschino cherries, drained, chopped
1 14-ounce can sweetened condensed milk
1/2 cup lemon juice
28 ounces whipped topping
3 9-inch graham cracker pie shells

Yield: 18 servings

Combine peaches, pineapple, maraschino cherries, condensed milk and lemon juice in bowl, stirring until slightly thickened. Fold in whipped topping. Spoon into pie shells. Chill until set. May freeze for future use.

Approx Per Serving: Cal 507; Prot 5 g; Carbo 65 g; Fiber 2 g; T Fat 27 g; 46% Calories from Fat; Chol 7 mg; Sod 350 mg.

Jane E. Davis

Ice Cream Pie

2 cups chocolate chips
1   14-ounce can sweetened
    condensed milk
4 cups miniature
    marshmallows
3/4 cup pecans, toasted
1   10-ounce package vanilla
    wafers
1/2 gallon vanilla ice cream
1/4 cup pecans, toasted

Yield: 8 servings

Melt chocolate chips in double boiler over boiling water, stirring frequently. Add condensed milk and marshmallows. Cook until smooth, stirring constantly. Remove from heat. Stir in 3/4 cup pecans. Layer vanilla wafers, ice cream and chocolate mixture 1/2 at a time in deep-dish pie plate. Sprinkle with 1/4 cup pecans. Freeze until firm.

Approx Per Serving: Cal 956; Prot 14 g; Carbo 133 g;
    Fiber 4 g; T Fat 47 g; 42% Calories from Fat;
    Chol 95 mg; Sod 295 mg.

Betty Day

Lemon Meringue Pie

1 cup sugar
1/4 cup (heaping) cornstarch
1/2 teaspoon salt
2 cups boiling water
3 egg yolks, beaten
1 tablespoon butter
Grated rind of 2 lemons
1/4 cup fresh lemon juice
1 baked 9-inch pie shell
3 egg whites
3 tablespoons sugar

Yield: 6 servings

Combine 1 cup sugar, cornstarch and salt in double boiler; mix well. Add boiling water. Beat with egg beater until smooth. Stir a small amount of hot mixture into egg yolks; stir egg yolks into hot mixture. Add butter, lemon rind and lemon juice. Cook over boiling water until thickened, stirring constantly. Spoon into pie shell. Beat egg whites in mixer bowl until foamy. Add 3 tablespoons sugar gradually, beating constantly until stiff peaks form. Spread over filling, sealing to edge. Broil for 3 to 4 minutes or until light brown.

Approx Per Serving: Cal 390; Prot 5 g; Carbo 60 g;
    Fiber 1 g; T Fat 15 g; 34% Calories from Fat;
    Chol 111 mg; Sod 392 mg.

Sharen Clark

Key Lime Pie

4 egg yolks, beaten
1   14-ounce can sweetened
      condensed milk
1/2 cup lime juice
6 egg whites
1/2 teaspoon cream of tartar
3/4 cup sugar
1 baked 9-inch pie shell

Yield: 6 servings

Combine egg yolks and condensed milk in bowl; mix well. Stir in lime juice. Beat egg whites and cream of tartar in mixer bowl until foamy. Add sugar 1 tablespoon at a time, beating constantly until stiff peaks form. Fold 6 tablespoons of beaten egg whites into lime filling. Spoon into pie shell. Spread remaining beaten egg whites over filling, sealing to edge. Bake at 350 degrees until brown. Cool. Chill until serving time.

Approx Per Serving: Cal 530; Prot 13 g; Carbo 78 g;
      Fiber 1 g; T Fat 20 g; 33% Calories from Fat;
      Chol 164 mg; Sod 307 mg.

Phyllis Stanley Stephens

Original Key Lime Pie

3 egg yolks, beaten
1   14-ounce can sweetened
      condensed milk
3/4 cup key lime juice
3 egg whites, stiffly beaten
1 baked 9-inch pie shell

Yield: 6 servings

Combine egg yolks and condensed milk in bowl; mix well. Stir in key lime juice. Fold in egg whites. Spoon into pie shell. Chill until set. May substitute lime juice for key lime juice.

Approx Per Serving: Cal 417; Prot 10 g; Carbo 53 g;
      Fiber 1 g; T Fat 19 g; 40% Calories from Fat;
      Chol 128 mg; Sod 278 mg.

Mary Lou Short

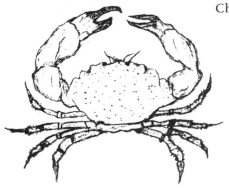

Another Original Key Lime Pie

4 egg yolks, beaten
1 14-ounce can sweetened
   condensed milk
1/3 cup lime juice
1 baked 9-inch pie shell
4 egg whites
Salt to taste
Cream of tartar to taste
1/4 cup sugar

Yield: 6 servings

Beat egg yolks and condensed milk in bowl until blended. Stir in lime juice. Pour into pie shell. Beat egg whites, salt and cream of tartar in mixer bowl until foamy. Add sugar gradually, beating constantly until stiff peaks form. Spread over filling, sealing to edge. Bake at 300 degrees until light brown.

Approx Per Serving: Cal 457; Prot 11 g; Carbo 60 g;
     Fiber 1 g; T Fat 20 g; 38% Calories from Fat;
     Chol 164 mg; Sod 288 mg.

Mary Lou Short

Delicious Peach Pie

1 1/2 cups flour
2 tablespoons confectioners'
   sugar
1/3 cup finely chopped
   pecans
1/4 teaspoon salt
1/2 cup oil
2 tablespoons milk
8 ounces cream cheese,
   softened
2 cups whipped topping
1 cup confectioners' sugar
3/4 cup sugar
2 tablespoons cornstarch
1/8 teaspoon salt
3/4 cup water
2 tablespoons (heaping) dry
   peach gelatin
1 teaspoon vanilla extract
2 cups sliced peaches

Yield: 8 servings

Combine flour, 2 tablespoons confectioners' sugar, pecans, 1/4 teaspoon salt, oil and milk in bowl; mix well. Pat into pie plate; prick side and bottom with fork. Bake at 350 degrees until brown. Remove to wire rack to cool. Beat cream cheese, whipped topping and 1 cup confectioners' sugar in mixer bowl until smooth. Spread over baked layer. Bring sugar, cornstarch, 1/8 teaspoon salt, water and peach gelatin to a boil in saucepan. Cook until of desired consistency, stirring constantly. Stir in vanilla and peaches. Cool. Spoon over prepared layers. Chill until set. May substitute strawberry gelatin and 2 cups sliced strawberries for peach gelatin and peaches.

Approx Per Serving: Cal 573; Prot 6 g; Carbo 68 g;
     Fiber 2 g; T Fat 32 g; 49% Calories from Fat;
     Chol 32 mg; Sod 196 mg.

B. Marty

Aunt Louise's Peach Pie Supreme

1 unbaked 9-inch pie shell
4 large peaches, sliced
2 eggs, beaten
1 cup sugar
2 tablespoons flour
2 tablespoons melted
  shortening

Yield: 6 servings

Line pie shell with sliced peaches. Combine eggs, sugar, flour and shortening in bowl; mix well. Pour over peaches. Bake at 400 degrees for 15 minutes. Reduce temperature to 325 degrees. Bake for 40 minutes longer. May substitute margarine for shortening.

Approx Per Serving: Cal 381; Prot 4 g; Carbo 56 g;
    Fiber 2 g; T Fat 16 g; 38% Calories from Fat;
    Chol 62 mg; Sod 182 mg.

Helene Wagner

Georgia Pecan Pie

3 eggs, beaten
1 cup sugar
1/2 cup light corn syrup
2 tablespoons melted butter
1 teaspoon vanilla extract
1 cup pecans
1 unbaked 9-inch pie shell

Yield: 6 servings

Combine eggs and sugar in bowl; mix well. Stir in corn syrup. Add melted butter; mix well. Mix in vanilla. Stir in pecans. Spoon into pie shell. Bake at 350 degrees for 35 to 40 minutes or until set. May substitute 1 cup packed brown sugar for sugar.

Approx Per Serving: Cal 566; Prot 6 g; Carbo 73 g;
    Fiber 2 g; T Fat 30 g; 46% Calories from Fat;
    Chol 104 mg; Sod 263 mg.

Verna Dekle and Shirley Gunn

Ode to St. George Island Volunteer Fire Department and First Responders

Words + Music
by Ellie J. Jones
© 1997

Healthy Recipes

West End Fire Station
by Sandra Thaxton

West End Fire Station

As proud as the residents of St. George Island were of receiving the "1992 Rural Community of the Year" award, they chose not to rest on their laurels. In July of 1992, Nick LaSlavic, a resident in St. George Plantation and representative from the St. George Island Fire Department, inspected our fire hydrants and pressure. The results showed both to be woefully inadequate, as was fire protection in general within our island community.

In 1993, Woody Miley spoke of the need for a fire station on the west end of St. George Island which would give better fire protection in St. George Plantation. As a result, a plan to purchase a new pumper ladder truck emerged. To support this cause even further was the fact that more island homes were being constructed nearly 40 feet in height, which made the existing fire equipment inadequate.

Discussion and negotiations continued until 1994 when Jay Abbott, Fire Chief, and the Plantation board examined plans to upgrade fire protection, as well as better serve the western part of the island, which includes the Plantation. This began the cost estimate process.

In 1995, the Board of Directors for the St. George Plantation Owners Association purchased a lot near the entrance gate for the purpose of building a third access lane into the Plantation, as well as providing a site for a new fire station. A fire station committee, comprised of Rod Davis, Guy Marsh, and Shirley Gelch, was formed to recommend plans and to take the necessary steps to make the fire house a reality.

Alice Collins, Vice Chairman of the Board of Directors of the St. George Island Volunteer Fire Department, served as liaison and worked with the committee. Rod Davis agreed to oversee the project. A long-awaited plan for a west end fire station was underway.

The building plan, drawn and donated by architect Bob Crozier, was for a three-bay, color-appropriate building. In January of 1997, the first shovel was turned to begin construction. In May of 1997, the St. George Island community enjoyed a ribbon cutting ceremony, officially welcoming and thanking all who contributed to the new West End Fire Station. The land and building, donated by the Plantation owners of St. George Island, was the largest single contribution ever made to the St. George Island Volunteer Fire Department. The most rewarding result of this dream, however, is that everyone on the island benefits.

Island Salsa

1/2 cup chopped peeled
   mango
1/2 cup chopped fresh
   pineapple
1/2 cup chopped peeled apple
2 tablespoons minced red
   onion
1 tablespoon minced ginger
1 jalapeño, seeded, minced
1 tomato, peeled, seeded,
   chopped
1/4 cup chopped fresh
   cilantro
2 tablespoons fresh passion
   fruit or pineapple juice
Juice of 2 limes

Yield: 10 servings

Combine mango, pineapple, apple, onion, ginger, jalapeño, tomato, cilantro and juices in bowl and mix gently. Chill until serving time. Serve with fish, meats or salads.

Approx Per Serving: Cal 21; Prot <1 g; Carbo 5 g; Fiber 1 g; T Fat <1 g; 5% Calories from Fat; Chol 0 mg; Sod 2 mg.

Connie Dehner

Do-Little Tuna Dip

1   6-ounce can water-pack,
   solid-pack white tuna
1 envelope Italian salad
   dressing mix
8 ounces reduced-fat sour
   cream

Yield: 12 servings

Drain and flake tuna in a bowl. Add salad dressing mix and sour cream; mix well. Chill for 8 hours. Serve with corn chips or melba rounds.

Approx Per Serving: Cal 42; Prot 5 g; Carbo 2 g; Fiber 0 g; T Fat 2 g; 37% Calories from Fat; Chol 10 mg; Sod 139 mg.

Barry Isenberg

Janie Burke's Low-Fat Cooking Tips

Use nonfat sour cream, cream cheese, cottage cheese, cheese, ricotta, etc., in your recipes. After a time or two, you will not know the difference.

Fat-free products are coming out all the time. Be brave and try them for things you eat often. It is difficult to change habits but you can substitute low- or fat-free varieties and get accustomed to them.

Veggie Dip

1/2 cup reduced-fat
  mayonnaise
1/2 cup reduced-fat cottage
  cheese
1/2 cup reduced-fat plain
  yogurt
1 to 2 tablespoons minced
  onion
2 teaspoons dried dillweed
1 teaspoon dried parsley
1/2 teaspoon sea salt

Yield: 12 servings

Combine mayonnaise, cottage cheese, yogurt, onion, dillweed, parsley and salt in bowl; mix well. Chill until serving time. Serve with bite-size fresh vegetables for dipping.

Approx Per Serving: Cal 39; Prot 2 g; Carbo 3 g;
    Fiber 0 g; T Fat 2 g; 52% Calories from Fat;
    Chol 4 mg; Sod 192 mg.

Judi Little

Skinny Gumbo

1 cup chopped onion
1 tablespoon olive oil
1/4 cup chopped garlic
1 cup chopped mixed red
  and green bell peppers
1   16-ounce can tomatoes
  or tomatoes with green
  chiles
1   10-ounce can each
  chicken broth and fiesta
  tomato soup
1   9-ounce package sliced
  okra
2 to 3 teaspoons Cajun
  seasoning
1 teaspoon lite salt
8 ounces turkey kielbasa,
  thinly sliced
12 ounces each peeled
  shrimp, scallops, fish
  fillets, shucked oysters
  and crab meat
2 teaspoons canola oil
Chopped parsley to taste
1 cup water
Salt, black pepper and red
  pepper to taste
2 tablespoons filé powder

Yield: 10 servings

Sauté onion in olive oil in large soup pot for 2 minutes. Add garlic and bell peppers. Cook for 2 minutes. Add undrained tomatoes, broth, soup, okra, 2 teaspoons Cajun seasoning and lite salt. Stir in sausage. Simmer, covered, for 20 to 30 minutes. Pat shrimp, scallops and fish dry with paper towels. Stir-fry shrimp, scallops and fish in canola oil in large skillet for 2 minutes. Add to vegetable mixture with parsley. Add water. Simmer, covered, for 20 minutes. Adjust seasonings. Add oysters and crab meat. Adjust liquid. Stir in filé powder; turn off heat. Let stand, covered, for 20 minutes. Serve in soup dishes with large spoonful hot cooked rice in center; garnish with chopped green onions. Add good wine, hot French bread with baked garlic and Laissez les Bon Temps roulez! Select seafood in any combination or amounts for your tastes and pocketbook to have about 4 pounds total.

Approx Per Serving: Cal 255; Prot 31 g; Carbo 15 g;
    Fiber 2 g; T Fat 8 g; 28% Calories from Fat;
    Chol 127 mg; Sod 1068 mg.
    Nutritional information does not include filé
    powder.

Eddie Lardent

Lentil and Pasta Soup

1 6-inch kombu strip,
   soaked
1 cup chopped onion
1 cup chopped celery
1 cup green lentils
1 cup chopped carrots
5 to 6 cups water
1 cup whole wheat elbow or
   shell macaroni
Sea salt to taste
1 cup chopped parsley

Yield: 8 servings

Cut kombu into 1/2-inch squares. Combine kombu, onion, celery, lentils, carrots and water in soup pot. Simmer for 45 minutes. Add macaroni and sea salt. Simmer for 15 minutes or until macaroni is tender. Ladle into soup bowl; sprinkle with parsley.

Approx Per Serving: Cal 134; Prot 8 g; Carbo 26 g;
    Fiber 8 g; T Fat 1 g; 4% Calories from Fat;
    Chol 0 mg; Sod 32 mg.

Lucy Goldman

Rockefeller Oyster Bisque

1 pint shucked oysters with
   liquor
2 tablespoons olive oil
3 tablespoons flour
2 cups skim milk
1/4 teaspoon Tabasco sauce
1 teaspoon garlic powder
1/2 teaspoon seasoned salt
1 10-ounce package frozen
   chopped spinach, thawed,
   drained
1/4 cup grated Parmesan
   cheese
2 tablespoons soy bacon bits

Yield: 4 servings

Sauté oysters in olive oil in large soup pot for 3 to 5 minutes or until oysters curl at edges. Sprinkle with flour; mix well. Stir in milk gradually. Cook until thickened, stirring constantly. Cook over very low heat for several minutes. Add spinach. Heat to serving temperature. Ladle into soup bowls. Sprinkle with Parmesan cheese and soy bacon bits.

Approx Per Serving: Cal 316; Prot 25 g; Carbo 22 g;
    Fiber 2 g; T Fat 15 g; 41% Calories from Fat;
    Chol 113 mg; Sod 840 mg.

Eunice Hartmann

Janie Burke's Low-Fat Cooking Tips

If you snack on chips a lot, try the fat-free type and even better, eat popcorn. Without butter, it is naturally fat free. Use Weight Watchers spray butter (no fat) on popcorn.

Oyster Potato Stew

4 large potatoes, peeled,
   chopped
1/2 cup butter or margarine
1 pint shucked oysters
1 teaspoon salt
1/2 teaspoon pepper
2 cups 2% milk

Yield: 6 servings

Cook potatoes in water to cover in large saucepan until tender; drain. Add butter, oysters, salt and pepper. Let stand, covered, until butter melts. Add milk; mix well. Heat until oysters curl at edges; do not allow milk to boil. Add seasonings such as celery seeds to taste. No additional thickening is needed; potatoes will cook down to thicken.

Approx Per Serving: Cal 345; Prot 13 g; Carbo 30 g;
      Fiber 2 g; T Fat 20 g; 51% Calories from Fat;
      Chol 102 mg; Sod 812 mg.

Ken Collins

Hearty Pasta Soup

4 1/2 quarts low-sodium
   chicken broth
8 ounces fresh cheese
   tortellini
1 pound fresh spinach,
   chopped
1 pound chicken breasts,
   cooked, chopped
1 red bell pepper, chopped
3 cloves of garlic, minced
1 cup cooked rice, couscous
   or orzo
Salt and pepper to taste

Yield: 10 servings

Bring broth to a boil in large soup pot. Add tortellini. Cook for 4 to 6 minutes or until al dente. Add spinach, chicken, red pepper, garlic and rice. Cook over high heat for 5 minutes. Add salt and pepper. Ladle into soup bowls. Garnish with Parmesan cheese; serve with garlic bread.

Approx Per Serving: Cal 227; Prot 23 g; Carbo 19 g;
      Fiber 2 g; T Fat 6 g; 23% Calories from Fat;
      Chol 34 mg; Sod 211 mg.

Jennifer Ficklen-Bucci

Janie Burke's Low-Fat Cooking Tips

You can thicken natural sauces with arrowroot.

Change from whole or 2% milk to skim. It has all the calcium as whole milk but just takes a little getting used to. You can save a lot of fat this way.

Summer Tomato Soup

2 cups chopped peeled fresh
    tomatoes
1 16-ounce can chopped
    tomatoes
1 tomato can water
Oregano, thyme and parsley
    to taste
1 cup plain nonfat yogurt
5 ounces nonfat sour cream
1 6-ounce can vegetable
    juice cocktail

Yield: 4 servings

Combine fresh and canned tomatoes, water and herbs in saucepan. Simmer for several minutes. Add yogurt, sour cream and enough vegetable juice cocktail to make the desired consistency. Heat to serving temperature.

Approx Per Serving: Cal 110; Prot 6 g; Carbo 21 g;
    Fiber 3 g; T Fat 1 g; 4% Calories from Fat;
    Chol 1 mg; Sod 356 mg.

Mary Isenberg

Cranberry Salad

1 6-ounce package
    strawberry gelatin
1 cup boiling water
1 15-ounce can crushed
    pineapple
2 tablespoons lemon juice
1 16-ounce can whole
    cranberry sauce
1 cup finely chopped celery
1 cup chopped pecans or
    walnuts

Yield: 15 servings

Dissolve gelatin in boiling water in large bowl. Add pineapple and lemon juice; mix well. Chill until partially set. Add cranberry sauce, celery and pecans; mix well. Chill until set.

Approx Per Serving: Cal 164; Prot 2 g; Carbo 29 g;
    Fiber 1 g; T Fat 6 g; 28% Calories from Fat;
    Chol 0 mg; Sod 42 mg.

Larry Kienzle

Dilled Cucumber Salad

1 cucumber, thinly sliced
1/2 red onion, thinly sliced
1/3 cup white vinegar
2 tablespoons vegetable oil
1/2 teaspoon seasoned salt
1 teaspoon sugar
1 teaspoon pepper
1/4 cup chopped fresh dill

Yield: 3 servings

Combine cucumber and onion in salad bowl. Add mixture of next 5 ingredients. Add dill; toss gently. Chill for 1 hour.

Approx Per Serving: Cal 111; Prot 1 g; Carbo 8 g;
    Fiber 1 g; T Fat 9 g; 71% Calories from Fat;
    Chol 0 mg; Sod 156 mg.

Connie Dehner

Reduced-Fat Broccoli and Cauliflower Salad

4 cups fresh broccoli
  flowerets
4 cups fresh cauliflowerets
1 medium red onion,
  chopped
2 cups cherry tomato halves
1 cup reduced-fat
  mayonnaise
1/2 cup fat-free sour cream
1 tablespoon vinegar
Garlic salt and pepper to
  taste

Yield: 12 servings

Combine broccoli, cauliflower, onion and tomatoes in salad bowl. Blend mayonnaise, sour cream, vinegar, garlic salt and pepper in small bowl. Add to broccoli mixture; toss to coat. Chill, covered, for 2 hours or longer.

Approx Per Serving: Cal 81; Prot 2 g; Carbo 10 g;
     Fiber 2 g; T Fat 4 g; 43% Calories from Fat;
     Chol 5 mg; Sod 126 mg.

Eunice L. Hartman

St. George—A Secret Spot

Sand and solitude is the offer
On this calm February day
Where the jewel shells trim the ocean
And morning footprints wash away.

Rise and fall the sparkle water
To touch the sun-streaked sky
Where the cadence of the sea
Is joined by a gull's mournful cry.

So magnetic the water's edge
It makes me stop and stare
The universe appears reborn
With the picture presented there.

Island surrounded with soft surf
Island of sunsets rare
Island of seabirds and beauty
Island so peaceful, so fair.

—Sarah J. Creason

Chinese Chicken Cabbage Salad

1 small head cabbage, finely
  chopped
4 boneless skinless chicken
  breasts, cooked, shredded
1 bunch green onions,
  chopped
1/2 cup (or more) shredded
  carrots
1 cup minus 2 tablespoons
  vegetable oil
6 tablespoons white vinegar
2 tablespoons soy sauce
2 tablespoons sesame oil
1/4 cup sugar
1 to 2 teaspoons salt
1 teaspoon white pepper
1 small can Chinese rice
  noodles
2 tablespoons toasted
  sesame seeds
1/2 cup sliced almonds,
  toasted

Yield: 8 servings

Combine cabbage, chicken, green onions and carrots in salad bowl; toss to mix. Chill until serving time. Combine oil, vinegar, soy sauce, sesame oil, sugar, salt and pepper in bottle or jar; shake vigorously. Sprinkle noodles, sesame seeds and almonds over chicken mixture. Add dressing; toss to mix. Serve immediately.

Approx Per Serving: Cal 463; Prot 18 g; Carbo 24 g;
    Fiber 4 g; T Fat 34 g; 66% Calories from Fat;
    Chol 36 mg; Sod 1001 mg.
    Nutritional information includes entire amount of dressing.

Darlyne Harper

Quick Cool Rice Salad

3 cups cooked brown rice
1 cup nonfat lemon yogurt
1   11-ounce can mandarin
  oranges, drained
1 kiwifruit, peeled, sliced
1/2 cup golden raisins
1/2 cup chopped peeled
  mango or apple
Grated fresh ginger to taste

Yield: 10 servings

Combine rice, yogurt, oranges, kiwifruit, raisins and mango in salad bowl. Sprinkle with ginger; mix gently. Serve with melon slices for lunch or brunch. Serve with jerk chicken or pork for dinner. May substitute white rice for brown or chopped dried dates, apricots or prunes for mango.

Approx Per Serving: Cal 141; Prot 3 g; Carbo 32 g;
    Fiber 2 g; T Fat 1 g; 4% Calories from Fat;
    Chol <1 mg; Sod 23 mg.

Eddie Lardent

Curried Rice Salad

1/3 to 1/2 cup olive oil
1/3 cup vinegar
1 tablespoon (or more) sugar
1 tablespoon lemon juice
1 clove of garlic, crushed
1 teaspoon to 1 tablespoon
   curry powder
Hot sauce to taste
2 cups freshly cooked warm
   rice
1 green bell pepper,
   shredded
2 tablespoons raisins
2 tablespoons chopped
   fresh parsley
2 tablespoons chopped
   green onions

Yield: 8 servings

Combine olive oil, vinegar, sugar, lemon juice, garlic, curry powder and hot sauce in covered jar; shake well to mix. Pour over warm rice in salad bowl; toss to mix. Add green pepper, raisins, parsley and green onions; toss to mix. Spoon into lettuce-lined salad bowl. Garnish with tomato wedges. May substitute finely chopped cucumber or broccoli for the green pepper.

Approx Per Serving: Cal 194; Prot 2 g; Carbo 17 g;
   Fiber 1 g; T Fat 14 g; 62% Calories from Fat;
   Chol 0 mg; Sod 2 mg.

Nora Collins

Tabouli

3/4 cup bulgur wheat
6 tablespoons fresh lemon
   juice
5 tablespoons extra-virgin
   olive oil
6 tablespoons chopped
   fresh parsley
1/4 cup chopped fresh mint
3 scallions, chopped
4 tomatoes, peeled, chopped
Salt and pepper to taste

Yield: 6 servings

Soak bulgur wheat in cold water to cover for 20 minutes. Drain and squeeze dry. Place in salad bowl. Add lemon juice, olive oil, parsley, mint, scallions, tomatoes, salt and pepper; mix well. Chill, covered, for 3 hours to overnight.

Approx Per Serving: Cal 184; Prot 3 g; Carbo 19 g;
   Fiber 5 g; T Fat 12 g; 54% Calories from Fat;
   Chol 0 mg; Sod 14 mg.

Ann Abbey

Janie Burke's Low-Fat Cooking Tips

There are a lot of wonderful fat-free salad dressings. Keep trying them until you find one you like and stick to it.

Creamy Chicken Primavera

1 cup chopped carrots
1 cup broccoli flowerets
1 cup tri-color rotini,
  cooked, drained
8 ounces cooked chicken,
  cubed
1/2 cup plain nonfat yogurt
1/4 cup chopped green onion
  tops
3 tablespoons nonfat
  mayonnaise
2 tablespoons grated nonfat
  Parmesan cheese
1/2 teaspoon crushed dried
  basil
1/8 teaspoon pepper

Yield: 4 servings

Microwave carrots and broccoli in microwave-safe bowl for 5 minutes or until tender-crisp. Combine with pasta in large bowl; toss gently. Combine chicken, yogurt, green onion tops, mayonnaise, cheese, basil and pepper in medium bowl; toss until mixed. Add to pasta mixture; toss gently to mix. Chill, covered, for several hours.

Approx Per Serving: Cal 215; Prot 22 g; Carbo 20 g;
  Fiber 2 g; T Fat 5 g; 19% Calories from Fat;
  Chol 51 mg; Sod 221 mg.

Jackie Mossburg

Poached Chicken with Spinach

4 large boneless skinless
  chicken breasts
Salt and pepper to taste
4 cups chicken broth
2 cups sour cream
1 cup red wine vinegar
2 tablespoons sugar
2 ounces pink peppercorns
1/2 cup (about) 1% milk
2 pounds spinach
3 mangos, peeled, chopped

Yield: 4 servings

Rinse the chicken; pat dry. Sprinkle lightly with seasonings. Arrange the chicken in skillet. Add broth. Bring to a simmer; cover with buttered parchment paper. Simmer for 7 to 10 minutes or until cooked through. Remove from heat; set aside to cool. Combine sour cream, vinegar, sugar, peppercorns and enough milk to make of the desired consistency. Rinse and tear spinach; pat dry and place in salad bowl. Add sour cream mixture; toss to coat. Drain and slice cooled chicken. Place spinach on salad plates. Add chicken slices and mangos. Serve with a glass of German Reisling. A glass of wine a day aids in the reduction of cholesterol.

Approx Per Serving: Cal 887; Prot 83 g; Carbo 56 g;
  Fiber 12 g; T Fat 36 g; 37% Calories from Fat;
  Chol 235 mg; Sod 1162 mg.

Chef Cole

Chicken and Black Bean Salsa

6 boneless skinless chicken
   breasts
1 tablespoon crushed garlic
1/3 teaspoon paprika
1/4 teaspoon pepper
1/2 teaspoon Beau Monde
3 tablespoons chicken broth
1   15-ounce can black beans
1/2 cup salsa
3 tablespoons thinly sliced
   scallions

Yield: 6 servings

Rinse chicken; pat dry. Spread with garlic; sprinkle with paprika, pepper and Beau Monde. Spray large skillet with nonstick cooking spray; preheat over medium-high heat. Arrange chicken in skillet. Cook for 2 to 3 minutes on each side or until brown. Reduce heat to low; add broth. Simmer, covered, for 12 minutes or until chicken is tender and juices run clear when pierced with fork. Place on serving platter; cover with foil to keep warm. Pour off liquid in skillet. Add undrained beans and salsa to skillet. Heat to serving temperature, stirring constantly. Spoon over chicken. Sprinkle with scallions. Serve with shredded lettuce and corn chips or hot cooked rice.

Approx Per Serving: Cal 208; Prot 31 g; Carbo 12 g;
   Fiber 4 g; T Fat 4 g; 16% Calories from Fat;
   Chol 73 mg; Sod 413 mg.

Janie Burke

Lemon Chicken Pasta

4 boneless skinless chicken
   breasts
Juice of 1 lemon
1 can roasted chicken or
   roasted garlic soup
Juice of 2 to 3 lemons
Salt and pepper to taste
Fresh parsley, basil or sage
   to taste
1 cup sliced mushrooms
12 ounces lemon-flavored
   linguine, cooked

Yield: 6 servings

Rinse chicken; pat dry. Cut into bite-size pieces. Marinate in juice of 1 lemon in refrigerator for 30 to 60 minutes. Spray nonstick skillet with nonstick cooking spray. Drain chicken. Sauté in prepared skillet. Heat soup and remaining lemon juice in saucepan. Add salt, pepper and herbs. Add sautéed chicken to soup mixture. Cook until chicken is cooked through. Sauté mushrooms in skillet. Add to chicken mixture just before serving. Pour over hot cooked pasta. Serve with Parmesan cheese if desired.

Approx Per Serving: Cal 201; Prot 22 g; Carbo 21 g;
   Fiber 2 g; T Fat 3 g; 12% Calories from Fat;
   Chol 50 mg; Sod 44 mg.

Sharon Odell

Southwest Chicken Lasagna

10 ounces lasagna noodles
4 egg whites, beaten
3 cups nonfat cottage cheese
1/3 cup chopped fresh
   parsley or cilantro
1 cup chopped onion
1 red bell pepper, chopped
2 tablespoons minced garlic
2   10-ounce cans tomato
   soup
1   10-ounce can enchilada
   sauce
1 tablespoon chili powder
1 teaspoon ground cumin
1 teaspoon freshly ground
   pepper
3 cups shredded cooked
   chicken
2 cups shredded reduced-fat
   Monterey Jack cheese
3 cups shredded reduced-fat
   Cheddar cheese

Yield: 10 servings

Cook noodles using package directions; rinse, drain and set aside. Mix egg whites with cottage cheese and parsley; set aside. Sauté onion, red pepper and garlic in large skillet sprayed with nonstick cooking spray until tender. Add soup, enchilada sauce, chili powder, cumin and pepper. Simmer for 10 minutes, stirring occasionally. Spray 9x13-inch baking pan with nonstick cooking spray. Alternate layers of sauce, noodles, chicken and cheeses until all ingredients are used, ending with cheeses. Bake at 375 degrees for 50 minutes. Let stand for 10 minutes before cutting and serving.

Approx Per Serving: Cal 448; Prot 43 g; Carbo 36 g;
   Fiber 2 g; T Fat 14 g; 28% Calories from Fat;
   Chol 73 mg; Sod 1026 mg.

John Shelby

The St. George Heron

Larry has long blue legs
He marches the beach as a castle guard
Serious, so very serious
A special look passes between us

Eyes left and eyes right
To guard the smorgasbord
The table a perfect sea of sand
And shells painted soft earth colors

His Majesty presides over paradise found
The cadence is done stiff and starchy
Hup, Two, Three, Four
Long blue limbs marking time

—Sarah J. Creason

Spicy Lemon Grass Chicken

2 tablespoons minced fresh
   lemon grass
1 tablespoon minced fresh
   ginger
1 tablespoon chili paste
1 tablespoon peanut oil
1/4 cup soy sauce
1 cup pineapple juice
1 tablespoon sugar
2 tablespoons tab nuoc mam
   (fish sauce)
2 tablespoons white vinegar
2 8-ounce boneless
   skinless chicken breasts
2 tablespoons peanut oil
1 yellow bell pepper, cut
   into thin strips
1 red bell pepper, cut into
   thin strips
8 ounces fresh snow peas
1 onion, chopped

Yield: 2 servings

Sauté lemon grass, ginger and chili paste in 1 table-spoon peanut oil in small skillet over medium heat for several minutes. Add soy sauce, pineapple juice, sugar, fish sauce and vinegar and cook until slightly thickened. Rinse chicken and pat dry. Cut each breast into 2 thin slices horizontally. Cook chicken in 2 table-spoons peanut oil in large skillet until cooked through; set chicken aside. Add bell peppers, snow peas and onion to skillet. Sauté lightly. Return chicken to skillet. Pour sauce over top. Heat to serving temperature. Serve with steamed rice. May substitute lite soy sauce.

Approx Per Serving: Cal 672; Prot 58 g; Carbo 52 g;
   Fiber 7 g; T Fat 27 g; 35% Calories from Fat;
   Chol 136 mg; Sod 3374 mg.

Pauline Jordy

Red Snapper Vera Cruz

4 4-ounce red snapper
   fillets
Salt and pepper to taste
Juice of 1 lime
1 white onion, thinly sliced
1 clove of garlic, minced
2 tablespoons olive oil
1 16-ounce can
   Italian-style stewed
   tomatoes
1 jalapeño, seeded, chopped
1/2 cup sliced green olives
1 tablespoons capers
1 teaspoon dried oregano
1/2 teaspoon sugar

Yield: 4 servings

Sprinkle fish with salt, pepper and lime juice; set aside. Sauté onion and garlic in olive oil in skillet until tender. Add tomatoes, jalapeño, olives, capers, oregano and sugar; mix well. Simmer for 15 minutes. Add fish; spoon sauce over fish. Cook for 7 minutes or until fish flakes easily. Serve fish and sauce over hot cooked yellow or white rice.

Approx Per Serving: Cal 219; Prot 18 g; Carbo 12 g;
   Fiber 2 g; T Fat 11 g; 45% Calories from Fat;
   Chol 28 mg; Sod 866 mg.

Shirley Redd

Sole with Cucumber Sauce

1 tablespoon melted
    margarine
1/4 cup packed minced fresh
    dill
1/2 teaspoon salt
1/2 teaspoon pepper
4   4-ounce sole fillets
1 cup plain yogurt
3 tablespoons lemon juice
2 teaspoons grated lemon
    zest
1/2 teaspoon dry mustard
2 inches cucumber, peeled,
    minced
1/4 cup minced red bell
    pepper

Yield: 4 servings

Combine margarine, 1 tablespoon of the dill, 1/4 tea-spoon of the salt and 1/4 teaspoon of the pepper in small bowl; mix well. Preheat broiler. Arrange fillets in lightly greased foil-lined broiler pan. Spread with dill mixture. Broil 4 inches from heat source for 7 minutes or until fish flakes easily. Combine yogurt, lemon juice, lemon zest, dry mustard and remaining dill, salt and pepper in small bowl; mix well. Stir in cucumber and red pepper. Serve fish with cucumber sauce.

Approx Per Serving: Cal 165; Prot 22 g; Carbo 5 g;
    Fiber 1 g; T Fat 6 g; 34% Calories from Fat;
    Chol 60 mg; Sod 432 mg.

Kim Norgren

Crab Manicotti

16 ounces reduced-fat
    ricotta cheese
1   6-ounce can crab meat
1 teaspoon parsley
1 clove of garlic, minced
1/2 teaspoon seasoned salt
1/2 teaspoon lemon pepper
1/4 cup shredded reduced-fat
    mozzarella cheese
16 large manicotti shells
1 small onion, chopped
1 green bell pepper, chopped
1 zucchini, chopped
1   16-ounce can stewed
    tomatoes
2 cloves of garlic, minced
1   6-ounce can tomato paste
Sugar to taste
Italian seasoning to taste
1/4 cup grated Parmesan
    cheese
1/2 cup shredded reduced-fat
    mozzarella cheese

Yield: 8 servings

Combine ricotta, crab meat, parsley, 1 clove of garlic, seasoned salt, lemon pepper and 1/4 cup mozzarella cheese in bowl; mix well and set aside. Cook manicotti using package directions; rinse, drain and set aside. Sauté onion, green pepper and zucchini in saucepan. Add undrained tomatoes, tomato paste, 2 cloves of garlic, sugar and Italian seasoning; mix well. Simmer until desired consistency. Stuff manicotti with ricotta mixture; arrange in baking pan. Spoon sauce over top. Sprinkle with Parmesan cheese and 1/2 cup mozzarella cheese. Bake at 350 degrees for 30 minutes or until bubbly.

Approx Per Serving: Cal 322; Prot 22 g; Carbo 41 g;
    Fiber 4 g; T Fat 8 g; 23% Calories from Fat;
    Chol 40 mg; Sod 637 mg.

Lana Heady

Oysters à la St. George

4 ounces saltine crackers,
   crushed
1 pint (or more) shucked
   oysters
1   16-ounce can cream-style
   yellow corn
1½ teaspoons salt
1½ teaspoons pepper
½ cup margarine, chopped
3 eggs, beaten
2 to 3 cups evaporated milk

Yield: 8 servings

Alternate layers of cracker crumbs, oysters, corn, salt, pepper and margarine in greased casserole until all ingredients are used, ending with cracker crumbs. Beat eggs with evaporated milk; pour over layers. Bake at 450 degrees for 30 minutes. This was a prize-winning recipe in 1967. May use egg substitute and evaporated skim milk.

Approx Per Serving: Cal 412; Prot 16 g; Carbo 33 g;
      Fiber 2 g; T Fat 24 g; 52% Calories from Fat;
      Chol 148 mg; Sod 1205 mg.

Dollie Cassel

Stir-Fry Scallops

½ cup chicken broth
2 teaspoons honey
1 teaspoon Chinese
   five-spice seasoning
2 teaspoons cornstarch
2 tablespoons vegetable oil
1 pound scallops, sliced
½ cup sliced celery
⅓ cup sliced green onions
1   8-ounce can sliced water
   chestnuts, drained
2   6-ounce packages frozen
   snow peas, thawed

Yield: 4 servings

Blend broth, honey, seasoning and cornstarch in small bowl; set aside. Heat oil in large skillet or wok. Add scallops. Stir-fry until cooked through; remove scallops and set aside. Add celery and green onions. Stir-fry for several seconds. Add water chestnuts, snow peas, scallops and broth mixture. Cook until thickened, stirring constantly.

Approx Per Serving: Cal 217; Prot 13 g; Carbo 21 g;
      Fiber 6 g; T Fat 9 g; 38% Calories from Fat;
      Chol 18 mg; Sod 355 mg.

Cheryl Cianciolo

Janie Burke's Low-Fat Cooking Tips

Think of chicken or vegetable broth as a substitute for oil. Anytime you need to sauté in a recipe use broth. (Substitute chicken or vegetable broth instead of oil. It works beautifully when cooking onions or garlic to add to chili, spaghetti, etc.)

Scallops in White Wine Sauce

1 large shallot, chopped
1 tablespoon chopped garlic
2 tablespoons olive oil
8 ounces bay scallops
2 tablespoons unsalted
  butter
1 teaspoon fresh lemon juice
1/2 cup semi-dry white wine
Salt and pepper to taste
9 ounces linguine
1/2 cup freshly grated
  Parmesan cheese
1 tablespoon chopped
  parsley

Yield: 2 servings

Sauté shallot and garlic in olive oil in large saucepan over medium heat for 3 minutes. Add scallops, butter, lemon juice and wine. Sauté for 5 minutes. Add salt and pepper; remove from heat. Let stand, covered, to keep warm. Cook linguine until al dente using package directions. Drain; add to saucepan with sauce. Toss until coated. Sprinkle with Parmesan cheese and parsley; serve immediately.

Approx Per Serving: Cal 987; Prot 39 g; Carbo 115 g; Fiber 10 g; T Fat 37 g; 34% Calories from Fat; Chol 69 mg; Sod 714 mg.

Barbara Yonclas

Scallop and Shrimp Pasta

1/2 cup margarine
1/2 teaspoon garlic salt
Juice of 6 lemons
1 pound peeled shrimp
1 pound scallops
1/2 cup white wine
1 pound angel hair pasta
1/4 cup (or more) grated
  Parmesan cheese

Yield: 8 servings

Melt margarine in large skillet. Add garlic salt, lemon juice, shrimp and scallops. Simmer until shrimp turn pink. Add wine. Simmer for 1 minute longer. Cook pasta using package directions. Drain and place on large serving platter. Spoon seafood mixture over top. Sprinkle with cheese.

Approx Per Serving: Cal 368; Prot 22 g; Carbo 35 g; Fiber 1 g; T Fat 15 g; 36% Calories from Fat; Chol 92 mg; Sod 708 mg.

Ticia Lipscomb

Janie Burke's Low-Fat Cooking Tips

Don't use butter in white sauce or cream sauce. Use Butter Buds mixed with water (recipe on package). Liquefied Butter Buds works as a substitute for melted butter for dipping or in recipes.

When you want a light cream sauce or gravy, use a few spoonfuls of low-fat cream of chicken, mushroom or celery soup.

Shrimp Canton

1 pound large shrimp,
  peeled, deveined
1/4 cup soy sauce
1/4 cup water
2 tablespoons sugar
1 green bell pepper, sliced
1 tablespoon grated fresh
  ginger
2 tablespoons margarine
1 cup sliced mushrooms
1 pound cherry tomatoes

Yield: 4 servings

Marinate shrimp in mixture of soy sauce, water and sugar for 30 minutes. Sauté green pepper and ginger in margarine in large skillet for 3 minutes. Add mushrooms and shrimp. Cook until shrimp are pink. Add tomatoes. Cook for 3 minutes longer. Serve over hot cooked rice. May substitute lite soy sauce.

Approx Per Serving: Cal 187; Prot 17 g; Carbo 15 g;
    Fiber 2 g; T Fat 7 g; 33% Calories from Fat;
    Chol 135 mg; Sod 1147 mg.

Shirley Redd

Angel Hair and Shrimp

6 cloves of garlic, minced
3 tablespoons olive oil
1 pound peeled medium
  shrimp
1 cup white cooking wine
8 ounces angel hair or
  capellini pasta
4 medium tomatoes, peeled,
  seeded, chopped
1 cup chopped fresh basil
Salt and pepper to taste
Crushed red pepper to taste

Yield: 4 servings

Sauté garlic in olive oil in large skillet over medium heat for 1 minute. Add shrimp. Sauté for 1 minute or until pink. Add wine gradually. Cook until slightly reduced. Cook pasta in large pot of boiling salted water until al dente, stirring occasionally to prevent sticking. Add tomatoes and basil to shrimp mixture. Cook just long enough to blend flavors. Season with salt, pepper and crushed red pepper. Drain pasta; add to sauce. Toss to mix and serve immediately with French bread toasted with garlic and olive oil.

Approx Per Serving: Cal 409; Prot 26 g; Carbo 40 g;
    Fiber 3 g; T Fat 13 g; 27% Calories from Fat;
    Chol 161 mg; Sod 393 mg.

Chef Tamara Suarez at Harry A's

Calypso Shrimp with Black Bean Salsa

1 tablespoon fresh lime juice
1 tablespoon vegetable oil
1/2 teaspoon grated lime rind
1 clove of garlic, minced
1 teaspoon minced fresh
    ginger
1 pound large shrimp,
    peeled, deveined
Black Bean Salsa

Yield: 4 servings

Combine lime juice, oil, lime rind, garlic and ginger in medium glass bowl. Add shrimp; mix until coated. Marinate for 15 minutes. Cook shrimp in large skillet over medium heat for 5 minutes or until pink and firm, turning once. Divide Black Bean Salsa among 4 plates. Arrange shrimp on salsa. Garnish with lime slices. May serve shrimp and salsa mixed together or arranged side by side.

Approx Per Serving: Cal 220; Prot 21 g; Carbo 24 g;
    Fiber 7 g; T Fat 5 g; 21% Calories from Fat;
    Chol 135 mg; Sod 484 mg.
    Nutritional information includes Black Bean Salsa.

Black Bean Salsa

1 15-ounce can black beans
1 cup chopped peeled mango
1/2 cup chopped red bell
    pepper
1/4 cup sliced green onions
1 tablespoon chopped fresh
    cilantro
1/2 teaspoon grated lime rind
1 to 2 tablespoons fresh
    lime juice
1 tablespoon red wine
    vinegar
1/4 teaspoon cayenne

Yield: 4 servings

Drain and rinse beans; drain well. Place in medium bowl. Add mango, red pepper, green onions, cilantro, lime rind and juice, vinegar and cayenne; mix well.

Barbara Yonclas

Janie Burke's Low-Fat Cooking Tips

Make a favorite casserole recipe substituting a vegetable for the meat. Add a meat seasoning such as Goya ham flavoring to give added taste. This is found in the spice section of most groceries.

Use nonstick cooking sprays (Pam, etc.) instead of greasing pans.

Baked Angel Hair with Shrimp

8 ounces angel hair pasta
12 ounces cooked peeled
  shrimp
1 green onion, chopped
1/3 cup chopped seeded
  peeled plum tomatoes
2 cloves of garlic, crushed
1/2 cup chopped fresh basil
  or 1 teaspoon dried
1/4 cup dry white wine
1 cup reduced-fat,
  reduced-sodium clam
  chowder
3 1/2 tablespoons grated
  Parmesan cheese

Yield: 5 servings

Cook pasta using package directions; drain and rinse. Drain well and set aside. Combine shrimp, green onion, tomato, garlic, basil, wine and clam chowder in large bowl. Mix in 3 tablespoons of the cheese. Add pasta; toss to mix. Spoon into baking dish sprayed with non-stick cooking spray. Sprinkle with remaining 1/2 tablespoon cheese. Cover with foil sprayed with nonstick cooking spray. Bake at 350 degrees for 20 to 25 minutes. Garnish with lemon wedges.

Approx Per Serving: Cal 253; Prot 23 g; Carbo 30 g;
    Fiber 1 g; T Fat 4 g; 13% Calories from Fat;
    Chol 138 mg; Sod 486 mg.

Katrena Plumblee

Shrimp Casino

3 10-ounce cans tomatoes
  with green chiles
2 tomatoes, chopped
1 purple onion, chopped
1 red bell pepper, chopped
1 green bell pepper, chopped
1/4 clove of garlic, minced
Juice of 1 lime
Salt to taste
1 1/2 pounds shrimp
1/4 cup (about) grated
  Parmesan cheese
3 (about) crisp-fried bacon
  strips, crumbled

Yield: 6 servings

Combine canned tomatoes, fresh tomatoes, onion, bell peppers, garlic, lime and salt in bowl; mix well. Peel shrimp, leaving tails intact. Devein and butterfly shrimp. Arrange on lightly greased baking sheet. Spoon generous amount of tomato mixture over shrimp; sprinkle with cheese and bacon. Bake at 450 degrees for 10 to 15 minutes. Serve on hot cooked yellow rice or angel hair pasta.

Approx Per Serving: Cal 155; Prot 19 g; Carbo 12 g;
    Fiber 3 g; T Fat 4 g; 22% Calories from Fat;
    Chol 141 mg; Sod 856 mg.

Mike Cates

Janie Burke's Low-Fat Cooking Tips

Sprinkle Butter Buds on hot cooked vegetables. It even comes in garlic, herb, cheese, and sour cream flavors.

Fisherman's Spaghetti

1 onion, chopped
1/2 cup minced celery
1/2 cup chopped red or
 green bell pepper
1 clove of garlic, pressed or
 minced
2 tablespoons olive oil
1 16-ounce can whole
 peeled tomatoes, chopped
1 8-ounce tomato sauce
1/2 cup dry white wine
1/2 cup water
1 teaspoon dried basil
1/4 teaspoon dried thyme
1/4 teaspoon dried sage
3 drops of hot pepper sauce
8 ounces crab meat
Salt and pepper to taste
12 ounces spaghetti, cooked
2 tablespoons chopped
 fresh parsley

Yield: 6 servings

Sauté onion, celery, bell pepper and garlic in olive oil in large skillet over medium heat until onion is tender but not brown. Add undrained tomatoes, tomato sauce, wine, water and seasonings. Simmer, uncovered, for 20 minutes or until slightly thickened. Stir in crab meat. Heat to serving temperature. Add to hot cooked spaghetti in large bowl; toss to mix. Sprinkle with parsley. May substitute scallops for crab meat. Cut large scallops into halves or thirds; cook for 2 minutes or until opaque.

Approx Per Serving: Cal 344; Prot 17 g; Carbo 52 g;
 Fiber 3 g; T Fat 6 g; 16% Calories from Fat;
 Chol 29 mg; Sod 499 mg.

Cheryl Cianciolo

Angel Hair with Broccoli

1 10-ounce can chicken
 broth
4 cloves of garlic, minced
1 large onion, chopped
1 cup sliced fresh
 mushrooms
Tabasco sauce to taste
Flowerets of 1 bunch
 broccoli
1 pound angel hair pasta,
 cooked
1/4 cup freshly grated
 Parmesan cheese

Yield: 6 servings

Bring broth to a boil in large saucepan. Add garlic, onion, mushrooms and Tabasco sauce. Simmer for 10 minutes. Add broccoli. Cook for 5 minutes or until tender-crisp. Serve over hot cooked pasta and top with Parmesan cheese.

Approx Per Serving: Cal 272; Prot 15 g; Carbo 47 g;
 Fiber 3 g; T Fat 3 g; 11% Calories from Fat;
 Chol 4 mg; Sod 638 mg.

Lorraine Knight

Penne with Three Peppers

1 large red bell pepper
1 large yellow bell pepper
1 large green bell pepper
1/3 cup fat-free balsamic
   vinaigrette
1 15-ounce can cannellini
   beans, drained
1/2 cup crumbled feta cheese
10 ounces penne pasta,
   cooked

Yield: 8 servings

Seed peppers; cut each into 4 pieces. Spray with non-stick cooking spray. Broil peppers 5 1/2 inches from heat source for 5 minutes, turning once. Cut into 1-inch pieces. Add peppers, vinaigrette, beans and cheese to hot cooked pasta; toss to mix. Serve immediately. Note: Cook pasta using package directions but omitting salt and fat.

Approx Per Serving: Cal 223; Prot 9 g; Carbo 40 g;
    Fiber 4 g; T Fat 3 g; 12% Calories from Fat;
    Chol 8 mg; Sod 302 mg.

Marilyn Bean

Fat Jack's Light Pasta

1 medium onion, chopped
2 cloves of garlic, minced
2 tablespoons olive oil
1 tomato, chopped
8 ounces fresh spinach,
   chopped
6 tablespoons white wine
1 pound fresh mushrooms,
   sliced
Salt and pepper to taste
Fresh chopped parsley to
   taste
1 pound linguine, cooked

Yield: 4 servings

Sauté onion and garlic in olive oil in large skillet until tender. Add tomato, spinach and wine. Cook until reduced by half. Add mushrooms, salt, pepper and parsley. Cook for several minutes. Serve over hot cooked linguine. Sprinkle with Parmesan cheese if desired.

Approx Per Serving: Cal 579; Prot 20 g; Carbo 101 g;
    Fiber 12 g; T Fat 10 g; 15% Calories from Fat;
    Chol 0 mg; Sod 57 mg.

Todd Baroody, Fat Jack's Eatery

Spinach Quiche in Potato Crust

1   10-ounce package frozen
    chopped spinach, thawed
1/4 cup minced onion
1 cup shredded reduced-fat
    Swiss cheese
1 cup dry curd cottage
    cheese
1 cup egg substitute
1 1/2 teaspoons Dijon
    mustard
1/8 teaspoon pepper
1/8 teaspoon garlic powder
2 medium potatoes,
    scrubbed

Yield: 6 servings

Drain spinach; squeeze dry. Combine spinach, onion, Swiss cheese, cottage cheese, egg substitute, mustard, pepper and garlic powder in large bowl; mix well and set aside. Slice potatoes 1/4 inch thick. Spray 9-inch deep-dish pie plate with nonstick cooking spray. Arrange potato slices in single overlapping layer over bottom and up side of prepared pie plate to form crust. Spoon in spinach mixture. Bake at 375 degrees for 45 minutes or until golden brown and knife inserted in center comes out clean. Let stand for several minutes before cutting.

Approx Per Serving: Cal 170; Prot 18 g; Carbo 11 g;
    Fiber 2 g; T Fat 6 g; 32% Calories from Fat;
    Chol 17 mg; Sod 172 mg.

Janie Burke

Spinach and Potato Scramble

3 tablespoons olive oil
1 small onion, chopped
2 cloves of garlic, chopped
3 medium potatoes, chopped
5 eggs, beaten
Salt and pepper to taste
3 cups chopped fresh
    spinach
1/4 cup shredded Monterey
    Jack or Parmesan cheese

Yield: 6 servings

Combine olive oil, onion, garlic and potatoes in large skillet over medium heat. Cook, covered, for 20 minutes or just until potatoes are tender, stirring several times. Beat eggs with salt and pepper. Add eggs and spinach to skillet. Cook until eggs are set and spinach is wilted, stirring gently. Sprinkle with cheese. Let stand, covered, for 5 minutes or until cheese melts. Serve with fresh tomato salad.

Approx Per Serving: Cal 207; Prot 8 g; Carbo 16 g;
    Fiber 2 g; T Fat 13 g; 54% Calories from Fat;
    Chol 181 mg; Sod 93 mg.

Cheryl Cianciolo

Pickled Beets

2   16-ounce cans sliced
     beets
1/2 cup sugar
1/2 cup cider vinegar
1/2 teaspoon salt

Yield: 8 servings

Drain beets, reserving liquid. Place beets in large bowl. Combine reserved liquid, sugar, vinegar and salt in saucepan. Heat until sugar dissolves, stirring frequently. Pour hot liquid over beets; mix gently. Chill until serving time. Beets may be combined with sliced sweet onion and hard-boiled egg slices arranged on lettuce-lined salad plates for a garnet and gold salad.

Approx Per Serving: Cal 82; Prot 1 g; Carbo 21 g;
     Fiber 1 g; T Fat <1 g; 1% Calories from Fat;
     Chol 0 mg; Sod 431 mg.

Ruth Guernsey

Fire Chief Broccoli

1   10-ounce package frozen
     chopped broccoli
1 1/4 cups shredded
     reduced-fat Cheddar
     cheese
1/2 cup reduced-fat
     mayonnaise
1/2 cup egg substitute
1   10-ounce can reduced-fat
     cream of mushroom soup
1 small onion, grated

Yield: 6 servings

Cook broccoli using package directions; drain and cool. Combine with cheese, mayonnaise, egg substitute, soup and onion in bowl; mix well. Spoon into greased casserole. Bake at 350 degrees for 30 minutes.

Approx Per Serving: Cal 148; Prot 11 g; Carbo 11 g;
     Fiber 2 g; T Fat 8 g; 44% Calories from Fat;
     Chol 14 mg; Sod 477 mg.

Jay Abbott, Fire Chief

Janie Burke's Low-Fat Cooking Tips

You can use mashed ripe bananas as a substitute for fat when baking muffins and brownies.

Instead of using whole eggs all the time, use some egg substitute from time to time. They are very good and cook in recipes very well.

Healthy Broccoli

1 large bunch broccoli
1/4 cup cold water
1 tablespoon extra-virgin
    olive oil
2 cloves of garlic
Salt and crushed red pepper
    to taste

Yield: 3 servings

Trim broccoli; cut into bite-size pieces. Rinse with cold water, drain and place in large saucepan. Add 1/4 cup cold water, olive oil, whole garlic cloves, salt and crushed red pepper. Bring to a boil; cover tightly. Steam for 5 minutes or less. Remove with slotted spoon; serve immediately. May add to cooked pasta and serve with grated Parmesan cheese.

Approx Per Serving: Cal 84; Prot 5 g; Carbo 8 g;
    Fiber 4 g; T Fat 5 g; 47% Calories from Fat;
    Chol 0 mg; Sod 40 mg.

Dr. Andrew Weil

Mushroom Stroganoff

1 quart fresh button or
    Italian mushrooms
1 pint shiitake mushrooms
1 pint oyster mushrooms
1/4 cup finely chopped onion
Finely chopped garlic to
    taste
Juice of 1/2 small lemon
1/2 teaspoon Beau Monde
    seasoning
1/8 teaspoon fines herbs
1   10-ounce can reduced-fat
    cream of mushroom soup
1/2 cup (about) chicken broth
1/4 cup sherry
1/2 cup fat-free sour cream
1/8 teaspoon white pepper
Salt to taste

Yield: 8 servings

Clean mushrooms; trim stems and place on paper towels to dry. Slice button and shiitake mushrooms medium-thin; cut large oyster mushrooms into halves or leave smaller mushrooms whole. Add onion and garlic to large skillet sprayed with nonstick cooking spray. Sauté lightly. Add button mushrooms and lemon juice to prevent darkening. Stir in shiitake mushrooms, Beau Monde seasoning and fines herbs. Sauté over medium-high heat for 2 minutes. Add oyster mushrooms; remove from heat. Remove mushrooms with slotted spoon to prevent overcooking. Add soup and broth to pan juices; blend well. Mix in sherry, sour cream, white pepper and salt. Return mushrooms to skillet. Heat just enough to warm through. Serve over hot cooked rice, couscous, small pasta shapes or toast points.

Approx Per Serving: Cal 308; Prot 22 g; Carbo 47 g;
    Fiber 9 g; T Fat 3 g; 10% Calories from Fat;
    Chol 2 mg; Sod 315 mg.

Janie Burke

Sugar-Free Fruit Bread

1/2 cup margarine, softened
1 cup Sugar Twin
2 eggs
2 cups cake flour
1 teaspoon baking soda
1 teaspoon cinnamon
1/2 teaspoon nutmeg
1/2 teaspoon ground cloves
1 cup applesauce
1 cup raisins
1 cup walnuts

Yield: 16 servings

Cream margarine and Sugar Twin in large bowl until light and fluffy. Beat in eggs. Sift dry ingredients together. Add to creamed mixture; mix well. Stir in applesauce, raisins and walnuts. Pour into greased tube pan. Bake at 350 degrees for 1 hour or until bread tests done.

Approx Per Serving: Cal 205; Prot 4 g; Carbo 25 g;
    Fiber 1 g; T Fat 11 g; 47% Calories from Fat;
    Chol 27 mg; Sod 155 mg.

Maxine Cobb

Whole Wheat Pancakes

1 1/2 cups Whole Wheat
    Pancake Mix
1 egg, well beaten
1 1/4 cups skim milk
1 tablespoon vegetable oil

Yield: 11 pancakes

Combine Whole Wheat Pancake Mix, egg, milk and oil in bowl; mix just until moistened. Do not overmix; batter will be slightly lumpy. Preheat nonstick skillet or griddle sprayed with nonstick cooking spray over medium heat. Pour 1/4 cup batter at a time onto hot skillet. Bake until bubbly on top and brown on bottom. Turn pancake over. Bake until brown.

Approx Per Serving: Cal 84; Prot 4 g; Carbo 13 g;
    Fiber 1 g; T Fat 2 g; 23% Calories from Fat;
    Chol 20 mg; Sod 151 mg.

Whole Wheat Pancake Mix

4 cups whole wheat flour
4 cups all-purpose flour
2 cups wheat germ
1 cup nonfat dry milk
    powder
1/3 cup baking powder
1 teaspoon salt

Yield: 11 cups

Combine all ingredients in large bowl; mix well. Store mixture in airtight container in cool place. Measure and use as desired.

Frank and Sue Latham

Fat-Free Chocolate Trifle

1 package fat-free brownie
  mix or fat-free chocolate
  cake mix
2 small packages fat-free
  chocolate pudding mix
4 cups skim milk
16 ounces fat-free whipped
  topping

Yield: 12 servings

Prepare and bake brownie mix using package directions. Cool and crumble into a large bowl. Prepare pudding mix with skim milk using package directions. Spoon over the brownie crumbs. Top with whipped topping. Chill until set.

Approx Per Serving: Cal 266; Prot 4 g; Carbo 59 g; Fiber 1 g; T Fat <1 g; 1% Calories from Fat; Chol 2 mg; Sod 296 mg.

Melanie Pinkerton

Fresh Fruit Buckle

1 cup sugar
1/2 cup natural applesauce
2 eggs
3/4 cup skim milk
3 cups flour
1 tablespoon baking powder
3/4 teaspoon salt
3 to 4 cups fresh blueberries
1/2 cup packed brown sugar
1/2 cup flour
1/2 teaspoon cinnamon
6 tablespoons butter,
  softened

Yield: 15 servings

Combine sugar, applesauce, eggs and skim milk in large bowl; beat until smooth. Mix 3 cups flour, baking powder and salt together. Add to applesauce mixture 1 cup at a time, beating well after each addition; batter will be thick. Fold in blueberries. Spoon into greased and floured 9x13-inch baking pan. Mix brown sugar, 1/2 cup flour, cinnamon and butter in small bowl until crumbly. Sprinkle over batter. Bake at 375 degrees for 45 to 50 minutes or until golden brown. Serve as dessert or coffee cake. May substitute peaches, apples or other fruit for blueberries or use any combination of choice.

Approx Per Serving: Cal 273; Prot 5 g; Carbo 52 g; Fiber 2 g; T Fat 6 g; 19% Calories from Fat; Chol 41 mg; Sod 282 mg.

Lola Seager

Peach Crisp

5 cups peach slices
3 tablespoons sugar
1 tablespoon all-purpose
   flour
1/2 cup rolled oats
1/2 cup packed brown sugar
1/4 cup whole wheat flour
2 tablespoons chopped
   walnuts or pecans
2 tablespoons Grape Nuts
   cereal
1/4 teaspoon nutmeg
1/4 cup buttermilk

Yield: 6 servings

Drain peaches; discard juice. Place in 8-inch round baking dish. Sprinkle with mixture of sugar and all-purpose flour; toss to mix. Combine oats, brown sugar, whole wheat flour, walnuts, cereal and nutmeg in small bowl; mix well. Drizzle buttermilk over mixture; toss with fork until crumbly. Sprinkle over peaches. Bake at 350 degrees for 30 to 35 minutes or until golden brown.

Approx Per Serving: Cal 247; Prot 4 g; Carbo 56 g;
   Fiber 5 g; T Fat 2 g; 8% Calories from Fat;
   Chol <1 mg; Sod 36 mg.

Mason Bean

Pecan Whip

1 envelope unflavored
   gelatin
1/4 cup cold water
3 egg yolks, beaten
2 tablespoons granulated
   sugar replacement
1/8 teaspoon salt
3/4 cup skim milk
1 teaspoon vanilla extract
1/2 cup finely ground pecans
3 egg whites
1/2 teaspoon cream of tartar
1 teaspoon vanilla extract

Yield: 6 servings

Soften gelatin in cold water for 10 minutes. Beat egg yolks in top of double boiler until frothy. Add sugar replacement, salt and skim milk; mix well. Cook over simmering water until mixture coats spoon, stirring constantly. Stir in 1 teaspoon vanilla and pecans. Remove top of double boiler from heat; set aside to cool. Combine egg whites, cream of tartar and 1 teaspoon vanilla in large bowl; beat until stiff peaks form. Fold into cooked mixture. Spoon into dessert dishes. Chill until serving time.

Approx Per Serving: Cal 106; Prot 6 g; Carbo 3 g;
   Fiber 1 g; T Fat 8 g; 66% Calories from Fat;
   Chol 107 mg; Sod 98 mg.

Maxine Cobb

Maxine Cobb suggests a **Fat Replacement** for baking that you make yourself. Process 12 ounces pitted prunes, 1/4 cup light corn syrup and 2 tablespoons sugar in a food processor for 5 seconds. Add 3/4 cup water, processing constantly until smooth. Store in an airtight container in the refrigerator for up to 2 months.

Gingerbread with Lemon Cream

1 14-ounce package
   gingerbread mix
1¹/₃ cups skim milk
2 egg whites or ¹/₄ cup egg
   substitute
2 tablespoons finely
   chopped crystallized
   ginger
¹/₃ cup reduced-fat lemon
   yogurt
¹/₃ cup reduced-fat sour
   cream

Yield: 8 servings

Combine gingerbread mix, skim milk and egg whites in bowl. Beat at low to medium speed until mixed. Beat at high speed for 3 minutes. Stir in half the ginger. Pour into 9-inch square baking pan sprayed with nonstick cooking spray. Bake using package directions. Cool slightly. Blend yogurt and sour cream in small bowl. Chill until serving time. Top individual gingerbread servings with yogurt mixture. Sprinkle with remaining ginger.

Approx Per Serving: Cal 257; Prot 6 g; Carbo 41 g;
    Fiber 1 g; T Fat 8 g; 27% Calories from Fat;
    Chol 5 mg; Sod 374 mg.

Mary Lou Short

Island Wedding Cake

2 cups flour
2 cups sugar
2 teaspoons baking soda
2 eggs or ¹/₂ cup egg
   substitute
1 20-ounce can juice-pack
   crushed pineapple
1 cup flaked coconut or
   shredded carrots
1 cup chopped walnuts or
   pecans
¹/₂ cup margarine, softened
8 ounces cream cheese,
   softened
1 cup confectioners' sugar
2 teaspoons vanilla extract

Yield: 15 servings

Combine flour, sugar, baking soda, eggs, pineapple, coconut and walnuts in large bowl; mix by hand until well mixed. Pour into greased and floured 9x13-inch cake pan or two 8-inch layer pans. Bake at 350 degrees for 45 minutes or until cake tests done. Cool. Combine margarine, cream cheese, confectioners' sugar and vanilla in bowl; beat at high speed until smooth and creamy. Frost cooled cake. Decorate with maraschino cherries. Best when refrigerated overnight.

Approx Per Serving: Cal 410; Prot 5 g; Carbo 58 g;
    Fiber 1 g; T Fat 19 g; 40% Calories from Fat;
    Chol 45 mg; Sod 307 mg.

Ellie Jones

Lemon Yogurt Cookies

1/2 cup margarine, softened
1 1/4 cups sugar
1/2 cup plain nonfat yogurt
2 egg whites
1 tablespoon grated lemon
    rind
1/2 teaspoon vanilla extract
2 cups quick-cooking oats
1 1/2 cups flour
1 teaspoon baking powder
1/2 teaspoon baking soda
1/4 cup (about) sugar
1/4 cup confectioners' sugar

Yield: 48 cookies

Cream margarine and 1 1/4 cups sugar in bowl until light and fluffy. Add yogurt, egg whites, lemon rind and vanilla; mix well. Add mixture of oats, flour, baking powder and baking soda gradually, mixing well. Shape into 1-inch balls; place on cookie sheet sprayed with nonstick cooking spray. Flatten to 1/8 inch with bottom of glass dipped in 1/4 cup sugar. Bake at 375 degrees for 10 minutes or until light brown. Cool on cookie sheet for 2 minutes. Remove to wire rack to cool completely. Sift confectioner's sugar over top. Store in airtight container.

Approx Per Serving: Cal 73; Prot 1 g; Carbo 12 g;
    Fiber 1 g; T Fat 2 g; 26% Calories from Fat;
    Chol <1 mg; Sod 50 mg.

Alice D. Collins

Reduced-Fat Sweet Potato Pie

2 small sweet potatoes
1   14-ounce can fat-free
    sweetened condensed milk
2/3 cup egg substitute
1 1/2 teaspoons apple pie
    spice
1 graham cracker pie shell

Yield: 8 servings

Bake sweet potatoes until very soft. Peel; mash in bowl. Add condensed milk, egg substitute and spice; mix well. Pour into pie shell. Bake at 375 degrees for 35 minutes or until filling forms dome in center and is light brown.

Approx Per Serving: Cal 319; Prot 9 g; Carbo 53 g;
    Fiber 1 g; T Fat 8 g; 23% Calories from Fat;
    Chol 4 mg; Sod 261 mg.

Sharon Odell

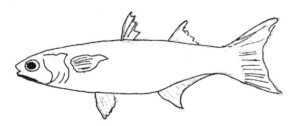

Index

Treasured Recipes from St. George Island

First Responder Unit
St. George Island Volunteer Fire Department
P.O. Box 682
Eastpoint, Florida 32328

Please send me _____ copies of **Treasured Recipes from St. George Island** at $18.95 plus $3.00 postage and handling per book.

Enclosed is my check or money order for _____

Name _____

Address_____

City _____ State_____ Zip_____

Treasured Recipes from St. George Island

First Responder Unit
St. George Island Volunteer Fire Department
P.O. Box 682
Eastpoint, Florida 32328

Please send me _____ copies of **Treasured Recipes from St. George Island** at $18.95 plus $3.00 postage and handling per book.

Enclosed is my check or money order for _____

Name _____

Address_____

City _____ State_____ Zip_____

Treasured Recipes from St. George Island

First Responder Unit
St. George Island Volunteer Fire Department
P.O. Box 682
Eastpoint, Florida 32328

Please send me _____ copies of **Treasured Recipes from St. George Island** at $18.95 plus $3.00 postage and handling per book.

Enclosed is my check or money order for _____

Name _____

Address_____

City _____ State_____ Zip_____

Order Additional Copies